JDoW
(9or)

KT-486-027

BRIDGES LIBRARY
S. MARTIN'S COLLEGE
LANCASTER

k Loan

Books are to be returned on or before
the last d

B 17401 NOV 2007

SCHOOL TRANSFER AND CURRICULUM CONTINUITY

SCHOOL TRANSFER AND
CURRICULUM
CONTINUITY

Brian T. Gorwood

CROOM HELM
London • Sydney • Dover, New Hampshire

© 1986 Brian T. Gorwood
Croom Helm Ltd, Provident House, Burrell Row,
Beckenham, Kent BR3 1AT
Croom Helm Australia Pty Ltd, Suite 4, 6th Floor,
64-76 Kippax Street, Surry Hills, NSW 2010, Australia

British Library Cataloguing in Publication Data

Gorwood, Brian T.
  School transfer and curriculum continuity.
  1. Education – England – Curricula
  I. Title
  375'.00942   LB1564.G7
  ISBN 0-7099-1177-7

Croom Helm, 51 Washington Street, Dover,
New Hampshire 03820, USA

Library of Congress Cataloging in Publication Data

Gorwood, Brian T.
  School transfer and curriculum continuity.

  Bibliography: p.
  Includes index.
  1. Students, Transfer of—Great Britain.
  2. Articulation (Education)—Great Britain.
  3. Education—Great Britain—Curricula. I. Title.
  LB3064.4.G7G67   1986   373.12'914'0941   85-22423
  ISBN 0-7099-1177-7

W 29940 /17.95. 6.86

Printed and bound in Great Britain
by Billing & Sons Limited, Worcester.

CONTENTS

TABLES AND FIGURES

ACKNOWLEDGEMENTS

I should like to thank the many teachers and local
education authority officials who have given me
information and advice. Because of the demands of
confidentiality, some cannot be mentioned; others
I have named in the text. This book could not have
been produced without the active support of the
teaching profession whose comments and criticisms
have been much appreciated.

I also express my thanks to Peter Sowden at Croom
Helm and Anne Petch of Bervatim Word Processing in
the preparation of the manuscript for publication.

Chapter One

THE PROBLEM OF CONTINUITY

In recent years, concepts associated with education
have been subjected to close scrutiny. 'Aims',
'values', 'indoctrination' and several other basic
concepts have been analysed over and over again.
Despite frequent reference in educational literature
and particularly in documents emanating from the
Department of Education and Science (DES) to the need
to establish continuity, there has been little
attempt to elucidate this and associated concepts.
Later, we shall examine strategies that have been
devised for the possible alleviation of continuity
problems but a prior consideration must be to clarify
what is understood by continuity.
    Education, like other enterprises, appropriates
language to its own practice. 'Comprehensive' as
applied to schools, for example, conveys a different
meaning from its use in an insurance context.
'Continuity' has specific meaning in several realms:
in the cinema, in law, in biology and physics, as
well as in education. General definition offers
some help but complex issues defy concise statements
of meaning. Indeed, general definition can sometimes convey a false impression. 'Continuity'
according to the Shorter Oxford Dictionary is
'uninterrupted connexion or succession', a state
impossible to achieve in education for there are
inevitable interruptions not only when a child moves
from school to school or class to class but in the
day to day changes of teacher or programme of work -
changes so often determined by an inflexible time-
table. Significantly, publications devoted
exclusively to educational definition offer little
assistance, for 'continuity' seems not to be one of
the 'key words' included in their lists despite its
now frequent use in the western democracies.
(Collins, 1973)

Dewey (1983) reminds us, 'every experience both takes up something from those which have gone before and modifies in some way the quality of those which come after'. But for education to be worthwhile, there must be the potential for growth and this implies that the mere acquisition of knowledge is not enough. The learning of a certaim amount of arithmetic, geography, history, etc., because it may be useful at some future time is not necessarily a preparation for 'later experiences of a deeper and more expansive quality.' This then, according to Dewey, is what constitutes educational continuity, that one experience of worth should follow another in a sequence of meaningful learning. The trouble with learning in school is that subject matter tends to be learned in isolation, 'put, as it were, in a water-tight compartment'. Even within subjects, little priority is given to making pupils aware of the relationship between what can seem discrete items of information learned merely to enable one to pass examinations. Identifying links between learning in different subjects presents even greater problems.

Education as a Continuum

Educational theorists who exhort us to teach for 'fundamental structure' (Bruner, 1960), 'cumulative learning (Gagne, 1965) or 'integrative reconciliation' (Ausubel, 1967) are concerned that learning should be seen as a continuum. By 'integrative reconciliation', Ausubel means 'that new ideas, once introduced, need to be deliberately related to old ideas, significant similarities and differences pointed out, real or apparent inconsistencies reconciled'. However carefully experienced teachers plan to ensure 'integrative reconciliation', spontaneous classroom interaction will cause breaks in continuity. Some classes, of course, become expert at encouraging teachers to digress. But minor deviations can usually be accommodated and pupils are brought back to the mainstream of learning. This will be easier to achieve in some areas of the curriculum than others. Much will depend upon the extent to which learning activities can be subjected to sequencing principles (Barnes, 1982).

Continuity is inherent in the linear structure of subjects in which the learning of new skills and concepts needs to be securely based on what has been learned at earlier stages. Mathematics, modern

languages and science are all to greater or lesser
degree linear; continuity of learning is achieved
when each individual pupil progresses along a fairly
well-defined course. In a sense, these subjects are
'teacher-proof' in that freedom to deviate from a set
structure is limited. This does not prevent linear
subjects presenting continuity difficulties. In
other areas of the curriculum, there are fewer
bounds. In subjects like history, music and
literature, teachers can exercise considerable
autonomy in determining not only the content of
courses but the order in which items within courses
are presented. In practice, it is at school or
department level that autonomy operates for syllabus
structure seldom devolves on individual teachers.
Yet even within a single teacher's course of work
with a given group of pupils continuity problems can
occur. There are inevitable interruptions in
continuity for the pupil absent frequently or for
long periods. The teacher who mistakenly assumes
that children have mastered an essential preparatory
skill or acquired a basic concept will be able to
rectify the error only at the expense of that
uninterrupted sequence deemed fundamental to smooth
continuity. Similarly, unnecessary repetition of
learning already achieved has an effect on sequence.
[Within a school, change of teacher can present
some continuity difficulties for pupils. Though
these are often caused by differences in teaching
style, they can also be related to curriculum.] In
secondary schools, continuity is usually maintained
within a close-knit department which can be seen 'as
a cell in a much larger structure representing the
interests of those with a common background in one
subject or specialism whether in schools, universities or outside the public educational scene'.
(Weston, 1979) With relatively few staff, of
kindred academic interest, usually teaching in the
same area of the school, the departmental structure
is one in which communication and collaboration can
be readily established. The occasional 'rogue'
teacher, out of sympathy with fellow members of a
department can present difficulties but major
discontinuities are unusual. Her Majesty's
Inspectorate (HMI, 1977) has suggested that it is
when departments combine to offer courses that
continuity and progression in the curriculum may be
disrupted. For example, 'a humanities course may be
introduced in year one without adequate adjustment
being made to the history and geography courses
which follow in year two'. In primary schools, the

main mechanism for promoting continuity is the
syllabus - often referred to as 'curriculum guidelines'. Some local authorities publish guidelines
in a limited number of subjects for all primary
schools under their jurisdiction. More often
schools are responsible for their own subject
planning - or non-planning according to a recent HMI
report on education in one authority in which it was
stated: 'few schools possess clearly conceived and
expressed schemes of work in social studies,
geography, history, environmental studies, science,
music, art, craft; work in these subjects frequently
lacks purpose and continuity.' (HMI 1980) The
overall verdict was that only in mathematics and
language, areas of the curriculum in which the
authority had published clear curriculum guidelines,
was planning for continuity adequate. Of course,
many of those involved in primary education
deprecate precise statements of policy which they
consider take spontaneity out of teaching. Only in
areas of the curriculum where it is important for
teachers to work in a similar way in order to
maintain continuity do they consider it necessary to
provide detail. Consequently, schemes of work in
all but sequential subjects tend to leave a great
deal to the individual teacher. (Dean 1983) There
are many advantages in allowing primary-school
teachers considerable freedom but the promotion of
continuity is not one of them.

Public Concern for Educational Continuity

The 'Great Debate' on education acknowledged
more widespread public interest in the content of
education. Concern about what was happening in
schools called for the teaching profession to be
more accountable to society and prompted the DES to
make increasingly more venturesome forays into what
had hitherto been the preserve of schools. It was
inevitable that attention would be focused on
transition between schools for whatever the
difference within, the disparities between them had
been shown to be extreme. As part of its survey of
local authority arrangements for the school
curriculum, DES Circular 14/77 asked local
authorities to describe procedures for ensuring
continuity when pupils moved from school to school.
We shall return to this circular later; it is
mentioned here as the document at the centre of
national concern about problems of curricular
discontinuity at change of school. Yet this is not

4

solely a British phenomenon.

In the USA, there has been concern for continuity for many years but particularly since the institution of the junior high school in about 1912. (Richardson, 1940) Though 'articulation', or more precisely 'vertical articulation' seems the favoured terminology in American literature, some authors do refer to 'continuity'. Oliver (1977) states, 'continuity refers to the conditions whereby the learner will move smoothly from level to level in an educational system'. Manning (1971) suggests, 'The design of a curriculum, whatever its form, should represent an articulated overall plan through which the learner can move from level to level smoothly, continuously, and with a minimum of institutional-ized confusion.' That this is a statement of aspiration rather than reality is indicated by several research studies which have, over the years, outlined the difficulties in relating courses and syllabuses between one school and another. (Michael, 1959) Summarising the continuity between American secondary schools and other institutional agencies, Gwynn (1961) comments, 'a fairly good job is being done in articulating the secondary school with institutions of higher education; ... not so good a job is being done in articulation with elementary school'. One of the major reasons for the development over the last twenty years or so of middle schools in the USA has been to increase educational continuity by bridging the original two levels, elementary and secondary. (Alexander, 1984) But as in this country, the innovative nature of underlying ideas and day-to-day practice in middle schools has created as well as solved continuity problems:

> Articulation with elementary schools and high schools is a persistent problem in middle schools.... After three years in a middle school one student may be performing at level 28 in mathematics, another at level 19. Unless the high school mathematics program is also non-graded, the high achiever may be obliged to mark time, while the low achiever may be required to take an extra course. (Lounsbury and Vars, 1978)

Although his enthusiasm about the prospects for middle level schooling in the United States is unabated, Alexander (1984) identifies certain 'acute but not insurmountable problems' of which

5

vertical articulation is one. He suggests that
despite the continuing emphasis on the bridging
function of the middle level, too many schools in
the middle tend to operate as the islands their
connecting schools were. Concern for continuity
between schools, then, is by no means confined to
Great Britain; it occurs in America, in Australia
(Connell, 1967) and indeed within a world-wide
context. (Parkyn, 1962)

Change of School

In response to Circular 14/77 (DES, 1979)
comparatively few authorities saw serious problems
in pupils' transition between nursery and infant or
between infant and junior schools, although it was
acknowledged that even in these situations and even
where schools occupied the same site, communication
difficulties could sometimes arise. It was transition between primary and secondary, and middle and
upper schools which most concerned local
authorities. It is at this level that change of
institution frequently involves changes in learning
style, the kind of skills to be developed, and even
the content of learning.
On entry to secondary education, a pupil may be
able to see a relationship between the mathematics
and English taught in primary school and that which
is now presented to him, but he may well wonder what
has happened to the thematic or environmental work
which was so much a feature of schooling before
transfer. Differentiated sciences may be new, as
may technical subjects and foreign languages.
Though much of the curriculum will be new to pupils,
some learning will be all too familiar. Unnecessary
repetition of learning already achieved can be a
cause of increasing school dissatisfaction which
seems to develop in the early years of secondary
education. Particularly in those areas of the
curriculum which are often introduced in the primary
school by means of topics or centres of interest, it
is difficult to avoid, within the secondary school
differentiated approach, repetition of factual
matter. A further cause of problems of this nature
is the practice maintained in some secondary schools
of starting all incoming pupils at the same stage of
instruction irrespective of previous learning
achievement. It is not unknown, too, for pupils who
have already read a given text in the primary school
to be required to re-read it in the secondary
school. The effects on pupils of curricular

discontinuity at primary-secondary transfer have
been specified by ILEA's staff inspector for
geography as 'boredom and bewilderment':

> The varied experience that pupils from
> different feeder schools bring to their first-
> form geography classes makes it extremely
> difficult to avoid the twin hazards of boredom
> and bewilderment. Some pupils invited to
> concentrate upon basic mapwork or local surveys
> are bored having done this sort of thing in
> their primary schools. Yet if the secondary
> school specialist abandons this tabula rasa
> approach and confidently asks first year pupils
> to extract information from the atlas, he is
> likely to produce bewilderment in at least some
> of the pupils. Either way, bored or bewildered
> we incur an unnecessary erosion of enthusiasm
> for learning. (Storm, 1979)

Attempts to discover pupils' capabilities after
transfer can present problems. Some testing is
inevitable but testing is not teaching; as one
adviser commented to the staff of an over-tested
school, 'You don't fatten a pig by weighing it.'
Prolonged diagnostic testing can interrupt
curricular continuity, as indeed can a pupil's
intense preoccupation with a quest to discover what
new standards are required of him. Given the major
leaps that have to take place at change of school it
would be surprising if standards at either side of
an interface were similar. According to Newsam
(1977) it is rare to find work in the first term of
secondary school that equals the standard achieved
by the same child in the previous year. Pupils and
teachers spend some time adjusting to each other,
inevitably causing setbacks in progress. Teachers
of top-year juniors tend to know more about what
their pupils can do and are in a better position to
insist upon it than most teachers of first-year
secondary children. 'There is nothing surprising
about this. For every hour an individual secondary
teacher will spend with a first-year child, the
primary teacher may have spent two, three or more.'
Another aspect of continuity is that of
differences in organisation inherent in the successive stages of education. In the primary school, the
pupil is in a basically self-contained situation,
one teacher being responsible for a class during
most of the day. A move to secondary school is to a
much more time-conscious community. A ring of bells

every 40 or 50 minutes signifies a different subject, a different teacher, a different room, and possibly a different style of teaching. Lady Plowden confessed herself to being baffled, when working on the Central Advisory Council Report, by the difference between what experts were calling the primary and secondary way of learning. She found it incomprehensible that within the space of two months a child should be faced with such an entirely different kind of teaching situation from what he had learned to accept. (Plowden, 1970) Organisational and pedagogical changes at time of transfer have been analysed by Hayling (1970) essentially in terms of a move from 'integrated to fragmentary' and 'pupil chosen to teacher dominated' techniques.

Emotional Implications of Transfer

[Any significant change is potentially traumatic.] The most dramatic change in a young child's way of life is that experienced in the move from home to school. [Subsequently, year by year there is a change of class, a change of teacher, and some adjustment to friendship patterns] - each in its way a preparation for the critical move that a child has to make from one school to another. Concern for continuity should not be narrowly conceived in terms of attainment but must also acknowledge the need to maintain pupils' emotional stability when they transfer school. Of course, these aspects of transfer are often related. White and Brockington's (1983) consumer's view of British education provides detailed evidence of this and other aspects of the 'juniors to seniors' effect. Janet, aged 17, comments:

> At primary school I was amongst the top people - clever I suppose you'd call it. But I can remember the first maths test we had at secondary school. I was near the bottom, which really upset me and I don't think I bothered after that. I was only eleven and up till then I thought I'd be something.

Another of the young people interviewed by Roger White is obviously puzzled by the change that took place:

> I still don't understand it. I was enjoying myself in the juniors and then I went to senior school and everything stopped. I suddenly

8

didn't want to go to school. In the juniors I
was reading books and everything.

Several paragraphs in the Plowden Report are
devoted to avoiding strain at the time of transfer.
It is pointed out that so strong is the myth that
'going up' must mean going to something better that
some children who are hopelessly bewildered by
secondary school work persist in saying that all is
well. There is then a 'harder work' dimension to
school transfer that can cause sufficient distress
to some pupils in effect to truncate their education
at the early secondary stage.
    Patterns of friendship change as a pupil moves
from primary to secondary education. (Blyth, 1960)
But if such changes are forced upon pupils they can
add to the trauma of transfer. Several of White's
interviewees reveal the distress experienced at
being parted from friends:

    - It's scary for the first week. I thought I'd
    be with my friends from middle school but we
    were split up;

    - My best friend went to a different school and
    I was split up from my other friends because we
    were put in classes according to how clever we
    were;

    -. The trouble is you make a lot of friends at
    primary school and then they split you up. I
    still see them to say 'Hello' to, but we used
    to be really friendly.

Research studies confirm the importance of
considering friendship patterns when arrangements
are being made for transfer. (Neal, 1975; Youngman
and Lunzer, 1979) Pupils have to adjust not only to
a change of school-fellows but of teachers too;
failure to make successful new relationships can be
a major cause of stress at the time of transfer.

Degree of Continuity

    To advocate continuity in education is not to
argue that there should be no change in successive
schooling. Differences between schools are
inevitable but they should not be so extreme that
pupils become emotionally disturbed or scholastically confused. Though complete continuity is
unattainable, a statement of what it would entail

9

provides a useful ideal by which to judge reality.
Sumner and Bradley (1977) have suggested such an
ideal:

> In broad terms, pupils in a continuous system
> would perceive little difference in school
> ethos; thus they would be given similar
> learning situations presented through a similar
> approach, using a basis of existing knowledge
> and skills and have their work judged by much
> the same standards. Classroom control, access
> to resources, freedom to move around the
> school, opportunity to use all these would be
> similar, as would methods of assessment,
> reporting to parents, notions of tidiness, and
> so on.

Very few pupils can attain such a measure of
continuity. Those within a sheltered special school
environment may stay in the same institution
throughout the period of compulsory schooling but
the majority of pupils within the state system in
England are subjected to at least one change of
school as an integral part of progression to a more
advanced stage of education. If the curricular,
pedagogical, material, or social features outlined
by Sumner and Bradley are dissimilar in the schools
involved at either side of the interface, it follows
that there must be some measure of discontinuity.
Complete continuity can never be a realistic
expectation if a school is to respect diversity of
philosophy and teaching style. (Manning, 1971) The
critical issue as far as this matter is concerned is
one of degree. Change there must be, but it is the
extent of change which determines whether or not a
measure of smooth continuity can be achieved. The
Plowden Committee accepted 'children, like adults,
enjoy and are stimulated by novelty and change', but
pointed out that such change must be carefully
prepared and not too sudden if it is to stimulate
rather than dishearten pupils. Ten years after
Plowden reported, the Secretary of State for
Education and Science identified transition between
schools as an area of weakness. (DES, 1977) Since
then, many documents have featured transfer, liaison
and continuity as aspects of education continuing to
present difficulties. One can only assume that
transfer between schools is too sudden and
insufficiently prepared.

THE PROBLEM OF CONTINUITY

Type of Transfer

The 1977 Green paper, <u>Education in Schools</u>
mentions two types of transfer between schools: that
between schools in different areas involving
children who have to move schools because of a
change of parental abode, and the more common
transfer of children arising from the successive
stages of education. The first of these, which
Sumner and Bradley refer to as 'migratory transfer',
usually involves a single child moving into an
established class. As an outsider, the pupil will
feel ill at ease for a short time but the others in
the class are familiar with the routine and usually
keen to look after the newcomer. Whilst the school
will do its best to help the pupil settle in, its
practice cannot be changed to suit an individual.
But much will be familiar, for schools within the
same stage of education have many features in
common. Problems can arise, however, if there are
significant changes in the content of curriculum.
Upper secondary school pupils preparing for external
examinations are at a particular disadvantage if they
have to transfer schools, for the various examining
boards, alternative papers and different syllabuses
offer such a wide range of choices that only by
chance will courses be matched. Organisational
transfer involving large groups of children in
change from one type of school to another as an
integral part of the progression to a new stage of
education has its own characteristics. The child
will be just one of many who are faced with the
trauma of transfer. there will be 'a corporate
feeling of newness' but little help or support can
be expected from classmates who themselves are
having to cope with change. The school, however,
will make special arrangements to integrate pupils
into its community as rapidly as possible.
Manifestly, different types of transfer present
different kinds of continuity problem. To the child
who spends his schooldays entirely within one area,
there may be but one major transfer to negotiate.
If the family home is in a 'three-tier' local
authority, the effects of two transfers may be
mitigated by a consciously transitional middle
school. Certain categories of pupil, however,
particularly the children of service personnel and
other highly mobile workers may suffer frequent.
school change. But one does not have to move far
for changes of system to produce some anomolous
effects. These are caused by the very complex

11

pattern of school provision that exists within this country.

At one time, a widely-held view of comprehensive education was that it would create a school system of dreary uniformity. In fact there are more than twenty different age-ranges in operation between the ages of five and eighteen. Since local government reorganisation the position has become particularly confusing in that many of the new authorities have variations within their enlarged areas inherited from former LEAs. (Williams, 1976) In Humberside, for example, depending upon locale, pupils can pass through an 11 - 18, 11 - 16 plus sixth-form college, 8 - 12 or 9 - 13 system. It is possible to transfer at eleven from a small primary to a large secondary school where a differentiated approach to curriculum operates. A move of parental home within the following year could return the pupil to more general work in a small middle school. At thirteen comes the usual organisational transfer to an upper school and a return to subject teaching. This is an exceptional but possible case and one which illustrates the potential for discontinuity now that we have such a complex pattern of educational provision. Of course, many LEAs encourage parents to leave pupils where they are if organisational transfer is to take place within a comparatively short period.

Sumner and Bradley (1977) note that 'transition' and 'transfer' are often used inter-changeably but suggest that 'transition' should apply to moves between recognised stages of education whilst 'transfer' can be used for any change of school. Stillman (1984a) takes a rather different view of the relationship between the two terms. 'Transfer' he suggests as a word to describe 'just the physical displacement of the child from one place of learning to another'. 'Transition' implies changes in the lives of pupils, in the teaching they receive and the expectations made of them.

The literature on transfer emphasises difficulties pupils face in making the transition but there are also advantages to change of school. There are times when we all welcome the opportunity of a fresh start and this need not only be for the negative reason of not having done very well. There are pupils who have acquired a bad reputation in primary school but there are also those who are ready for more specialised, intellectually demanding

12

work; indeed, one study suggests that bright children actually benefit from the stimulation of the new environment after transfer. (Whalen and Fried, 1973) There are, of course, cogent arguments for relating forms of school organisation to pupils' developmental stages; furthermore, organisational transfer enables teacher expertise to be used economically. (Spelman, 1979) School transfer is not without advantages and it would be misleading not to mention them. It is also important to keep the extent of continuity difficulties in perspective. Research findings will be considered further in chapter four; suffice it here to note that though difficulties caused by school change are likely to be experienced by just over half the pupils, they are remarkably short-lived for the majority. Several research studies attest to most pupils being well-integrated into new schools within a term of transfer.

Transfer from one stage of education to another presents a crisis point in a child's school career. The change at its most extreme can be likened to taking an icy cold shower after a warm bath - an invigorating experience for some, but for others sufficiently distressing to discourage or even alienate them. The child who has been used to learning by discovery, who has been accustomed to handling materials and working with real objects can so often be plunged into a verbal world in which it is assumed that merely to read about something or have it explained in the abstract is to understand it. [Successful transition presumably involves the pupil in a process of adjustment] to his or her new school but if continuity is to be meaningful, this should not involve total abnegation of previous experience. Undoubtedly some schools secure rapid adaptation of protean pupils to an educational approach irreconcilable with what they have known hitherto. Such deceptively effective practice can in no way contribute to continuity of educational experience for it repudiates the value of previous learning. The title of this chapter seems to imply that a precise statement can be made as to the nature of 'the problem of continuity'. Clearly, no such simple statement is possible for problems are manifold, but at the core of many difficulties is failure of teachers in one sector of education to get to know and respect what colleagues across the divide are doing. As Andy Stillman (1984a) comments, 'There is no point in reaching curriculum agreement across transfer if the receiving teacher

13

still feels the necessity to go over the material
again just to make sure the pupils have learnt it
"properly" this time!'

Chapter Two

CONTINUITY IN ITS HISTORICAL CONTEXT 1870-1944

Recent expansion of interest in continuity of
educational experience seems to be related to the
increasing complexity of educational provision.
When the system of schooling was simpler, one would
expect a pupil's educational continuity to be more
easily achieved. In the early days of compulsory
education, children of the labouring classes spent
five or six years within one institution. Board
schools 'were self-contained and not preparatory to
a grammar school or any other education'. (Lawson
and Silver, 1973) 'Continuity' is an inappropriate
word to describe a pupil's progress through the
'standards', for a limited curriculum, the
mechanical routine and rote learning, inspected and
paid for according to the Code of Grants laid down
by Government, produced an effect which a former
inspector described as having been 'devised for the
express purpose of arresting growth and strangling
life'. (Holmes, 1911) A system so minutely
prescribed and rigidly controlled by Whitehall,
however, could never display any of the curricular
intricacies modern educationalists recognise. The
system of schools for the upper and middle classes
was in no way co-ordinated by Government; the
curriculum in such schools was vastly different from
that provided in the elementary school, being
predominantly literary in content to match the
aspirations of those who were of or wished to be
associated with the liberally-educated group in
society. Transfer from an elementary school to any
higher institution would have involved not only a
major change in curriculum but a reorientation in
the concept of the meaning and purpose of education.
Continuity, then, was maintained only within each of
the strictly demarcated systems.

The Scholarship Ladder

In the last quarter of the nineteenth century, attempts were made to organise for able pupils a systematic scholarship 'ladder' from elementary to grammar school education. The higher-grade school, still within the elementary tradition, sometimes acted as a transitional stage in the journey to the grammar school but ultimately the scholarship boy had to adjust to a major change in educational approach. The gap between what was regarded as sufficient for the lower-class child and what was regarded as the minimum for middle and upper-class children was enormous. For a minority of pupils transferring from elementary to secondary education, then, a sharp break in continuity occurred somewhere around the age of eleven. The Education Act of 1902 reaffirmed the pattern of parallel systems of elementary and secondary education that was to survive for a further thirty years. By the Regulations of 1904, affirmation was given to secondary education's highly academic curriculum devoid of technical or vocational bias. Three years later, secondary education became open to a much larger number of scholarship pupils from the elementary school when the Free Place Regulations of 1907 were evolved. For pupils gaining the much sought after places in secondary schools, the change in curriculum after transfer was extreme.

Liberalising of Elementary Education

In the first decade of the twentieth century was seen the start of that liberalising process which was to develop later into a primary school philosophy. The publication in 1904 of the Elementary Code and a year later of the associated Suggestions for the Consideration of Teachers marked the establishment of a freedom to determine the approach to curriculum cherished by a later generation of primary school teachers. The Suggestions were particularly significant since they established the right of any elementary school to determine for itself the methods and curriculum to be followed:

These suggestions as to methods are issued by the Board in the belief that they are calculated to lead to good results. They are not, however, intended to condemn the use of any methods which a teacher believes to be

> useful, more especially when his belief is
> confirmed by experience . . . . . The only
> uniformity of practice the Board of Education
> desires to see in the teaching of the Public
> Elementary Schools is that each teacher shall
> think for himself and work out for himself such
> methods of teaching as may use his powers to
> the best advantage and be best suited to the
> particular needs and conditions of the school.

For the first time, elementary school teachers were
not required to follow a uniform course of study:

> The number and the character of the subjects
> chosen and the extent to which the subjects
> chosen may be developed in the teacher's hands
> are left sufficiently open to enable individual
> authorities, managers and teachers free to
> adapt the instruction to local requirements.

No doubt it took time for elementary teachers to
grasp opportunities offered by this change in
policy; as Lowndes (1969) puts it, the Code was 'a
manifesto stating an ideal rather than describing
the average school'. From this period onwards,
however, the autonomy enjoyed by elementary schools
allowed them to develop a diversity impossible in
the secondary schools. The regulations for
secondary schools made very detailed recommendations
about what the curriculum must contain and the time
to be allocated to each subject. The development of
University-based school-leaving examinations acted
as a further influence for uniformity of curriculum
in the grammar schools.

By the beginning of the twentieth century,
then, no legislative or administrative action had
been taken to narrow the gap between the curriculum
of the elementary and that of the secondary school.
From 1907 onwards, as the scholarship ladder
widened, an increasing number of children
transferred from elementary to secondary education
at the age of eleven. Secondary schools depended
for their grant upon providing a quarter of their
places without fee for pupils from elementary
schools, but there was no extension for such pupils
of their elementary courses to fit them for the
higher school. Entrance was conditional upon
passing an attainment test after a 'thorough
grounding in the ordinary elementary subjects'. At
a time when the sharp contrast between elementary
and secondary education was being perceived at first

hand by those working-class children who had started
up the ladder, it is significant that successive
Board of Education annual reports should affirm the
unity of the educational process. Typically, the
Report for 1905-6 stated, 'Education is one. Any
dislocation of its course is at best but a necessary
evil. It ought to be continuously progressive from
the time when a child first goes to school up to the
time when school life ceases.' Yet there was an
admission within the reports that the secondary
school curriculum presented serious initial
difficulties to elementary school children. 'Range
of knowledge in some specific subject' was considered to be less important than a scholar's
'capacity and quickness of mind' and since the
elementary school pupil was selected from a wide
field of competitors, it was thought he would be
'adaptable and clever enough after a few months'
special attention to the subjects in which he is
deficient to hold his own without difficulty among
pupils of his own age'.

Secondary Education for All

In the first two decades of the twentieth
century there was increasing pressure from the
Trades Union Congress and the National Union of
Teachers for the development of some form of
secondary education for everybody. The slogan of
the period 'secondary education for all' was used as
the title of a Labour Party policy document of 1922
edited by R.H.Tawney, who was later to become a
member of the Hadow Committee. The Education of
the Adolescent, the Hadow Report of 1926,
recommended a major revision in the relationship
between elementary and secondary schools. No longer
should there be two parallel systems in which pupils
moved along separate and distinct paths; instead,
all pupils were to pass from a 'primary' to a
'secondary' stage of education at about the age of
eleven. The Consultative Committee recommended,
indeed, that the move should be to a new
institution:

> We desire to mark as clearly as possible the
> fact that at the age of 11 children are
> beginning a fresh phase in their education,
> which is different from the primary or
> preparatory phase, with methods, standards,
> objectives and traditions of its own.

What reservations there were about change of school were concerned with the disadvantages to the 'decapitated' elementary schools rather than to the promoted scholars. By losing their older and brighter pupils, teachers at the primary stage might be deprived of a source of interest and stimulus. The transferred pupils, however, would benefit by moving to new buildings, completely separated from their previous schools, by meeting new staff and by being introduced to a curriculum 'new and different from anything in the existing schools'. The new post-primary schools were, of course, to be additional to existing academic secondary schools. Following Hadow reorganisation, all pupils, not merely those passing the scholarship, were to change school. The need for continuity of primary and post-primary school curricula did not warrant particular emphasis. Far more concern was given to practical aspects: the buildings to be used, problems of transporting pupils in rural areas and the cost of the whole exercise. Some commentators have seen continuity as implicit in Hadow's recommendation that the curriculum should be planned as a whole but one must also accept it as approving the first breach in continuity of educational experience for pupils of average or below-average ability.

The Primary School

The Consultative Committee's next task, completed in 1931, was to inquire and report as to the courses of study suitable for children between the ages of 7 and 11 in elementary schools. In its report, The Primary School, specific reference was made to the need for continuity:

> The process of education, from the age of five $\flat$ to the end of the secondary stage, should be envisaged as a coherent whole, . . . there should be no sharp division between the infant, 'junior', and post-primary stages, and . . . the transition from one stage to the succeeding stage should be as smooth and gradual as possible.

This was stated, however, in the context of a declaration that the primary stage could be regarded as 'forming so marked a period in the physical and mental development of the average child' that it demanded 'special treatment and special methods of

teaching'. That special treatment was to be thought
of in terms of 'activity and experience rather than
knowledge to be acquired and facts to be stored'.
    The Hadow Report on the Primary School,
reflecting as it did much of the progressive movement at work in education during the inter-war
period, offered the elementary school teacher
official endorsement of further release from
curricular constraint. It is difficult to assess
the extent of the adoption of less formal techniques
advocated at the time, particularly since there was
no obligation upon teachers to accept official
recommendations. Such approaches, however
influential at primary school level, were 'resisted
at the level of secondary education, which was more
firmly wedded to academic courses, formal teaching
and examination requirements'. (Lawson and Silver,
1973) Thus the gap between the approach to
curriculum in the progressive primary school and the
traditional secondary school widened and the
potential for discontinuity at transfer increased.
Undoubtedly, this was the very antithesis of the
Consultative committee's intentions. It is
significant that one of their principal recommendations was that 'teachers in all types of secondary
school should keep in close touch with the teachers
of contributory primary schools and departments'.
As we shall see, little resulted from this
recommendation. Indeed, over 40 years later, a
Schools Council research group in its initial report
on a Middle Years of Schooling Project was to show
that little had been done to effect successful
transfer from primary to secondary schools:

> In some cases a secondary school will receive
> no more than a set of record cards from
> contributory primary schools, in other areas
> these will be supported by tests of
> intelligence and attainment set by the local
> authority. Personal contact between schools is
> likely to be minimal or even non-existent, and
> attitudes cordial, suspicious or even hostile.
> (Badcock et al, 1972)

Selection for Secondary Education

    Following the Hadow Report, interest in
continuity between successive stages of education
was centred on methods of selecting primary-school
pupils for the available kinds of secondary
provision. Paradoxically, Hadow had both a

liberating and a constraining influence on the
primary-school curriculum. Though encouraged to
adopt informal methods, the primary teacher was
also, by Hadow's endorsement of the hierarchical
structure of secondary education, inevitably
involved in selection procedure. In that the
selection examination was commonly limited to
testing proficiency in English and arithmetic,
schools concentrated on these two subjects and more
narrowly upon their 'testable' aspects. (Perkins,
1936) In 1937, a grammar-school headmaster was so
concerned about the effects of selection testing
that he conducted a survey of his scholarship
winners to discover whether their junior-school
curriculum 'had been narrowed to meet the requirements of the impending examination'. He concluded
that 'for the scholarship candidates, the curriculum
consisted of very little besides English and
arithmetic'. In an extreme case, 'not even
scripture' was included in the course of study.
(Hecker, 1937) In the most liberal of elementary
schools, examination pressure exerted a powerful
influence on the curriculum. A headmistress,
commended by Susan Isaacs for her innovative
approach to junior-school work, could admit that her
arithmetic schemes contained more than was of
practical use to her pupils solely because in
entrance and scholarship papers far too much was
expected. (Warr, 1937) Typical of elementary
teachers of the period, she cautioned against making
the junior stage merely a preparation for the next
one. Many teachers in the secondary sector,
however, took a contrary view. Their attitude was
effectively reported by the editor of the 1937 Year
Book of Education:

> The whole educational system must be viewed as
> a unit into which the Junior School is placed
> to perform a definite function. That function
> is two-fold: to complete the work of the
> Infant School, and at the same time to prepare
> for all forms of post-primary education.

That the junior school was failing to fulfil this
role there seemed no doubt. It was claimed there
was a difference not only in degree but in kind
between the education provided in the primary and
post-primary sectors. Further, it was suggested
that within a group of junior schools there should
be 'some definite agreement as to syllabus and
methodology'. (Usill, 1937)

The Spens Report

It is the Consultative Committee's recommended policy of tripartite selection by which the 1938 Spens Report on secondary education is best known. Although it made no direct comment on the need for co-operation between successive stages of education, nevertheless, some of its conclusions and recommendations have implications for curriculum continuity. Because of its advocacy of a possible second transfer at about the age of 13, it recommended the curriculum for pupils in the first two years of secondary education should be broadly identical in different types of post-primary school. It was felt that a second transfer was necessary to eliminate initial mistakes in allocation and to encourage special aptitudes particular pupils might have developed. But this could only be achieved smoothly if common curriculum was provided for children between the ages of eleven-plus and thirteen-plus. Although the primary school would have to pass its pupils on to three different types of secondary school, at least, theoretically, it could envisage an initial unified approach to post-primary curriculum at the time of transition. Consonant with the Hadow Report's recommendation that the curriculum of the primary school be thought of in terms of activity and experience, Spens suggested secondary-school studies should be seen as 'modes of activity to be experienced' rather than 'bodies of facts to be stored'. It was argued that the content of the curriculum in some secondary schools was 'such as to distort the teaching in the primary schools' and to improve the situation, Spens urged 'in the secondary school the pupil's studies must be retrospective in so far as they are based on what has gone before' as well as 'prospective in so far as they look forward to maturer studies'.

Appearing as it did only nine months before the outbreak of the Second World War, it is unlikely the Spens Report could have had anything like the impact of its predecessors. When the Government did eventually formulate proposals for educational reconstruction, the only Spens Committee recommend-ations to be influential were those related to the establishment of grammar, modern and technical schools. Those of the Consultative Committee's proposals that would have had effect on curriculum continuity were restated in official literature but not activated by local authorities.

1939-1945 War

At the beginning of the 1939-1945 war, the Government concentrated efforts on saving lives of as many children as possible; the continuation of an education service was an important though inevitably secondary matter. For many months it was impossible to guarantee continuity in a child's education. The Government Evacuation Scheme effected a complete dislocation of the system: in evacuation areas, schools were often completely closed; in reception areas, shift systems were frequently operated, the separate organisation of junior and senior schools occasionally abandoned, and alternative, often unsuitable premises utilised to accommodate an expanded school population. (Padley and Cole, 1940) A particular cause of difficulty was the difference in development in terms of Hadow reorganisation between urban and rural areas. Practice operating in receiving schools was frequently different from that in evacuating schools. As the war intensified, retired teachers were reinstated to replace younger ones drawn into the armed services, replacements for worn-out text books and materials became difficult to obtain, and pupils came to lessons tired on account of the exigencies of living in a country at war. Curriculum activity was low in the list of priorities. Evacuation had been devised as a contingency for saving lives. Undoubtedly it had this effect but of greater long-term significance was its influence on post-war social reform. Differences in educational provision were not as readily tolerated by those who had been sensitized to the inequalities inherent in the system.

Education Act of 1944

The Education Act of 1944, eighteen years after Hadow's recommendations, recast the system into one of continuous stages: 'primary', 'secondary' and 'further' were to replace 'elementary' and 'higher' education. The Ministry of Education's interpretation of the Act's provision that there should be 'variety of instruction and training' to suit 'the different ages, abilities and aptitudes of pupils' was that there should be distinct types of secondary education provided in different schools:

> Everyone knows that no children are alike. Schools must be different too, or the Education Act of 1944 will not achieve success. They

23

> must differ in what they teach and how they
> teach it, just as pupils differ in tastes and
> abilities. (Ministry of Education, 1947)

Obviously, such a prescription could present
difficulties to the primary school if it were to
have to co-ordinate its curriculum with three
distinct types of secondary school. The Ministry
confirmed, however, the Spens recommendation that
the first two years of secondary education should be
general in all types of school; the curriculum
should contain many common elements in order that
transfer from one school to another could be
effected smoothly.

In reality, grammar schools did little or
nothing to adjust their courses in order to achieve
some overlap with work appertaining elsewhere in the
secondary sector, whilst the modern school's
'watered down' academic curriculum for pupils in the
first years after transfer seems far removed from
the notions of equivalence contained in Government
statements following the 1944 Education Act. The
main types of secondary school developed in
isolation. It would have been impossible, therefore
for primary schools to undertake specialised
preparation for the secondary stage. In any case,
such a practice was not deemed desirable in that the
role of the primary school was merely to provide a
very broad preparation for a later stage; as a
teacher-training text of the day put it: 'Junior
education must open up new fields of study and lay
the foundations for the pursuit of knowledge focused
along particular channels during the secondary phase
of school life.' (Daniel, 1947)

Though the Butler Act of 1944 conceived of
education as 'a continuous process' there was felt
to be no incongruity in accepting there should be a
decided break at about the age of eleven. The
primary school's functions were regarded as being to
broaden, consolidate and stabilize a child's basic
skills before classifying him for what was deemed to
be the most suitable form of secondary education.
The process of classification bore a remarkable
resemblance to that of selection, the effects of
which had provoked the Board of Education's
disapproval hitherto. 'The curriculum is too often
cramped and distorted by over-emphasis on
examination subjects' complained the White Paper on
Educational Reconstruction of 1943. Sixteen years
later, that statement was reiterated in the Ministry
of Education's updated Handbook of Suggestions.

Eleven-plus

The dominance into the late 1950s of the eleven-plus examination and its lack of relevance to work in schools at either side of the age divide has been documented by pupils and teachers. Razzell's comments seem particularly pertinent. As a practising teacher, he argued that the qualities which had to be trained and developed for pupils to be able to answer abstruse questions devised by examining officials bore no relationship to philosophies postulated in Government documents. An over-concentration on speed, quick-thinking and accuracy in arithmetic, and the writing of essays in English within a short time-span 'was scarcely the best way to begin a study of mathematics or creative writing. It gave a wrong concept of what these disciplines were about.' (Razzell, 1968)

For those pupils who failed the test, most local authorities gave the opportunity of a 'second chance' at the end of their first year in a secondary modern school. Partridge catalogued the disruption which this caused, with pupils being shuffled around the ability streams in mid-term in order to group together all those who stood any kind of chance in the second attempt at the eleven-plus. His verdict on this system was that pupils had spent at least two years of their schooldays cramming for the eleven-plus, or at least had been neglected for two years while their brighter brothers had been so prepared. (Partridge, 1966) For the less-able child, the eleven-plus acted as an irrelevant interruption to education whereas for the brighter pupil it marked a significant change in approach; for both it effected a break in curricular continuity.

One of the major effects of the 1944 Education Act was to establish the age of eleven as the administrative watershed between primary and secondary stages of education. At eleven, pupils crossed 'as straight a frontier in time as the 49th parallel is in space'. (Central Advisory Council for Education, 1963) The move to secondary schools often required children to make rapid adjustments to markedly different kinds of study from those they had experienced hitherto; this was particularly so for pupils who gained places in a grammar school. Jackson and Marsden (1966) have described the uncertainty and confusion experienced by working-class children on grammar-school entry. Many of their problems were caused by having to cross social boundaries but insecurity was heightened by changes in routine:

> On top of this came the new subjects, the new vocabulary (not 'kept in' but detention, not 'playtime' but 'break' - and was it 'yard' or 'playground' or 'cloisters'?) the masters' gowns, the prefects, the whole body of customs, small rights and wrongs, that any well-developed grammar school holds. Some of the schools made a practice of teaching the new children aggressively for the first weeks to 'break them in', and presumably, to nip behaviour problems in the bud. The effect on children already bewildered was to knock them off balance.

The vestiges of this approach can still be observed in some of our schools today. During my research on continuity and liaison I was invited to observe the way one comprehensive school introduced new pupils to secondary education. Head, deputy head and first-year co-ordinator had anticipated many of the pupils' anxieties. First years arrived an hour before the rest of the school to avoid being over-whelmed in the company of over a thousand, sizeable fellow pupils for the first time. There was a welcoming talk, a gentle introduction to the few 'essential school rules' and a warm reception by form tutors. After break, regular time-tabled lessons began. The group I joined met their mathematics teacher for the first time. He left them in no doubt that what they had done previously would not satisfy him. Slipshod and untidy work would result in detentions and they would be well-advised to get into his way of doing things rapidly or they would be 'for it'. The teacher concerned had used the same approach to initiating pupils for many years, in fact since he started teaching in the same building, then a grammar school in the 1950s.
    Passing the eleven-plus was the uppermost educational issue for many pupils and even more parents during the post-war period. The prevailing issues discussed at length in documents emanating from Government and the academic world were those of differentiation of curricula and dominance of selection procedures; both of these affected continuity adversely. Continuity of curriculum, if it was considered at all, was seen to be peripheral to ideological concerns that had exercised educationalists throughout the twentieth century -

equality of educational opportunity and secondary
education for all.

HAROLD BRIDGES LIBRARY
S. MARTIN'S COLLEGE
LANCASTER

Chapter Three

CONTINUITY AS AN ISSUE OF IMPORTANCE AFTER 1944

Accepting 'progressive' schools were still in the
minority, the Plowden Committee noted 'the extent as
well as the profundity of the changes' that had
taken place in primary education since the war. In
the secondary sector, changes had been different in
character albeit fundamental in effect, involving
widespread experiment in reorganisation strategies
leading towards a comprehensive system of schools
and replacement of tripartism of the immediate post-
war period. Scholastic segregation based on
examination at the age of eleven-plus became
increasingly suspect as research results were
published. These developments impinged on the
nature of transition from one stage of schooling to
the next and further complicated issues of
curriculum continuity.

Demise of the eleven-plus

    Mention has already been made of dominance up
to the late 1950s of the selection examination but
whereas formal written papers in basic subjects had
been the main constituent of tests in the 1930s,
there was an increasing dependence upon determining
intelligence in the post-war period. As Richmond
(1978) puts it:

    For hard-pressed administrators, faced with
    the ticklish problem of allocating 'special
    places' which were always in short supply, the
    Intelligence Quotient was a godsend. Here, it
    was thought, was an infallible, exact and
    objective yardstick **and** a perfect predictor
    of a pupil's academic performance.

Doubts about the validity of intelligence testing
arose, however, during the 1950s. A particularly
influential report from the British Psychological
Society refuted the notion that such tests were
solely a measure of inborn ability but stated that
they were partly dependent upon educational
experience. (Vernon, 1957) Published in the same
year, a report by the NFER showed that even when the
most sophisticated and costly selection techniques
were used, it was not possible to eliminate a ten
per cent error in the allocation of children at the
age of eleven. (Yates and Pidgeon, 1957) The error
would be even greater in those local authorities
whose restricted finances prohibited such thorough
testing. Indeed, it was calculated that to ensure
the academically-able minority was given a chance to
work for external examinations, 70 per cent of the
eleven-year-old age group would need to be admitted
to grammar school. (Yates, 1971) Psychologists
clearly refuted the use of intelligence testing as a
regulator, 'a turnstile through which people are
allowed to pass only in single file on production of
standardized credentials'. (Pedley, 1964)
    Sociologists contributing to the debate
expressed concern that the eleven-plus examination
discriminated against working-class children.
(Floud, Halsey and Martin, 1956) It seemed there
were inequalities of educational opportunity
inherent in the system of selective schooling. In
some areas there were moves to abolish the eleven-
plus more as a gesture of reform than as a solution
to the problem. (Shipman, 1972) Official recognition of the eleven-plus problem was voiced in the
Ministry of Education's 1958 document, Secondary
Education for All:

> We must eradicate a more general defect in our
> system of education - a defect which is the
> root cause of the concern that is currently
> felt over what has come to be known as the
> '11-plus examination'. The fact is that there
> are today, too many children of approximately
> equal ability who are receiving their
> education in schools that differ widely both
> in quality and in the range of courses they
> are able to provide. And this means that a
> number of these children are not getting as
> good opportunities as they deserve.

Clearly, the selection examination had failed to
classify pupils into academic, technical and

practical groups with any degree of scientific accuracy, as Norwood had imagined it could. Now it was acknowledged that in grammar and modern schools there could be overlap in the orientation of pupils. Further support for critics of the secondary selection process appeared in 1959 when the Central Advisory Council report 15 to 18 provided a measure of the inefficiency of the eleven-plus test:

> The longer the period for which a system of selection is asked to predict, the greater the subsequent need for redistribution. Much careful research work has shown pretty clearly that a fresh classification after four years i.e. about the age of 15, would have redistributed between selective and non-selective schools about 14 per cent of the pupils. By the time they join up for National Service this 14 per cent has become 22 per cent among Army recruits and 29 per cent among the more homogeneous group of RAF recruits, according to the evidence of the National Service Survey.

Widespread anxiety among parents, stimulated by exposure of the issue in the press, together with a growing concern expressed professionally, led to a gradual change in LEA policy. But it was over a decade before a significant number of authorities had abandoned selection procedures altogether. It was evident from the four-yearly surveys conducted by the NFER into local authority procedures for allocating pupils to secondary education that it was not until 1968 that major changes were noted. By then, 16.6 per cent of local authorities had completely abolished allocation procedures whereas only 1.5 per cent had done so at the time of the previous survey in 1964. (NFER, 1969) It was anticipated that the pace of change would increase after 1968 for of 131 authorities still using selection tests, 104 stated that they had plans to abolish allocation altogether. In fact, only 24 of those authorities, 31 per cent of the total, did abolish allocation procedures by 1972 when the next survey was conducted, although a further 35 per cent abandoned selection procedures in part of their areas. The effects of the eleven-plus, so dominant in the early post-war period, faded away only gradually. With the election of a Labour Government in 1964, early abolition of eleven-plus examinations seemed assured but the adoption of political persuasion rather than governmental legislation considerably delayed the process, (Parkinson, 1970)

Changes in Primary Education

The restrictive effect on the junior-school curriculum of the selection examination has already been mentioned. There is no lack of commentary in support of this view. According to Blyth (1965), 'the backwash effects of the eleven-plus examination, with their encouragement to teachers to limit themselves more and more to basic skills reinforced a tendency to ignore the wider potentialities of language and mathematics'. Marsh (1970) wrote of the examination's 'depressing effect on a teacher's expectations'. Richmond (1978) felt that the stresses and strains experienced by those concerned with eleven-plus selection 'vitiated and distorted the work of junior schools'. It was accepted by the Plowden Committee that the selection system had been partly influential in bringing about 'less enterprising primary schools' yet its National Survey suggested that the worst effects of selection, including a narrowing of the primary-school curriculum, were lessening 'perhaps because teachers' estimates were tending to replace externally-imposed attainment tests'. In 1968, the NFER Survey noted a pronounced decline in the use of attainment tests and essays and this trend continued during the next four-year period.

It is tempting to ascribe the development of informal methods in primary schools - and therefore, as we shall see, a further divergence from secondary-school practice - to a reduction in eleven-plus pressure. This is the opinion of many commentators and is voiced particularly by American observers of the English progressive primary school in the early 1970s. (Fisher, 1972) As Deanne Boydell (1978) points out, however, forces underlying the dramatic change in primary education over the past twenty years or so 'are not fully understood although factors like disillusionment with eleven-plus and streaming undoubtedly played some part'. Whatever the reasons, there is no doubt that there has been a gradual increase in informality in primary schools over recent years. This change is often designated 'progressivism', sometimes in approbation, more often pejoratively (Bantock, 1975) It is unfortunate that such a term has been used frequently to describe any form of education other than that which conforms to

traditional attitudes. Although owing something to
the 'New School' and 'New Education' movements, most
primary schools are not as radical as the term
'progressive' implies. (Skidelsky, 1969) Indeed,
the Plowden Committee refrained from using the term
at all preferring to categorise schools as 'quite
clearly good'. In such schools the content of
courses would be the same as in more traditionally-
organised establishments but the approach, the
motivation, the emphasis and the outcome different:
children's own interests were central to the Plowden
ideal and the teacher was to be 'alert to provide
material, books or experiences for the development
of their ideas'. The most explicit statement of its
basic philosophy was presented in the chapter on
aims of primary education. The school should be 'a
community in which children learn to live first and
foremost as children and not as future adults'. It
should set out deliberately 'to devise the right
environment for children, to allow them to be
themselves and to develop in the way and at the pace
appropriate to them'. It should 'lay special stress
on individual discovery, on first-hand experience
and on opportunities for creative work' and should
insist that 'knowledge does not fall into neatly
separate compartments'.

Thus, paradoxically, the Plowden Report, which
devoted a whole chapter to continuity and
consistency between stages of education, can be seen
by its apparent encouragement towards progressivism
to have widened the gap between the free primary
school and the essentially formal secondary school.
(Peters, 1969) But as Wright (1977) has pointed
out, 'it was not so much a **cause** of progressivism
as a legitimisation; its major impact was probably
to make people already doing it feel more confident
about doing it'. Almost a decade before Plowden was
published, the tenor of official comment on the
primary school indicated a promotion of child-
centred and discovery methods. The Ministry's
updated handbook of suggestions maintained that
'concern with children as children' was a salient
feature of primary education and that concern
involved 'being aware of the child as a whole with
inter-dependent spiritual, emotional, intellectual
and physical needs'. Further, children's efforts
were most effective 'when sustained by some urge
within themselves - by curiosity, interest (whether
direct or caught from someone else) or the urge to
express, make or do'. (Ministry of Education, 1959)
Clearly, long before Plowden's endorsement of

progressive methods, emphasis in many primary
schools was firmly placed upon the child as an
active participant in the learning process.

Although the change that had occurred had been
gradual, it was nevertheless fundamental involving a
move away from a teacher-directed, text-book
dominated approach to one that was open-ended and
child-centred. As Plowden noted, there was a
decided lack of educational theory to support many
of the developments in primary education which were
more in response to teachers working intuitively and
being sensitive to the needs of children. Compared
with secondary colleagues, primary teachers were,
and still are, in a better position to experiment
and introduce new organisational and curriculum
change. Working independently within their own
classrooms, they have a freedom denied to secondary
teachers who need to persuade departmental
colleagues and engage school administrators in
sometimes long and tedious negotiations before
significant change can be effected. From the 1950s
onwards, primary schools experienced change upon
change. Razzell identifies the fluctuating pattern
of junior education in terms of 'the breakdown of
time-table tyranny', an increasing self-discipline
in children who became more involved in learning how
to learn rather than in being taught, and an
increase in the facets of a teacher's task because
of new techniques and the proliferation of
equipment.

To catalogue the many changes that took place
in primary education during the 1950s and 1960s is
beyond the scope of this work but mention must be
made of some of them for they helped to accelerate
the movement, already well under way, from a
relatively uniform system to one so heterogeneous
that contact between primary and secondary schools
inevitably became random. There were fundamental
changes in primary-school design. The old type of
school with its self-contained classrooms for each
teacher-group of children was superseded by open-
plan buildings of a more flexible nature with shared
teaching areas, small quiet rooms and work bays for
specific activities. Though the major thrust in
open-plan building did not occur until the early
1970s, there was continuing debate in the previous
decade about the implications of working in an open
environment. As far as organisation was concerned,
there was a steady reduction in streaming. The
Plowden Committee noted that while 85 per cent of
primary teachers favoured streaming in 1962, replies

to their own survey indicated that 'only 34 per cent
approved of streaming for all or most junior
children, 25 per cent approved of streaming for
older pupils and 30 per cent were hostile'. In
spite of Plowden's reservations, there was some
development of 'family' or 'vertical' grouping.
Miss E. Moorhouse (1970) one of those who submitted
evidence to the Plowden Committee, subsequently
wrote that such grouping was 'spreading rapidly in
many parts of Britain'. She suggested that the
typical approach being adopted in a primary school
of 560 children aged five to eleven involved a
change from the standard 'two classes of children in
each of the seven age-groups in A and B streams' to
'six parallel classes of children from five to seven
years of age, four parallel classes of seven-plus to
nine-plus and four parallel classes of nine-plus to
eleven-plus'. Plowden accepted there could be
advantages to vertical grouping in the infant school
but was not convinced that junior children would
benefit from being taught in a 'double age group'.
It was more enthusiastic about team teaching,
although not quite sure how to define it. There is
no evidence to suggest that the more developed forms
of team teaching on the American pattern were in use
in British primary schools in the 1960s but there is
no doubt that there was much collaborative teaching.
Indeed, the development of open-plan building almost
made a team approach obligatory. We have to
recognise the interdependence of different
innovations: 'Changes in curriculum, in methods of
teaching and examining, in school organisation, and
in school buildings, are all interrelated. (Bassett,
1970)
     As far as curriculum in the primary school is
concerned, the dominant trend during the 1960s was
undoubtedly towards 'the unified method'. Over
thirty years of development from Hadow's conception
of the 'activity and experience' curriculum had led
to a proliferation of project approaches aimed at
developing in pupils skills, insights and attitudes
rather than absorption of factual material. Plowden
welcomed such practices in that they made good use
of the interest and curiosity of children, but
warned they need not always lead to active
participation in learning. In that 'children's
learning does not fit into subject categories' the
undifferentiated curriculum was preferred. It was
suggested that one of the most effective ways of
integrating the curriculum was to 'relate it through
the use of the environment to the boundless

34

curiosity which children have about the world about them'. Following Plowden, there was a rapid development of interest in the educational use of the environment with further promotion by both official agencies and individual teachers.

Plowden recommended the curriculum should be dealt with in terms of 'broad areas' and suggested language, science and mathematics, environmental study, and the expressive arts. Undoubtedly flexibility of approach was reflected in the practice of many junior schools in the 1960s but the majority were much more traditional, tending to organise the curriculum into separate activities if not into discrete subject divisions. Teachers who preferred to work in this way, however, were not absolved from making decisions about curriculum change for this was taking place within the subjects themselves. The growing complexity of primary teaching presented problems, as one commentator has noted:

> Despite the courses established by many LEAs to allow teachers to become more familiar with changing techniques, the spate of new information not only in mathematics but in science, English and French to say nothing of the creative arts has resulted in many teachers feeling that there is too much to absorb all at once. (Hughes, 1968)

For a century at least, mathematics in the primary schools had been 'largely arithmetic or, to be even more honest "doing sums"' (Boucher, 1970) Modern mathematics had extended this into a consideration of mathematical principles and relationships. The old arithmetic book with its hundreds of examples to labour through had become an anachronism. Science, which in the past had merely involved nature study, was broadened to include the physical sciences but adapted to suit a child-centred philosophy, as the basic tenets of the Nuffield Junior Science Project testify. In English, too, the emphasis had moved towards informal approaches with creative writing, 'themes', and the spoken word predominating. French, of course, was an entirely new subject as far as the majority of primary schools were concerned, having developed rapidly after the Nuffield Foreign Languages Teaching Materials Project was set up in 1963. The 1960s then was a period of radical ferment in primary school curriculum.

Diversity

The many innovations in curriculum and organisation combined with the lack of external controls, particularly after the demise of the eleven-plus test, led to great diversity in the primary sector. Schools of vastly different ethos could be found within walking distance of each other. In some schools radical changes had been made during the sixties; in others there had been few, if any, innovations. The possibility of such variety was in large measure owing to what Peters (1966) has described as the 'astonishing degree of autonomy accorded to headmasters, at every level in the school system in England, over matters to do with curriculum, syllabus, discipline and school organisation'. Though some have disputed that primary-school heads have such a degree of autonomy, there is no doubt of their 'strong discretion' and the fact that they are the major source of educational innovation in primary schools. (Kogan, 1973) Of course, some heads were innovative but others were reluctant to endorse 'new-fangled ideas'. To some extent, this accounts for the unevenness of curriculum provision across English primary schools.

For the primary teacher who does not diverge too far from the broad path determined by head-teachers, there are few constraints. According to Blackie (1967) a former member of HM Inspectorate, the class teacher in England has a freedom 'unparalleled in any other country in the world'. Morrish (1976) taking an extreme point of view suggests that within their own classrooms, teachers have 'full autonomy' resenting 'the intrusion of virtually any outsider whether headmaster, their peers, advisers or just parents'. A teacher's professional autonomy is the cornerstone of education in England; there is freedom to formulate curriculum objectives, to adopt or reject informal methods, to determine the emphasis to be placed on particular aspects of the syllabus - any influence exerted will be merely friendly and advisory. It is, for example, a salient feature of nationally-promoted curriculum projects that the professionally-mature, autonomous teacher is ultimately responsible for directing the course of pupils' learning. Suggested approaches and resource materials in a typical project are 'merely crutches' for interim use until teachers have made adaptations to suit their own situations. (Blyth et al, 1976)

Inevitably, this leads to extreme diversity.
The uniformity characteristic of elementary
education in the past is no longer evident in
primary schools. The layman's notion that such
schools can be thought of as either 'traditional' or
'progressive' can be expanded into a broad spectrum
within the bands of which there are further
differences. Mitchell (1970) a primary-school headmaster favouring modern methods found it impossible
to define such methods for so often the old and the
new were intermingled. Nash (1973) informs us that
whilst the Scottish schools in which he conducted
his research were generally organised along
traditional and formal lines, there were differences
of degree within schools: 'some classes were run
much more formally and strictly than others'.
Plowden's classification of primary schools into
nine categories would seem to be an oversimplifica-
tion of an extremely complex situation. The
diversity of approach that exists is perhaps
understandable given that the focal point of the
system is the child in contact with a teacher.

Differences in teacher orientation

The prevalent organisational structure of
primary schools - the class with its own teacher -
favours an inclination towards child-centred
education. Even when a school uses some alternative
arrangement such as vertical grouping, it tends to
retain the class base for 'membership of a class,
relationship with a class teacher, and territorial
security of the classroom are seen as basic needs of
the primary-school child'. (Ayerst, 1969) The
primary-school teacher has little to divert him from
the individual child, whereas within the secondary
sector, the variety of available responsibility can
be appreciated merely by considering status
terminology: 'Head of Year', 'Head of House', 'Head
of Department' etc. Furthermore, unlike teachers of
young children, secondary-school teachers are not
interchangeable; they mostly specialise in one or
two subjects which they teach to many children in
several classes. It is unlikely that a specialist
teacher will be required to teach outside his or her
own specialism, but the very nature of expertise can
mean that teachers become involved with hundreds of
pupils in a week. Moreover, a teacher may well come
into contact with these pupils only in relation to
their performance in one subject and so have a
narrow view of their intellectual and personal

characteristics. Thus there are sharp differences
of ethos between primary and secondary sectors
despite attempts that have been made to offset some
of the inherited inequalities arising from systems
of teacher education and training. In a study of
educational practice in member countries of the
OECD, differences in professional preparation in
different segments of an educational system were
suggested as a major cause of discontinuity. The
authors of the OECD's (1975) <u>Handbook on Curriculum
Development</u> were convinced that 'any attempt to
provide continuity between the primary and secondary
curriculum, if it is to be at all successful, must
include deliberate steps to bring teachers'
attitudes and practices closer together'.

Developments in the Secondary School

In the immediate post-war period, whereas
administratively there was homogeneity of primary
education, no distinctions being made between young
children, in the secondary sector, different types
of schooling emerged to meet the differences that
were considered to exist between children. Though
it was intended there should be parity of esteem
between grammar, modern and technical schools, there
was never any doubt they would be different types of
institution. In reality, so few technical schools
were developed that the essential differences
related not to three types of pupil but two - the
selected and the non-selected.

It was assumed that by virtue of long-standing
prestige, its graduate teaching force and its
striving after academic excellence, the grammar
school would continue much as before. No Ministry
guidance on curriculum was thus needed, for the
external examination structure would determine
grammar-school courses of study, which would become
increasingly more specialist as a pupil approached
entry to university, training college or one of the
professions. In the first few years, a pupil would
study at an elementary level an academic core of
subjects one at least of which might be pursued
eventually at university. In all probability, the
logical structure of the subject as a form of
knowledge would take precedence over its relevance
to the pupil at that early stage of post-primary
education. Thus, the approach in the grammar school
was the very antithesis of that in the typical
primary school.

The modern school, mainly for those who had
failed the eleven-plus examination, was to have a
practical and realistic rather than an academic
bias. There was to be a decided emphasis on workshop skills, domestic subjects, painting, modelling
and other forms of artistic expression. Social
studies would provide a more practical context for
the study of man than traditional history and
geography syllabuses. Conventional subjects were
not to be neglected, however, but a child-centred
approach was to be used in their presentation. In
contrast with the grammar school, the modern school
was to have something in common with the primary
school but as Baron (1969) pointed out: 'From their
earliest days many secondary-modern schools
struggled to free themselves from the ideological
factors responsible for their shaping.' They
attempted to gain prestige not only by adopting
higher-status rituals such as house systems and
school prefects but by entering some of their pupils
for external examinations. Initially, the
examination used by grammar schools, the GCE, was
not accessible to secondary-modern pupils for it had
been decreed that no one could enter for it unless
he had attained the age of sixteen by 1st September
of the year in which he proposed to take the
examination - a device designed by the Minister and
her advisers to ensure the modern school would not
be 'defiled by examinations'. For some time, an
external measure of a pupil's attainment was met by
using examinations set by such bodies as the College
of Preceptors or the Royal Society of Arts, but
eventually a change of regulations opened the GCE to
secondary-modern pupils. Some time later, the
Certificate of Secondary Education was developed for
their use.
For that increasing number of modern school
pupils who were entered for external examinations
during the 1960s, the subject-orientated curriculum
they followed probably represented a major contrast
with primary-school experience. It may be argued
examination courses are not followed by younger
secondary pupils but there is some evidence that
externally-validated examinations have the effect
of producing early specialization. (Barnard and
McCreath, 1970) A further consequence of the
introduction of examinations into the secondary-
modern school was, paradoxically, to promote both
unification and diversity: by reducing the
distinction of purpose between grammar and modern
schools, external examinations brought the two

institutions closer together while they added another variant to the type of secondary-modern school. By the time the Newsom Committee reported in 1963, half the secondary-modern schools in the country possessed fifth forms. There was some concern that the schools had veered too far from their intended course; the curriculum of non-academic pupils was being unduly influenced by the examination system. Hence the Advisory Committee's warning that schools 'should resist external pressures to extend public examinations to pupils for whom they are inappropriate'. It was thought academic courses were influencing an excessively large part of the programme for many pupils. The modern school had a special responsibility to offer non-examination pupils an educational experience which was worth while. 'Worth while' in Newsom terms meant 'deliberately out-going - an initiation into the adult world of work and leisure'.

Lawton (1978) suggests that in regard to curriculum theory and practice there are at least three popular sets of assumptions held by teachers, sometimes referred to as 'the child-centred view of education, the subject-centred or knowledge-centred view, and the society-centred view, i.e. education justified in terms of the supposed needs of society'. The secondary-modern school has traditionally been associated with the last of these theories; it has been categorised as the school in which pupils were offered 'life adjustment courses'. It was conceived, however, in the Hadow child-centred tradition and influenced by the grammar-school knowledge-centred curriculum; it therefore offered more diversity than its stereotype would suggest.

On transition from primary to secondary education, pupils inevitably encountered fundamental change irrespective of the particular type of school to which allocated. Organisational and social changes occurred whether transfer was to a secondary-modern or grammar school. The senior primary-school pupil became a junior secondary-school pupil. One class teacher was exchanged for several subject specialists. There were changes in school ethos. Expatiating on these changes, Blyth (1965) likened them to rites of passage from childhood to adolescence in preliterate societies. In some respects, greater change was involved in making transition from primary to grammar school than from primary to secondary-modern. Unlike the latter, the grammar school had a distinctive image.

There were, of course, differences of detail but the
'grammar ethos' was similar throughout the nation.
Jackson and Marsden (1962) have provided detail of
the ways in which pupils were given 'training in
tone which distinguished the grammar school from the
general community'. Indeed, they commented on the
aggressive approach to teaching in the first few
weeks to 'break pupils in'. The modern school had
no equivalent set of basic values to impart.
Because there were about three modern schools to
every grammar school, they tended to serve a more
limited locality. As neighbourhood schools they
would have found it difficult to impose values out
of sympathy with those of the immediate community. A
secondary-modern pupil would be less likely to
undergo difficulties such as those encountered by
children in the Jackson and Marsden sample when they
moved out of their neighbourhood to the grammar
school. Whereas the grammar-school entrant was
inevitably faced with the task of making new peer
relationships, the modern pupil would generally have
the support of friends, for classes often moved en
bloc from the primary school. Another advantage
related to the type of teacher encountered by the
modern pupil, for the majority of secondary-modern
teachers received professional preparation in the
same type of institution as primary colleagues.
Furthermore, their courses, according to a college
principal writing in the mid-sixties, were very
similar if not the same: 'the colleges have resisted
the introduction of any sharp division between
students preparing for service in primary and
secondary schools and the course for both follows
broadly the same pattern'. (Peirson, 1965) Though
the secondary-modern school child was presented with
much that was new in his extended environment, he
could expect similarity of attitude between new
teachers and those in the former school. For the
eleven-plus failure, there could be some advantage
vis-a-vis the transitional process over more
successful counterparts entering a prestigious
grammar school.

The development of comprehensive schools

The validity of segregation by use of eleven-
plus tests was increasingly open to question during
the 1950s and early 1960s. As a viable form of
organisation, tripartitism had a brief life but it
resulted in the development of a system of schools
related to its underlying philosophy. In making its

41

request to local authorities in Circular 10/65 to
produce schemes for reorganisation, the Labour
Government had to accept that many comparatively
small but by no means outdated buildings would have
to continue in use within a comprehensive plan. The
result was that six varieties of reorganisation were
approved. Although the DES stated its preference
for all-through comprehensive schools for pupils
aged eleven to eighteen, it had to accept alternative tiered-school systems which were already either
in operation or proposed through local authority
initiatives. The strong tradition of allowing
autonomy to local authorities was maintained and
indeed enhanced for there was a lack of central
advice on comprehensive reorganisation, resulting in
approval being 'bewilderingly various from area to
area'. National similarities in tripartite development could be attributed not only to guidance
contained in documents such as the Spens and Norwood
Reports but to information supplied by central
authority. No such guidance was offered in the
1960s (Benn and Simon, 1972) Given the range of
schemes sanctioned by government, there would be
great diversity of provision even after comprehen-
sivisation was completely effected, but by making
reorganisation permissive rather than mandatory,
Circular 10/65 protracted transition, allowing
schools of the tripartite era to coexist with
comprehensives for a considerable time. This
resulted in there being 'a range of provision of
perplexing variety with more than twenty different
age-ranges in operation between the ages of 5 and 18
years' (Williams, 1976) Following local government
reorganisation after the report of the Royal
Commission on Local Government was published in
1969, further complications arose. Many of the
enlarged authorities inherited a variety of patterns
of provision when they absorbed their smaller
predecessors. As a result, diversity was evident
not only between different local authorities but
within a single authority. The children of highly
mobile workers and of service personnel were
particularly disadvantaged in the possibility of
their having to move between totally different kinds
of school but similar problems could also occur when
pupils moved within a confined area. For example, a
pupil who had already spent a year in a large 11-18
comprehensive school, with a fully specialized
approach to the curriculum, could be transferred to
a 9-13 middle school of a third the size, in which
class teaching predominated. After a year in the

middle school, organisational transition returned
the pupil to a large institution in which he would
again be exposed to a differentiated approach to
curriculum. As such anomolies came to light, many
local authorities took steps allowing pupils to
remain in a school to which transfer had been recent
but parents were not always co-operative, particularly when the move of home had taken them some
distance from the school.
       Problems of this nature would seem to be
inevitable given that by the late 1970s only 12 of
105 local authorities in England and Wales had a
clear-cut 11-18 pattern of provision (DES, 1978)
The Director of Education for Humberside revealed
the extreme diversity existing within his authority
when he spoke at the DES Comprehensive Education
Conference held in York in December 1977. Fourteen
age ranges were in operation within the LEA, a
result of its having incorporated five former
authorities. It was pointed out that similar
curriculum objectives could be pursued in schools
with different age ranges but nevertheless, the
ethos of the schools would be different and to
pupils and their parents the age range of the school
assumed great importance as they moved about
the country or within one authority but between
different systems. Parents were usually anxious if
their children moved to a school with a younger age
range than the one to which they had been
accustomed. Of course, problems of this kind could
occur only when families moved into an area with
schools of a different age range but such mobility
is by no means uncommon between an inner city and
its urban fringe. Bower concluded: 'Study of an
area in Humberside involving a former county borough
and a surrounding country area found that
difficulties could generally be met by allowing
pupils to continue at existing schools if the
parents wished.' It is presumably as a result of
ad hoc solutions to the diversity problems
revealed at the York conference that a concluding
statement included the comment 'less importance
needs to be placed on particular patterns of
provision than has hitherto been thought necessary.
More important than the precise age at which pupils
transfer schools is the need to establish
continuity.' (DES, 1978b)   Though diversity of
provision must have an effect upon continuity of
educational experience, it is of concern to
relatively few pupils.

Table 3.1: Schools - changes in size and emphasis

	1950			1965			1976		
	a	b	c	a	b	c	a	b	c
Primary	23,133	171	100	22,882	187	100	22,685	213	95.6
Middle (deemed primary)	-	-	-	-	-	-	645	341	4.4
Middle (deemed secondary)	-	-	-	-	-	-	509	438	5.6
Modern	3,227	339	64.5	3,727	417	55	1,002	558	15
Grammar	1,192	422	30	1,285	559	25.5	477	619	7.5
Technical	301	241	4	172	492	3	23	652	0.4
Comprehensive	10	799	0.5	262	915	8.5	2,878	957	70
Other secondary	35	485	1	417	530	8	93	641	1.5

Key: a = The number of schools in each category
b = The average size of school in numbers of pupils
c = The percentage of pupils in each category of school, primary and secondary being considered separately

Another feature of the growth of comprehensive education, that of size of schools, affects the majority of pupils. There has been little development of the very large schools thought necessary in the early days of comprehensive schooling but there can be no doubt that schools have been getting bigger. (Bellaby, 1977) Between 1950 and 1976, there was an increase in the average number of pupils attending all types of school, whether primary or secondary (Table 3.1). At the point of transfer from primary to secondary, however, a really significant change occurred. Whereas in the 1950s, for the majority, this involved a move to a school with twice as many pupils, by the mid 1970s, secondary schools had, on average, increased to over three times the size of their contributory primaries. This, of course, masks the extreme possibility of a move from a two-teacher primary school to a comprehensive with over 2,000 pupils.

Although there are undoubted curricular advantages in a large school, there are major disadvantages in respect of the personal development of pupils. After considering much research evidence, Elizabeth Halsall (1973) concluded that the social environment of small schools was more favourable than that of large schools; in particular there was more pupil participation in activities and greater school satisfaction. She also gave support to those who have argued that large schools have great difficulty in providing adequate pastoral care for pupils. In a comparison between a fourteen-form-entry and a three-form-entry school, it was shown that 'close knowledge of children inside and outside the classroom was at most over twice as difficult . . . and at the very least one-and-a-half times as difficult' in the larger school. There was an even greater disparity between schools in the degree of difficulty experienced in exercising control and supervision outside the classroom: it was found to be at least three times as difficult in a fourteen-form-entry school as in a three-form-entry, at most nine times as difficult. When teachers had to contend with large numbers of children in a large school building, they suffered such an increase in the burden of control and supervision that they had insufficient time and energy to cope adequately with pastoral care, which was therefore less likely to be effective in this respect in a large school than in a small 'with all that this probably implies for the sense of security of the average pupil'. It would seem that discontinuity of educational experience is

inevitable when a pupil moves from a small primary
to a large secondary school, albeit for the
majority, as we shall see, this may be but a
temporary phase.

A further effect of secondary schools becoming
larger in relation to schools in the primary sector
has been the increased number of primary schools
from which comprehensive schools receive pupils. In
the 1950s, most secondary-modern schools received
their intake from some three or four primary schools
within the same locality. With the exception of
those few pupils who passed the selection examination, whole classes were received together.
Transfer of this kind had two major effects related
to continuity. Firstly, pupils of average ability
who were surrounded by many familiar faces felt more
secure than their brighter companions who often
faced a completely changed situation without the
support of friends. Secondly, in that so few
schools were involved, curriculum continuity was at
least possible. Blyth (1965) has shown how
'patterns of social grouping and norms of behaviour
and motivation may be carried forward when children
transfer with close friends from the same neighbourhood'. In his study of eight first-year classes in
a comprehensive school, he noted, 'for the first
half of the year, the children appeared to be
re-establishing something of the social and even
physical pattern which they had known in their
primary schools, often choosing as desk-partners
members of the previous classes'. Children who were
not members of one of the larger primary-school
contingents had a more difficult transition into
secondary-school society.

With the development of the large, all-through
comprehensive school, there was an inevitable
increase in the number of contributory primaries.
It was, of course, still probable that a pupil would
move with classmates when the allocation policy
involved the use of specific feeder schools or was
devised to associate a group of schools within a
confined catchment area. In their survey of methods
of allocation, Benn and Simon (1972) showed that 63
per cent of the then existing comprehensive schools
used such a 'feeder-school' or 'catchment-area'
approach. In some parts of the country, however, it
was felt that in order to achieve the comprehensive
school ideal, there should be a balance of intake to
obtain a cross-section of ability in each school;
occasionally, attempts were also made to achieve a
social and racial mix. Although this was a minority

approach - 11 per cent in the Benn and Simon survey
- it had a profound effect on continuity in that the
number of primary schools from which a comprehensive
could receive its pupils was increased considerably.
Burrows (1968) commenting on the difficulties faced
by secondary teachers in their attempts to achieve
smooth continuity, revealed that he had visited
schools which received pupils from more than 50
primary schools.

Manifestly, when a secondary school receives
its pupils from as many as 50 contributory primary
schools it is not going to be possible to achieve
close liaison to try to ensure continuity of
curriculum. Whilst there is some evidence that the
very size of schools had focused attention on
problems of transition, it seems that most effort is
directed towards familiarising pupils with the
schools they are about to join and to ensuring
adequate information about pupils is transmitted
between schools. Benn and Simon found that whilst
there was general agreement that the content and
methods of education were the joint concern of both
primary and secondary sectors, few arrangements had
been made for co-ordinating teaching method or
curriculum by those who responded to their
comprehensive-school survey. They saw it as
'symptomatic of the gulf between primary and
secondary education' that only one in four of their
survey replied to a question on curriculum
continuity:

> Those who did so referred to joint meetings and
> discussions (sometimes to study groups) on the
> teaching of mathematics, languages and science.
> But only two schools reported special arrange-
> ments involving, in one case, freeing heads of
> departments for one afternoon a week to visit
> feeder primary schools principally to discuss
> and ensure continuity of method in English,
> mathematics and French.

Again, such a commendable approach could only
operate with a limited number of feeder schools.
The head of a large urban comprehensive school
responded to one of the survey questions by stating,
'full information is passed on about pupils but co-
ordination of teaching methods or even subjects is
impossible'. The combination of large school size
and balanced-intake policy in allocation -
characteristic features of early comprehensive
development - exacerbated many of the continuity

problems already evident in the move from primary to secondary education.

Development of diverse approaches to the curriculum

During the 1960s there were several initiatives to change schools' curricula. Agencies such as the Nuffield Foundation and the Schools' Council undertook to plan and support major new curricula in the sciences, in mathematics, in English, in modern languages, and in the humanities. Of course, teachers were free to retain traditional methods and content if they so wished; indeed, the stated aim of the Schools' Council was 'to make available a wide range of materials and suggestions which schools might adopt or adapt as they felt to be desirable'. One result of the permissive nature of curriculum reform was to promote variation from school to school. In one school, history might be taught as a subject in its own right whilst in another it was incorporated into an inter-disciplinary course perhaps designated 'modern studies'. Similarly, religious education might be absorbed into the humanities or biology into environmental science. Changes in science and mathematics, the earliest of traditional disciplines to be considered for revision, were particularly difficult to assimilate. New curricula were not accepted without challenge. Typically, a critic of Nuffield Science complained, 'in the attempt to bring chemistry teaching up to date the Nuffield authors have produced a scheme of work which is so strained and ambitious that, like a piece of overstretched cloth, it has torn itself into holes. Little coherent remains'. (Bradley, 1971) Modern mathematics, too, divided the teaching profession. In the late sixties, Lyness (1969) HMI for mathematics, asserted that too many innovations had been introduced for the ordinary teacher who was expected to change content at too great a pace. 'It is better to teach well what one knows and has found to be of value than to fall victim to "modernisation" and teach badly what is unfamiliar and of doubtful value.' But there were those who claimed that in a time of rapid social and economic change it was incumbent on schools to make a positive response: 'surely it is time that we moved away from orthodox subject teaching with its content determined in a great measure by the demands of the Universities, and experimented with other and new approaches to the curriculum', was the comment of a grammar-school headmistress at a conference on the raising of the school-leaving age. (Lack, 1967)

Just as perfunctory reform in primary schools resulted in extreme diversity, so in the secondary sector there were differences from school to school. As polemic from the Black Papers testified, views concerning education are tenaciously upheld. The tendency to 'binary opposition' - the conflict between formal and informal, or traditional and progressive - which Lawton (1973) stated to be one of the most distressing features of educational discussion, certainly increased the possibility of discontinuity between primary and secondary sectors. There was a tendency when mentioning transfer difficulties caused by differences in ethos to characterise the primary school as 'progressive' whilst the secondary school was seen as a stronghold of traditionalism. Burrows (1968) for example, having itemized ways in which the primary school had been liberated from 'the restricting and distorting effect' of the eleven-plus, went on to lament the change which a pupil would face when he came into contact with secondary teachers, most of whom would be University graduates well-qualified in their subjects but lacking a working knowledge of psychological and sociological theory to enable them to understand the child. According to the Plowden Committee, one of the major virtues of the establishment of middle schools would be that they would enable the extension into what up to that time had been considered the secondary sector of 'the curriculum, methods and attitudes' of junior schools. Middle schools were certainly not to be dominated by secondary-school influences. Yet the very existence of secondary schools which were experimenting with curriculum innovation and of primary schools which were 'traditional' rather than 'progressive' admitted the possibility of an inversion of the discontinuity stereotype. The study by Nash (1973) of pupil transition in Scotland illustrated the way in which notions of primary and secondary modes of working could become confused. Primary teachers prepared pupils for a supposed strict secondary regime; secondary teachers introduced pupils gently through techniques abandoned by primary colleagues. Incorrect assumptions were being made at either side of the primary-secondary divide. Significantly, teachers were anxious to facilitate transition for their pupils but either through disinclination or lack of time they had been unable to speak to each other.

The potential for discontinuity was never greater than during the sixties and seventies when comprehensive reorganisation combined with curriculum innovation to produce extreme diversity of educational provision. Teachers were too busy contending with difficulties in their own schools to give much attention to relationships with other institutions. And even when they had shown an inclination to develop links with others, organisational complexity was a potent barrier, as the comments of a primary-school headteacher testify:

> We do not talk to one another. I mean talk -
> not communicate through a system of educational
> smoke signals. I know that some secondary
> schools have developed links with their
> contributory primary schools but the main
> obstacle to progress is always the same.
> So many schools are involved that it becomes
> organisationally impossible to achieve the
> closeness of contact that everyone desires.
> Methods vary so greatly between primary schools
> that plans for a smooth transition to secondary
> school must needs be a miracle of compromise.
> Whatever we do it seems that we must accept
> discontinuity as something inherent in the
> system. (Orsborn, 1977)

During the 1960s there was an increasing awareness of continuity problems. Within the Plowden Report, more consideration was given to this topic than there had ever been in a previous government-funded advisory report. In a full chapter devoted to continuity, such established issues as the avoidance of pupil strain at times of transfer, the need for contacts between teachers in successive stages of education, and the use of record cards were further discussed. By the implementation of one of its major recommendations, however, that of a change in the age of transfer and the establishment of middle schools, it was thought that many of the solutions to problems of continuity might be found. We shall consider middle school development in chapter six.

Chapter Four

THE NATURE OF THE PROBLEM

In spite of ubiquitous references to the need for establishing more effective continuity between progressive stages of education, there has been little direct research into the subject. There have been, however, several studies involving some consideration of school transfer. In this chapter, continuity will be reviewed from a research perspective in an attempt to clarify the nature of the problem.

When curriculum continuity has been mentioned in the past it has often been a marginal feature of research into some other aspect of transfer between successive educational stages. Early research was mainly concerned with selection processes. In order to find a procedure which would improve accuracy of selection, investigations were conducted into the predictive validity of assessments at the transfer stage. In the 1960s, research effort turned towards elucidating desirable ages for transfer. In the 1970s studies were concerned with pupil adjustment to secondary education after transfer. It is only in comparatively recent times that researchers have confronted curriculum continuity directly. Reflecting as they do contemporary dominant concern, it is interesting to note changes of emphasis in research studies. There has been a gradual but marked shift from investigations mainly concerned with administrative efficiency at time of transfer to those acknowledging that individual children experience difficulties during the whole transition period. Research into curriculum can appear remote from pupils; it is important to recognize 'whether the formal and wider curricula are devised for a class, a school or a people, and whatever variations they permit, still each individual constructs his or her own version of the curriculum'. (Blyth, 1984a)

THE NATURE OF THE PROBLEM

In the context of transition, research into
continuity must focus on pupils for they are the
only ones who can experience continuity - or the
lack of it.

Social Aspects of Transfer

The work of Nisbet and Entwistle (1966 and
1969) provides a useful starting point for a review
of associated research. Their study was established
in 1963 at the behest of the Scottish Council for
Research in Education to examine the question: 'At
what age should children in Scotland transfer from
primary to secondary education?' A five-year
research programme was set up to follow an age-group
of children, 3,000 in all, through the transition
period from the later years of primary to the end of
the second year of secondary school. At each age
from ten to thirteen, assessments of the performances and attitudes of children were collected. A
first report based on their preliminary findings was
published in 1965 in time to be considered by the
Plowden Committee. It recommended:

> A change of education - the transfer to a new
> curriculum and style of teaching - should be a
> gradual process extending over the whole period
> from age 10 to 13. These years should be
> regarded as a period of transition. Secondary
> education must develop naturally out of primary
> education throughout the period.

Though they could find no psychological evidence to
justify sudden changes in teaching method dependent
upon the age of a child, Nisbet and Entwistle
accepted such changes occurred on transfer from
primary to secondary schooling.

One of their concerns was to find whether
transition had any effects on the children concerned
and, if so, what these were. Their main analysis
was based on data obtained from a number of psychological tests but, additionally, children's
attitudes to transfer were obtained from analysis of
essays written by a representative sample of pupils.
The importance of social factors in relation to
primary-school attainment had already been noted in
the Plowden Report. Not only were these findings
reinforced by Nisbet and Entwistle but it was
suggested 'the social factor becomes even more
important at the stage of transfer into the
secondary school'. Clearly, differences in pupils'

52

background characteristics influence their experience of transfer. This study found that levels of parental education, type of accommodation, attitudes towards literacy and to some extent parental occupation - all distinguished significantly between pupils who improved after transfer and those who did not. This could account to some extent for the wide range in opinion of headmasters whose views on transfer had been surveyed as a first stage in the study. While some found the sharp division between primary and secondary education imposed a severe strain on some pupils and was for a few 'a traumatic experience from which they hardly recover', others felt that for the vast majority of youngsters, irrespective of ability, far from presenting difficulties, transfer was a stimulant. Nisbet and Entwistle suggested that such extremes of opinion could reflect head-teachers' liberal or conservative attitudes but it could be that their views were influenced by the predominant social background of their pupils.

Disadvantages obtaining to pupils from deprived home backgrounds were expounded in this study. Transfer, it was considered, adversely affected the attainment of the working-class child whose poorly-educated parents failed to give him the right sort of encouragement and could not appreciate the need for a quiet place to study. The typical child showing signs of difficulty lacked ambition and had a poor attitude to work in the primary school; this was paralleled by low academic motivation after transfer. Pupils particularly at risk at the time of transition, then, are those from low socio-economic backgrounds. This finding was endorsed by Spelman's (1979) study of pupil adaption to secondary education in Northern Ireland. He found that pupils most alienated in their attitudes to education after transfer were those of low verbal reasoning ability, those from manual backgrounds, those with no family connection with grammar school and those with no aspirations other than to do manual work.

One point that can be made, then, about problems of transfer is that deterioration is more pronounced among children from the lower socio-economic classes. Yet, in some local authorities, these children are subjected to an additional burden. In poor inner-city areas, old schools could be refurbished to house primary children from the immediate locality but very few buildings could be converted to accommodate the large secondary

population within a single comprehensive school.
Comprehensive schools were built mainly on the outer
fringes of cities where there were open fields and
plenty of space. Children from the poorest
districts in city centres were therefore the ones
required to travel furthest from home. To parents
of such children, school is geographically remote;
bus journeys are long and expensive; parent-school
contact is minimal.

The Extent of Problems

It is not surprising that an analysis of essays
written as part of the Nisbet and Entwistle study
revealed that children from the higher social
classes tended to adjust to secondary schooling more
quickly than other children. Although the essays
provided only a subjective and retrospective
impression of pupils' perceptions of transfer, they
gave an indication not only of the class of pupils
at risk but the extent of problems: 'It was possible
to estimate that as many as 57 per cent of the boys
and 64 per cent of the girls had experienced
identifiable problems in adjustment.' A term or so
after transfer, however, 80 per cent of the sample
preferred the secondary to primary school.
Indications from this study would seem to suggest
that for the majority of pupils, the trauma of
transfer was short-lived.
It is worth emphasising that some pupils experience no difficulties. Reporting on a small study
of continuity and liaison practices between a
Cambridgeshire 11-18 community school and its feeder
primaries, Frances Findlay (1983) observed that of
sixteen children interviewed prior to transfer only
one showed real anxiety about moving school. For
this girl, a half-day visit to the school was a
crucial experience which raised her confidence.
Visits by fourth-year primary-school pupils to their
future secondary schools are fairly standard; 92 per
cent of schools in the primary survey made such
arrangements. (DES, 1978a) Practice varies: sometimes pupils visit with their parents; more often
they are taken in class groups. Secondary schools
usually take the opportunity of imparting a large
amount of information on these occasions. Findlay
observed that pupils returning from such visits
could remember very little of what they had been
told. Though visits were successful in raising
confidence, they could have been used to better
effect if children had been able to ask more questions.

Further evidence of the transience of difficulties at the time of school change was presented
in a study conducted by Youngman and Lunzer (1977).
Based in Nottinghamshire, the research was concerned
to follow two large groups of pupils, one from urban
and one from rural schools, through and beyond the
transfer period. The majority of the first-year
intake to six schools were assessed in June,
September and December of the year in which they
transferred. The researchers were supplied with
measures of IQ, reading and mathematics ability, and
children were asked about areas of schooling which
they felt were particularly enjoyable or
disappointing. Towards the end of the first year in
the secondary school, 70 per cent of pupils agreed
with the extreme statement: 'This school is great',
78 per cent found lessons interesting and 94 per
cent thought their teachers were at least 'all
right'.

A local authority based study, similarly
concerned with a comparison of pupils' attitudes to
schooling before and after transfer also found that
the majority of pupils settled into secondary school
fairly soon. The Educational Development Centre of
Birmingham Education Department conducted research
into several aspects of continuity between the
primary or middle and the secondary stage of
education. (Neal, 1975) In one investigation, of
269 pupils interviewed at the end of the first year
at secondary school, 240 indicated that they had
enjoyed the experience. But the 29 who were
presumably less-contented present a sufficiently-
sizeable group to cause concern. Youngman and
Lunzer found that ten per cent of the children in
their research group positively disliked secondary
school when questioned towards the end of the first
year. An even larger proportion - 23 per cent of
the urban sample and 40 per cent of the rural sample
- wished they were still in primary school.

As we have already noted, the extent of
problems occasioned by school change varies
according to several factors, of which a pupils'
social background is one of some importance. It is
therefore difficult to determine norms for a
particular school but research offers an indication
of the likely incidence of difficulty when
considered within a large comprehensive catchment.
Problems of some kind are likely to be experienced
by just over half the pupils immediately after
transfer but for the majority of these pupils
difficulties are remarkably short-lived. For some-

thing like 10 to 30 per cent of pupils, the first
year after transfer is not satisfying enough to
remove a lingering wish to be back in primary
school. One in ten pupils' find transfer, or more
correctly the secondary school, a distressing
experience, and this is a feeling which persists for
at least two terms'. (Youngman and Lunzer, 1977)

Causes of Anxiety

With minor exceptions, research studies are
consistent in their specification of causes of
anxiety to pupils who failed to settle into
secondary school, Birmingham researchers found
children were worried about the size of school and
complexities of organisation. They were anxious
about school work and apprehensive about relationships with older pupils. Friendships were
particularly important to them and many felt lonely
when they were separated from primary-school
friends. Significantly, these anxieties were
expressed by a small group of pupils whose
experience of transfer had been unsuccessful. (Neal,
1975) A more general study, again within the
Birmingham Continuity in Education project, of a
larger group of pupils produced somewhat different
findings. In a comparison of pupils' attitudes to
secondary school both before and after transfer,
researchers had expected to find as potential
sources of unhappiness such factors as bullying,
homework, school size, organisation and discipline.
Surprisingly, these features were seldom mentioned
by pupils. It was relationships with teachers that
really mattered. Before transfer, children were
asked: 'What will you miss most about this primary
school?' In over 44 per cent of replies, individual
teachers were mentioned. A year later when asked
what they had missed most about their primary
school, 33 per cent still said they missed their
teacher. In the secondary school, they recognised
that relationships with teachers had changed; some
pupils mentioned 'adult treatment'. The majority of
children approved of this change; their own
peception of growing towards adolescence made them
more appreciative of being treated differently.
Socially-mature pupils, particularly those who had
passed through primary school relatively untroubled
settled into secondary school with little difficulty
but an occasional nostalgic backward glance.
A small-scale but significant study by a group
of Norfolk middle-school headteachers (1983) also

compared pupils attitudes before and after transfer. Asked in their final middle-school year what they found apprehensive about transfer to the high school, pupils mentioned most frequently, 'bullying', followed by 'size of school and getting lost'; new teachers, new subjects and homework were also represented in the list of anxieties and, to a lesser extent, getting to school, punishments and separation from friends. Pupils' responses were similar irrespective of the five middle schools in which research was conducted except that when they were to be transferred to a high school with an extended catchment area, 'making new friends' became a more significant area of concern. After transfer most of the anxieties were allayed before pupils had been in school for very long; many pupils stated they had overcome them in a few days. Supplanting their previous major anxieties concerning relationships with others, however, pupils became more worried about curricular matters. The level of work to be done caused stress, sometimes because it was too easy but on occasions because of excessive difficulty. High-school teachers took a long time to find a common starting-point. Homework, tests, new subjects and new styles of teaching - all were mentioned as problems after transfer.

Pupil Types

Clearly, the extent to which transfer causes problems varies significantly. For a socially-insecure child, bullying may be the predominant anxiety whereas for someone who has found learning difficult throughout primary school, the main worry may well be about harder work. The tendency for research studies to summarise and generalise can hide important individual aspects of school adjustment. Recognising this deficiency, Youngman and Lunzer (1977) tried to identify groups of pupils by type. Table 4.1 details their research groups from urban and rural schools further classified according to ability and attitude to school.

Table 4.1: 'Types' of children identified by Youngman and Lunzer

Type	Label	Rural (N = 290)		Urban (N = 454)		
		%	N	%	N	
1.	'Academic'	19	55	18	83	High ability
2.	'Disenchanted'	12	34	13	61	pupils
3.	'Uncertain'	12	36	6	29	
4.	'Contented'	20	58	13	59	
5.	'Non-academic'	13	39	17	77	Low ability
6.	'Worried'	12	34	14	65	pupils
7.	'Despairing'	5	15	-	-	
8.	'Disinterested'	-	-	12	55	

Pupils within the three 'high ability' groups all rated highly on intelligence measured while they were still in primary school. The 'academic' type consisted of pupils who showed little anxiety and were high achievers with a favourable attitude to secondary school. These were the pupils for whom transfer presented fewest problems. This is not to say that they were entirely trouble-free. In a case study of a pupil from this group, the researchers pointed out that during the first term after transfer, the girl failed to settle mainly because she was parted from a close friend. As she widened her friendship circle, however, anxiety ceased and she settled into school. The essential character-istics of this group were high achievement and strong personal self-concept involving ability to get on well with others and a feeling of security in their own competence. Though most research studies recognise the transfer advantage obtaining to able pupils, ability alone is no guarantee of successful transition. Youngman and Lunzer's 'disenchanted' group had higher than average intelligence scores but their academic involvement was low. Indeed, motivation deteriorated after transfer. Increasing disenchantment with school and lack of enthusiasm, despite above-average ability is obviously a cause of considerable concern. The other high-ability type in this research study, classified 'uncertain', though strongly committed to school, lacked confidence.

Of the low-ability types, the 'contented' group were slightly below average in both ability and attainment but from their attitudes it would seem they were generally contented; indeed they settled in well to secondary school. The 'non-academic' group, whilst being low achievers, were not unduly anxious reflecting, according to the researchers, 'an acceptance of the impossibility of secondary-school success'. In a case study of a pupil of this type it was suggested that the cause of difficulty was the pupil's being made aware of his own low ability by the teaching approach used in the secondary school. The dominant characteristic of the 'worried' group was high anxiety. They did not adjust well to transfer and children of this type from rural schools suffered a drop in achievement in comparison with primary-school performance. The type which was identified only within the rural sample was labelled 'despairing' because of its low ability, total lack of interest in secondary schooling, very high anxiety and extreme longing to be back in primary school. The city 'disinterested' group was also of low ability and poorly motivated, but unlike the rural children, these pupils were not unduly anxious nor did they lack self-assurance.

The complicated nature of school transfer is well illustrated by Youngman and Lunzer's research. Bullying caused concern for 30 per cent of the pupils they studied but was not randomly inflicted; some pupils were more susceptible to being bullied than others. Sixty per cent of their sample were worried about examinations, and schoolwork caused anxiety for 29 per cent of rural and 43 per cent of city children. But once again, there were differences according to type. The specific associations presented in their typology suggest the possibility of forecasting the extent of pupil adjustment to transfer. Indeed, most primary-school teachers know pupils sufficiently well to make an estimate of their chances of successful transition. But the vast amount of knowledge acquired during a pupil's primary years cannot be readily assimilated by secondary teachers, even if it is accurately transmitted and some, of course, is very difficult to record. Decisions about placing children at the time of transfer should be made on the basis of interacting characteristics. Allocating pupils to classes merely according to attainment or ability is inadequate because it fails to take account of other important attributes. The point is aptly illustrated by one of Youngman and Lunzer's case studies. Frank's attitude to school was good during the primary years but did not continue immediately after transfer. The researchers commented:

> There can be no doubt about the reason for this deterioration. On entering secondary school Frank was placed in the same tutor group as a rather wayward friend and the effect was disastrous. Both behaviour and work suffered until the obvious remedy, separation, was effected. . . . As well as the unsuitable start to secondary school, certain family circum- stances could have induced a degree of anxiety. By the end of the second year, however, his teacher did tend to observe a more settled personality.

It is doubtful whether problems of the kind illust- rated in this case study could have been anticipated but they needed to be recognised quickly. As the researchers commented, poor adjustment may be

associated with specific causes for which simple
remedies exist. The key to successful transition is
close vigilance over individual adjustment,
particularly during the first term in secondary
school. It is immediately after transfer that the
many changes with which they have to contend are
most likely to produce behavioural changes in
individual children. Youngman and Lunzer's
identification of a disenchanted ten per cent,
pupils of high ability without concomitant
application to school, suggests a potential waste of
talent that could possibly be prevented by closer
monitoring of pupils at time of transfer.

Liaison

Change of school can cause problems for some
pupils but is a stimulus for others. Even were it
feasible for secondary schooling to continue in the
primary pattern, it would not be desirable (although
the Plowden Report seemed to recommend this).
Pupils need to feel they have progressed to a new
kind of experience. They can expect change but this
need not involve depreciation of previous schooling.
Though seldom explicitly stated, the message sometimes transmitted is: 'In the secondary school,
things are so different that much of what you did
before transfer can be forgotten.' Between these
two extremes, continuance of previous practice and
abrupt change, there is the approach to learning
designed to be even and gradual, to ease pupils from
one kind of learning to another over a protracted
period. Only in recent times have such issues been
subjected to research scrutiny.

One of the areas of enquiry investigated by the
Birmingham Educational Development Centre was
liaison between primary and secondary schools and a
comparison of curriculum. (Neal, 1975) Liaison was
generally considered to be inadequate because of
staffing difficulties which hampered visits between
schools. Very few primary staff were able to visit
receiving secondary schools; when headteachers of
primary schools made visits, there was no evidence
that any information gleaned was passed on to class
teachers. Rather more visits were made by secondary
staff to feeder primary schools because of their
better staff-pupil ratios but there was little
evidence that such visits had any impact on
curriculum. No curricular discussions took place
between schools in half of those sampled by the
survey and even when there was some liaison, this

was achieved through informal contacts which appeared to be haphazard, and varied according to individual interest. No examples could be found of systematic attempts to promote continuity of learning when pupils transferred schools although some consultation took place about mathematics, remedial teaching and French.

A disturbing feature of the Birmingham research was that a few headteachers were apathetic about liaison, which was 'sometimes hampered by mutual lack of sympathy between the two types of school'. Very similar comments were made by Stillman and Maychell (1984) in a report on their Isle of Wight research into school transfer involving middle schools. Quoting responses to a survey of head-teachers on both island and mainland, who were asked to express their views on curriculum liaison, such terms as 'apathy' and 'human inertia' were used. The root of the problem, it was suggested, lay in a lack of mutual trust between the sectors. 'We do not have the time to get to know each other', said one middle-school head. Not knowing about the work of colleagues in the other stage led to false assumptions being made; the researchers found little or no substantiating evidence for discrepancies in material and staffing resources between sectors. It seems that the extent to which institutions can promote educational continuity is dependent on the attitude of the teachers concerned but these are somewhat ambivalent. Though most teachers in Stillman's study believed in some form of educational continuity, few were actually involved in achieving it.

The author's research in Hull suggests that reticence rather than apathy was the cause of lack of liaison. (Gorwood, 1981) Upper-school staff were generally prepared to concede more autonomy to middle schools than they sought for themselves. Only seven of 48 responding senior-high-school staff were concerned that middle schools 'should give a thorough grounding for work in senior high schools' whilst 20 of 38 middle-school headteachers accepted that pupils should have been 'introduced to skills needed for secondary work'. Only three middle-school headteachers asserted the right of schools to adopt appropriate organisational and curricular modes irrespective of upper-school attitudes. Middle schools accepted that they had a preparatory function and, as the following comments testify, complained that receiving schools did not give enough guidance:

- If only they would tell us what they wanted of our pupils, we could prepare them properly;

- In the days of eleven-plus we had a common measure. Now we look on secondary schools to set standards but they do not seem able to agree among themselves;

- How can we pack their suitcases if we do not know what journey they are going to take?

The survey revealed that communication between teachers in different phases of education was spasmodic. Informal ad hoc meetings served to deal with continuity problems but there was a lack of 'positive and systematic co-operation' advocated by HM Inspectorate (1977b). Some teachers with common subject interests and responsibility for the same pupils at a different stage of their education had never met.

Manifestly, there is need for schools at either side of an interface to communicate about curriculum. The problem seems to be one of starting discussions. Stillman and Maychell (1984) discerned that though many teachers perceived a need for liaison, they did not consider it their responsibility to take the initiative:

> Contributory school teachers often expressed the view that it was the responsibility of the receiving school to make the first move in setting up liaison and indicating what was expected from the contributory schools' curricula. Conversely, receiving school teachers, particularly those in high schools, often indicated a reluctance to appear to dictate to colleagues in contributory schools by calling meetings and making demands.

As the researchers commented, there would seem to be a need for some kind of intervention by local authorities to provide a stimulus for schools.

Continuity Impeded by Organisational Complexity

Even if teachers were enthusiastic about communicating with colleagues in associated schools, insuperable problems can face them if they are involved in a system with a large number of inter-related schools. Stillman and Maychell concluded that if the majority of middle and high schools set out to liaise with all their receiving and contributory schools across transfer there would be little time left for teaching. These researchers argued, however, that there was no need for liaison between all related schools. Approximately 94 per cent of the pupils in their sample transferred in 24 groups representing an average of less than five feed school groups to each high school. Liaison, they claimed, would not present an insuperable problem between one upper school and the five or six contributory schools providing the majority of its pupils. The author's own research, however, suggests that when many contributory and receiving schools are involved in a transfer system, irrespective of whether liaison is theoretically feasible, it is practically almost non-existent.

Gannon and Whalley (1975) compared transfer and continuity arrangements between a pyramidal system and what they termed a 'city-borough' pattern of organisation. In the pyramid approach, all pupils in a sector go to one upper school which is fed by several junior or middle schools each with its own infant or first schools. As all pupils eventually arrive in the same school, those negotiating curriculum continuity need be very few. In the city-borough system, not only do several upper schools receive pupils from many feeder schools, but eacher feeder school supplies a number of those upper schools. The resulting complex network of interrelationships demands the involvement of many teachers to arrange a co-ordinated curriculum policy.

A survey in Hull in the 1970s of transfer arrangements and attitudes to liaison showed that teachers in upper schools considered excessive number of feeder schools to be the major barrier to continuity. (Gorwood, 1983) The average number of middle schools from which 13 responding upper schools accepted pupils was 18, the range being from 7 to 28. Each upper school, however, could expect to receive the majority of its pupils from no more than six feeder schools, so on the surface, it would seem that continuity could be achieved at this interface if agreement was reached between only seven schools. But a feeder school could be a main supplier to more than one upper school, which would need to be involved in consultation together with all its contributory schools. Schools were so enmeshed that curriculum continuity needed to be discussed on a city-wide basis. The problem can be illustrated by the difficulty one middle school faced in trying to achieve mathematics continuity with its receiving schools. Of some 90 children transferring, about 40 went to one upper school, 30 to another and the remainder in smaller groups to a further four senior schools. One of the high schools to which pupils went in a sizeable group used a traditional approach to mathematics, the other had adopted the modern Schools Mathematics Project. Adequate preparation for transfer to either of these upper schools was thus almost impossible; the middle school's mathematics teacher was perforce required to introduce pupils to both modern and traditional syllabuses.

The survey by Stillman and Maychell (1984) suggests that the majority of schools are within a pyramidal system; 88 per cent of respondents to their middle and secondary school questionnaire regularly sent a sizeable proportion of pupils to or from a small number of schools. One can assume that this situation also applies to systems involving transfer at eleven. As parents increasingly take advantage of recent legislation allowing freer choice of schools, however, it will be more difficult to maintain pyramidal systems. Their demise will require an extension of LEA curriculum policy making to try to achieve consistency within the many feeder and receiving schools as a prior condition to promoting continuity between them. In very large local authorities, an organisational strategy of the kind used in Birmingham could help alleviate difficulties caused when an excessive number of schools are involved in transfer schemes. In the Birmingham area, schools are organised into a number of 'consortia', each consortium consisting of about six secondary schools and their twenty or so contributory primaries. (Denton, 1975) The affairs of each consortium are conducted by a committee of headteachers and inspectors. One of their responsibilities is towards 'achieving the optimum level of co-operation on such matters as curriculum, planning and development, time-tabling, the sharing of facilities and staff and the continual assessment of the appropriateness of educational provision available for the individual child at each stage of his secondary education'. Because of the commitment to working towards compatibility of curricula in a consortium's schools, liaison between the two sectors of education is greatly enhanced.

THE NATURE OF THE PROBLEM

Variations in Attainment

Ross (1975) has discussed the improbability of one course following directly after another at change of school. It is unrealistic, for example, to expect all pupils to reach the same pre-determined stage in a mathematics course before transfer so that all can start at the same stage after transfer. However well co-ordinated a curricular scheme, there are going to be differences in pupils' attainment. The strategy favoured by many receiving schools, however, of starting all pupils at a fairly low but commonly acceptable level can hardly be considered an adequate solution to continuity difficulties. Yet so diverse can pre-transfer learning be that secondary schools face daunting problems. Upper-school respondents to my Hull survey were convinced there was 'extreme diversity' of curricular provision in contributory schools. (Gorwood, 1981) Yet little difference was evident between subjects taught in these schools; even in the humanities, generally recognised as displaying diversity, there was surprising similarity. There were, however, differences in emphasis. From data supplied by 36 of Hull's 51 middle schools, a calculation was made of time-tabled hours allocated to mathematics, science and French during a pupil's four-year middle-school stay. Results are shown in Table 4.2. At age-13 transfer, a pupil from the school with the most generous share of science time had spent over three

Table 4.2: **Differences in time spent on three key subjects in Hull middle schools over a period of four years (N=36)**

	Mathematics	French	Science
Mean number of time-tabled hours	610	337	254
Maximum number of time-tabled hours	798	443	487
Minimum number of time-tabled hours	443	202	152
Proportional difference between maximum and minimum	1.8	2.2	3.2

times as long being exposed to the subject as a
pupil from the school with the minimum science time
allocation. Even in the basic subject, mathematics,
there were large differences in time allocation
between schools. It would have been surprising if
such differences had no effect on pupils' levels of
attainment. A follow-up study of six main contributory schools to one senior high revealed that though
pupils followed the same mathematics course, their
teachers had very different expectations: in one
school, the target was completion of SMP Book B
whereas in another pupils were expected to finish
Book D. Similar disparities were evident in middle-
school French teaching. The possible variety of
pupil experience of French before transfer can be
discerned from comments made by an upper-school head
of department:

> I receive pupils mainly from six junior high
> schools (i.e. middle schools). Five of them
> use En Avant, the sixth uses a scheme devised
> by the French teacher who taught in a grammar
> school before re-organisation. She concen-
> trates on written work but her pupils lack
> confidence in spoken French. In one of the
> other schools, pupils go through En Avant
> mechanically; they have staffing problems there
> and it's a struggle to keep French going. In
> Alpha Junior High they have two French lessons
> a week and are only starting En Avant Stage
> Three when they transfer; in Beta Junior High,
> they have five lessons a week and are up to
> stage four when they arrive here. With two
> lessons a week there is very little time for
> written work. Of course, a few pupils haven't
> done any French at all because they were in
> low-ability classes in junior high but mixed
> French groups here.

In subjects of a linear nature, there is need for a
greater degree of consistency in pre-transfer
learning than pertains at present. Obviously there
would be differences in attainment at transfer even
if pupils had been exposed to identical learning but
disparities become more extreme when there has been
no attempt at co-ordination of contributory schools.

Repetition

Close correlation between pre- and post-
transfer learning is less imperative in subjects not

demanding a sequential approach. Pupils are rightly perturbed if they are required to go back over mathematics or French course books already completed but are less likely to be as immediately aware of repetition in areas of the curriculum such as the humanities or aesthetic subjects. There have been no research attempts to correlate school rejection with incidence of repeated learning but it is interesting to note a general impression that it is during the early years of secondary education that the disenchanted ten per cent becomes readily identifiable, and during the same period duplication of work already accomplished is prevalent. In an unpublished discussion document, the Norfolk Association of Middle School Head Teachers (1983) reported that after transfer curricular worries were uppermost in pupils' minds: some work was too hard but there was also 'endless revision to find a common starting point'. A case study in a similar document produced in a Midlands local authority identified several topics in history and geography that recurred so frequently that parents had protested. A study of the Vikings was a regular feature of a secondary school's first-year history syllabus so the head of department arranged a visit to the Viking exhibition and issued worksheets prepared by the museum service. Pupils from two of the school's contributory primaries had made the same visit and used the same worksheets less than six months previously. It was no consolation to parents that this visit was free whereas the primary schools had required a contribution to transport costs. One parent suggested that his son had studied the Vikings four times during six years of schooling. A local authority investigation revealed similar repetition in geography. Projects in primary schools on 'forests', 'timber' and 'paper-making' had been followed in secondary school by work on Canada with very similar content. Teachers consulted by Stillman and Maychell (1984) defended duplication by referring to the 'spiral curriculum', but as the researchers pointed out, to operate effectively, such an approach should involve an advance on the previous teaching and a planned lapse of time before further exposure of the same topic.

HMI Surveys

In recent years, comprehensive consideration of transfer between schools has been undertaken by Her Majesty's Inspectorate in both primary and middle school surveys. Though there were differences in scale, the primary survey being of 542 schools whilst the middle survey was of 48, similar sentiments were disclosed. Commendable efforts were made to ease children's transition from one school to another but curriculum continuity was less successful. It was noted that in 92 per cent of primary schools surveyed, pupils visited their future schools before transition took place; but in only 29 per cent of schools were there joint meetings of teachers for discussion about the curriculum. Indeed the primary survey noted, 'the importance of continuity in the curriculum of schools was largely overlooked'. Only with 'regular and systematic consultation between teachers from associated schools' could effective curriculum planning take place so that schemes of work should take account of requirements in both the next and previous stages of education. This seldom happened. Much more curriculum consultation was reported between middle and upper schools. In mathematics, French, science and English over four-fifths of middle schools surveyed reported consultations with all or some of their upper schools. Indeed, in half the schools the same mathematics texts were used as in the receiving upper school. Despite these greater efforts by middle schools, curriculum continuity was difficult to achieve because a system of parental choice resulted in children being transferred to a large number of upper schools. HM Inspectorate's conclusion on continuity between schools involved in the middle-school survey was that consultation over the curriculum was not as well established as procedures for familiarising children with the schools to which they were about to transfer.

Conclusion

There has been criticism of the subjective nature of much that appears in HMI surveys but it has to be conceded that inspectorate opinion can be supported by more objective research findings. It is in curricular matters that transfer causes most problems. The anxieties pupils experience before transfer are fairly soon allayed in most cases. For a minority, the main cause of disenchantment with secondary education is inability to adapt to changes in curriculum. Changes of some kind are unavoidable but if there are large disparities in practice between associated schools, pupils may become

disorientated scholastically and troubled
emotionally. Several researchers consider the chief
cause of curriculum problems to stem from lack of
communication between primary and secondary
teachers. Efforts to being together those
responsible for pupils' education at either side of
a transfer interface are spasmodic. Individual
teachers sometimes take the initiative in establishing links with related schools; the tendency then is
for liaison to be effective in some subjects whilst
in others there is no agreement. When whole schools
are involved, continuity schemes can be more
effective but if many schools are interrelated in
transfer schemes it is difficult to gain agreement
except on very general issues.

Recent studies have commented on the desirabil-
ity of a third party being involved in liaison
schemes. It is difficult for teachers in their
individual schools to gain an overall impression of
liaison needs and possibilities. Many local
authorities give active support to initiatives taken
by their teachers but some researchers feel that
LEAs should themselves take the lead. Lois Benyon
(1984) suggests we might follow the example of a
scheme in Belgium. In the province of Liege, a
special Centre de Liaison has been set up with the
task of establishing and applying effective methods
for making smooth the transition from primary to
secondary education and in solving problems of
curriculum continuity in French and mathematics.
Given the autonomy of British schools and
particularly the key factor, headteacher leadership,
local authorities need to approach very carefully
the task of intervention to promote curricular
continuity. But they can count on support from the
research community, pehaps most explicitly expressed
in the NFER's report on transfer in the Isle of
Wight (Stillman and Maychell, 1984):

> It was felt that the LEA has an important part
> to play in helping to promote and maintain
> continuity by assuming the role of mediator
> between schools and by centrally co-ordinating
> a coherent policy of liaison across the LEA.

Chapter Five

THE IMPORTANCE OF CONTINUITY

'Schools stand to gain by working in close
professional consultation with each other.' This
statement from Her Majesty's Inspectorate seems
incontrovertable. (DES, 1980b) It reiterates a
theme so frequently expressed in recent years that
it has almost become an educational shibboleth. Yet
there are those who doubt the worth of efforts to
bring schools closer together. Marland (1977) has
suggested it is 'one of the romantic vaguenesses
peddled frequently in educational exhortation . .
that we should create a close liaison between
educational institutions. In fact it is one of the
hardest things to achieve and can consume
considerable time to little effect'. Marland, of
course, does not advocate that there should not be
liaison. Indeed, he proposes a 'community of
schools creating a broad plan, within which specific
details were agreed, and individual pupils' work
known'. Yet by drawing attention to lack of
functional continuity within school organisation, he
calls into question the worth of liaison efforts.
Certainly, there are differences in method and
content which children have to face at times of
transfer but whether these cause such serious
interruptions in a pupil's educational experience
that schools should attempt a closer liaison is open
to question. We need to consider to what extent
continuity, or more importantly discontinuity, is a
matter of importance.

Non-school Factors

At the conclusion of his report on pupil
adaptation to secondary school in Northern Ireland,
Spelman (1979) commented that many of the
difficulties experienced by children in their

71

transition and adaptation to secondary education
were 'a function of differences in their socio-
cultural characteristics, whether linguistic,
perceptual or aspirational, prior to entering
secondary school'. One could infer from such a
statement that since many factors affecting
successful transition are outside the control of
schools, there is little point in making great
efforts to achieve liaison. Several research
studies have commented on social implications of
transfer. Nisbet and Entwistle (1969) found that
children from poorer homes were likely to be
adversely affected by transfer. Dale and Griffith
(1965) in their study of failure in the grammar
school noted that deterioration was most pronounced
amongst children from the lower socio-economic
classes. Factors which have been found to correlate
positively and significantly with pupil adjustment
to secondary schooling include the type of education
parents received, parental encouragement, size of
family, pupil personality and pupil ability. The
extent to which each of these is susceptible to
school influence varies. Nothing can be done about
parental education or size of family; schools can
try to persuade parents to encourage their children;
pupil personality and ability may be slightly
influenced by schooling but most researchers
consider the school effect to be minimal. Indeed,
the extent to which primary-school experience can
have an effect on a pupil's adjustment to secondary
schooling is called into question by several studies
into school effectiveness.

School Effectiveness

Much research into school effectiveness has
been conducted in the United States of America. The
most influential study was that published by the US
Office of Education, generally termed The Coleman
Report (1966) after its principal researcher. Based
on a sample of 645,000 students in both elementary
and secondary schools, the research was concerned
with a number of problems related to equality of
educational opportunity for different ethnic groups
in the USA. At the conclusion of a study of pupil
achievement and motivation, the following statement
was made:

THE IMPORTANCE OF CONTINUITY

> One implication stands out above all: That
> schools bring little influence to bear on a
> child's achievement that is independent of his
> background and general social context.

Such a clear and unequivocal statement resulting
from a research study involving over 4,000 schools
would seem firmly to have established that schools
have a minimal effect upon a child's achievement.
A review of a further 19 American research studies
confirmed that there was little evidence of a
powerful impact of school resources on student
outcomes. (Averch, 1972) It would seem that if
successful transition is to be measured in terms of
pupils' achievements then the function of schools in
this process is limited. Given evidence on school
effectiveness, curriculum continuity becomes a
matter of importance only if its absence causes
pupils anxiety. Yet the evidence on school
effectiveness is problematical. As Averch has
pointed out, results cannot be interpreted as
indicating that schools **do not** affect pupils'
achievements but only that they have failed to show
that schools **do** have a positive effect.
    Research into school effectiveness is difficult
not only because of many variables that can be
involved but because there are no universally-
accepted norms for what constitutes educational
achievements. Rutter et al (1979) have indicated
some of the inadequacies in major studies which have
influenced opinion on effectiveness. Coleman is
criticised for relying on a single measure of verbal
ability which underestimated the importance of
schooling; indeed, Rutter claims, measures of
scholastic attainment in American studies were
unrelated to subjects taught in school. Studies in
Britain based on pupils' results in external examinations have shown greater effects. There are
differences, too, according to subjects. For
example, effects of schooling seem to be more
evident in mathematics and science than in social
studies and English literature. Two further factors
in large-scale surveys caused Rutter to question
their acceptability as indicators of school effectiveness. There was a lack of information on what
children were like when they entered school and so
no accurate indication of incremental achievement
was possible. Secondly, the studies emphasised
measurable resources such as average expenditure per

pupil, number of available books and teacher-pupil
ratio. In massive questionnaire surveys factors
such as style or quality of teaching, classroom
interaction and the social climate of the school
could not be taken into account. These aspects of
school life may well have an impact on pupils'
achievements; to neglect them but draw general
conclusions about school effectiveness on the basis
of a narrow range of school variables is misleading.

Many of the assumptions about school effectiveness have been based on research into the relative
importance of home and school influences on a
child's development. Peaker's analysis of the
National Survey carried out on behalf of the Plowden
Committee showed that pupil achievement was far more
affected by home factors than by school performance.
(Central Advisory Council for Education, 1967)
Summing up results, Peaker commented:

> Before the inquiry it was plain, as a matter of
> common-sense and common observation, that
> parental encouragement and support could take
> the child some way. What the inquiry has shown
> is that 'some way' can reasonably be
> interpreted as 'a long way'.

The significance of parental encouragement at the
time of transfer, it will be remembered, was
mentioned by Nisbet and Entwistle (1966). Following
Plowden, parental support was seen as more
influential than school factors in promoting pupil
achievement. Yet in Peaker's study, school attainment was assessed entirely on the basis of a
comparatively short reading test. It was performance
in a reading test rather than general attainment
that was measured. Yet Peaker emphasised one should
not infer that schooling was unimportant from the
fact that school variables accounted for so small a
part of a child's progress. He pointed out that
variation between schools was much less than that
between parental attitudes: 'If the least
co-operative parents rose to the level of the most
co-operative the effect would be much larger than if
the worst schools rose to the level of the best.'
This point was also made by Rutter who noted that
since schools probably varied less than homes then
their statistical effect on children's attainment
would also appear less.

Manifestly, Coleman's notion that schools bring
little influence to bear on a child's achievement
that is independent of social background is itself

open to question. Rutter's research, reported in
Fifteen Thousand Hours, categorically refuted the
notion that schools were relatively ineffectual in
influencing a child's achievement. The research
involved a longitudinal study of pupils in twelve
non-selective secondary schools serving socially-
disadvantaged inner-city areas. Social climate,
social organisation and teaching contexts in the
schools themselves were subjected to extensive
study. School effectiveness was judged in terms of
pupil attendance, behaviour, public-examination
results and delinquency rates. Clearly, these were
not the only measures by which effectiveness could
have been assessed but they provided a more
comprehensive appraisal of schooling than any
attempted in previous studies. In fact, marked
variations were evident in each of the indicators
even when differences in pupils' backgrounds were
taken into account. When these variations were
compared with school characteristics such as the
availability of pupil incentives, degree of academic
emphasis and teachers' actions during lessons, there
was found to be a systematic relationship. The
total pattern of findings indicated the strong
probability of a causal relationship between school
processes and outcomes.

The research by Rutter and his team was
subjected to considerable criticism, some serious
but some inconsequential. Objections centred on
technical and ideological issues but no clear-cut
verdict on the study emerged. Significantly, even a
harsh critic could accept that the basic idea behind
the study was a useful one 'with prima facie
evidence that genuine schools differences may
exist'. (Goldstein, 1980) In recent years, several
studies have pointed to the relationship between
home environment and scholastic attainment. Because
it has been thought the characteristics that pupils
bring to the school from outside have a powerful
influence on their achievement, the effects of
schooling have been underemphasised. Research by
Rutter and his colleagues has changed that
situation. Their findings have shown that school
differences are not merely a reflection of intake
patterns. In the context of considering liaison
between schools, Rutter's study suggests the
possibility that some 'sending' schools may be more
effective than others in preparing pupils for work
in the receiving school. This notion prompted the
author to pursue an investigation to monitor the
progress of a group of pupils at time of transfer

from junior to senior high schools in Hull.

Effects of Differential Pre-transfer Experience

The research was conducted in Hull, a city with a three-tier system of educational provision. Transfer from first to middle schools at age nine presented few problems as most pupils at this stage moved in their neighbourhood within a group of five or six schools which had long-standing liaison arrangements. At the middle to upper interface, at age 13, parental choice and maintenance of a balanced intake in pupil cognitive ability determined school allocation and resulted in many feeder schools to each upper school. A city-wide survey of teachers involved in the upper-age transfer was conducted mainly to determine the extent of differences between and within the two stages of education. Whilst there were found to be many similarities among schools, there were also significant differences not only across the transfer divide but between equivalent schools. The survey concentrated on key subjects identified by Her Majesty's Inspectorate as needing special attention. (HMI 1977b) In mathematics, science and French there were substantial differences not only in the content of middle-school courses but also in time allocations. Although disparities were not as extreme in upper schools, there were differences particularly in course starting points. Pupil transfer could be extremely varied involving, at one extreme, a move to a school of similar size, organisation, curriculum and general ethos, at the other, fundamental changes in educational experience. Middle-school teachers protested the impossibility of adequately preparing pupils for entry to several upper schools with different curricular schemes. Upper-school teachers generally expressed the opinion pupils had received such disparate preparation for secondary work that it was difficult to establish common ground. Indeed, some claimed there was evidence in pupils' attainments after transfer of differences in schooling during the middle phase. This claim was investigated by a study of pupils' attainments according to feeder schools. (Gorwood, 1983)

The study concentrated on pupil attainment to pre-transfer school, level of ability and social background. As a lone researcher, the author was limited in the size of sample he was able to keep under observation: 400 pupils transferring from ten

middle to two upper schools were followed in an
enquiry lasting four years. The question to be
resolved was whether upper-school teachers were
right in relating differences in attainment after
transfer to factors inherent in pre-transfer
schools. In fact, statistically significant
differences in first-year attainment among feeder-
school cohorts were demonstrated in several areas of
the curriculum. Teachers were therefore correct in
perceiving attainment to vary according to
contributory school, but whether disparities were
due to factors inherent in school was problematical.
When account was taken of pupil ability and home
background, apparent disparities across middle
schools were reduced considerably. Indeed,
significant variation was retained only in
mathematics in one upper school, but in mathematics,
physics, chemistry and geography in the other. Six
months after transfer, when these measures were
taken, in most subjects influences attributable to
factors inherent in pre-transfer schools were over-
whelmed mainly by pupils' levels of ability.
Clearly, however, attainment in mathematics could be
related to the schools previously attended, as could
some science in one of the upper schools. This
finding is consonant with researches reported by
Rutter (1979):

> Subjects such as mathematics or science which
> are generally learned mainly at school show
> greater school differences than do those such
> as reading which a child may learn in part at
> home from his parents, or those like English
> literature or Social Studies where a child's
> learning from television or from books at home
> as well as family conversation are all likely
> to play a part.

With effects of pupils' verbal reasoning ability and
social class controlled, significant differences in
mathematical attainment presumably resulted from
variations in middle-school learning. Though it was
not possible to gain direct access to all involved
middle schools, some were visited and information
obtained through secondary sources for others.
Enough was gleaned to suggest that schools producing
the most competent mathematics pupils had placed
extra emphasis on the subject.
    The study was extended beyond the first year by
taking measures of mathematical attainment in both
upper schools and English attainment in one of them.

77

Eighteen months after transfer little trace remained
of effects that could be attributed to pre-transfer
schools. One can speculate that since feeder-school
influence had faded in mathematics, the subject
displaying the greatest initial attainment
variation, little or nothing attributable to pre-
transfer schooling would remain in any academic
measures. As Nisbet and Entwistle (1969) noted in
their study, in the second year pupils had left
behind not only the school previously attended but
also the stage of transition. Pupil adjustment to
secondary schooling has been documented by several
researchers; despite differences in detail, all
agree the process is accomplished by most pupils
within a year. It is interesting to note that
within a similar period, attainment measures in the
Hull study showed diminution of effects traceable to
learning in the previous school.

An immediate response to research suggesting
that pre-transfer schooling has little impact on
post-transfer attainment could be to question the
need for continuity. Since the main determinant of
long-term achievement seems to be pupil ability, it
could be argued that there is little to be gained by
striving for liaison between schools. Yet we do not
know whether and to what extent effective curriculum
continuity would influence pupils' attainments for
there has been no longitudinal study of this issue.
Indeed, there is so little instance of planned
curriculum continuity that such a study would be
difficult to set up. As Stillman and Maychell
(1984) found, though the majority of teachers are in
favour of a linked curriculum across transfer, the
level of liaison between sectors is generally low.

Though it is unrealistic to expect all pupils
to start in one school where they left off in
another, common sense suggests that if that happened
there would be an improvement in post-transfer
attainment. In this context, it is instructive to
compare two of the ten middle schools in the Hull
study. The first school is located in a part of the
city in which many professional people live and
there is keen interest in education. Pressure from
an articulate group of parents indirectly influences
the curriculum. In the year in which transfer tests
were monitored, the mean verbal reasoning score of
pupils from this schools was significantly higher
than that of any other feeder school with 70 per
cent achieving a score in excess of 100 and none
below 80. The second school was designed to serve a
local authority housing estate but now receives

pupils from a wider area with older council property
and owner-occupied dewellings of considerable
variety. It is well-equipped and well-organised
with an enthusiastic staff whose efforts, as in the
previous school, are mainly given to the achievement
of good acadamic standards. Pupils, however, are of
lower ability; in the year measures were taken,
there was an eleven-point difference in mean verbal
reasoning scores of pupils from the two schools.

It was anticipated that when results of
transfer mathematics tests were considered, pupils
from the 'higher-ability' feeder school would
achieve higher scores. Local folk-lore reinforced
this assumption for in the era of selective
education this was the school consistently obtaining
the largest number of eleven-plus successes. In
fact, pupils from the 'lower ability' school
realised higher scores. This situation continued
for a short time after transfer for when the first
examinations were taken, the 'less-able' pupils
still had a discernible advantage not only in
mathematics but in several other subjects too. The
overall conclusion from an examination of these data
appeared to be that pupils were enabled to
compensate for significantly lower ability by some
factor at work in the feeder school. Further
investigations revealed that the 'low-ability'
school was used for mathematics demonstration
purposes by teacher-training institutions; its
deputy head had run, at the local authority's
behest, a mathematics course for local teachers.
As a pioneering school it was well-resourced for
mathematics being the first middle school in the
area to be equipped with mini-computers. Whilst no
causal connection could be implied, there seemed to
be support for the notion that pupils at this school
transferred with an advantage in mathematics.

Pupils were examined again during their second
year, eighteen months after transfer. The initial
advantage in mathematics enjoyed by lower-ability
pupils was lost to pupils from the higher-ability
feeder school. This trend continued in the third
year as pupils moved towards external examinations.
It is open to conjecture what caused a spectacular
loss of mathematics advantage by pupils from a
school that gave intensive preparation for secondary
work. They may have been deprived of close teacher-
supervision, less feasible in the upper school,
after transfer. Pupils may have become disorientated if confronted with a different approach to
mathematics. Whatever the cause, early in secondary

school, pupils' attainments became very clearly
related to ability whereas previously their
schooling had given them some advantage. One of the
findings of the study was that those who had
progressed furthest in middle-school courses were
the ones required to make the biggest leap back-
wards; upper schools seemed incapable of coping with
higher achievers. Because of variety of curriculum
content and disparities between levels of attainment, pupils' pre-transfer experiences provide a
weak basis for future work. But the strategy of
starting anew with everybody is analogous to
stopping a race when some runners have forged ahead
for all competitors to toe a new starting line. The
need for continuity cannot be dismissed on grounds
that research findings suggest attainment to be
little affected by early schooling. The influence
of pre-transfer schooling is likely to be obscured
if planned continuity is lacking.

Pseudo Continuity

Spelman (1979) concluded that 'schools have a
significant role to play in facilitating the adjustment of their pupils'. [The ways in which schools
organised physical, transitional, social and
academic environments had an influence on the
psychological dispositions of pupils. The quality
of relationships between teachers and pupils was 'a
consistently significant concomitant of successful
pupil adjustment'.] Manifestly, many schools make
decided efforts to ease pupils into secondary
education but this is rather different from planning
for transfer from school to school. Several
standard research studies into transition and
continuity reveal concern that pupils should adapt
to changed circumstances but little evidence of
effective strategies crossing school boundaries.
Early secondary practice may be modified to include
'primary' techniques (Philip, 1968); pre-transfer
schooling may be imbued with 'secondary' methods.
(Nash, 1973) But, as was revealed in Nash's study,
teachers tend to take their model for the mode of
working in the other stage of education from
theories presented in books rather than practice in
associated schools. There is almost reluctance to
step outside one's own school. Strategies in which
teachers presume to be promoting liaison and
continuity without making an effort to discover what
happens at the other side of a transfer interface
are merely cosmetic. Continuity is important, but it

has to be genuine.

Misconceptions about curriculum and teaching methods of the kind exemplified by Nash are understandable for teachers have little scope for discovering how associated schools deal with such matters. Visits between staff of schools are few and seldom involve those who teach primary leavers or first-year secondary pupils. The sporadic visiting that does occur tends to involve primary headteachers, secondary heads of department and first year co-ordinators. (Neal, 1975) Their main concern for transfer administration and documentation has little effect on curriculum continuity yet their visits are usually mentioned in this context.

Autonomy

Diversity of practice is the cornerstone of British education. Though subject to informal influences from outside, the curriculum is to a great extent the responsibility of teachers themselves. A correspondent, in answer to a question on the extent of dialogue with contributory schools commented: 'What would be the point? They are all very different but we couldn't interfere. What they do in their schools is their concern.' There can be little progress towards continuity if such attitudes prevail. School governors, the legal custodians of the curriculum, seldom comment on such professional matters, while local authorites are loathe to intervene. (Kogan and Van Der Eyken, 1973) Until the mid 1970s, central government seemed content with this situation but though there has been pressure for almost a decade for a nationally-agreed framework for the curriculum, there has been little impact on the practice in schools. According to a conference of the British Educational Administration Society in 1977 (Glatter) the practising teacher is no longer as determined as he once was to cling to control of the curriculum. Yet the overall determination of curriculum is more in the hands of headteachers than classteachers. Burrows (1978) affirms the actual extent of communication between schools 'depends in the main on the temperament of the two head teachers where they wish it to happen contact is close'. One head-master of insular attitude can obstruct attempts to achieve continuity as Dickinson's (1975) research shows. He quotes the extreme example of a head who introduced Latin into the curriculum of his middle

schools in spite of HMI disapproval, attempted
proscription by the local authority and the fact
that only a minority of girls transferring to one of
his upper schools would ever learn Latin again.
Further evidence of the decisive influence of headmasters upon curriculum and continuity is provided
by a letter to the Times Educational Supplement
(21 June 1974):

> We take pupils from several middle schools,
> each with its own character, aims and problems,
> and our maths, science and language depart-
> ments find it very difficult to build on the
> uneven and sometimes shaky foundations laid in
> these middle schools. Liaison between schools
> is much talked of, but attempts to forge links
> between the high school and the middle schools
> are squashed in the name of 'headmaster's
> prerogatives'.

It may be that diversity of practice and school
autonomy are worth preserving no matter what the
cost. The question to be asked is whether
continuity is sufficiently important to allow
erosion of the traditional freedom schools have
enjoyed.

The Sporadic Nature of Continuity

Commenting on the basically informal approaches
to curriculum continuity revealed by their survey,
the Norfolk Association of Middle School Head
Teachers (1983) observed that dependence on
personalities made them sporadic. Similar statements have appeared in several local authority
documents. Successful liaison frequently seems to
depend upon individual enterprise. The effectiveness of teacher initiatives may be assessed by
reference to examples given in chapter eight.
Clearly, many pupils have experienced smoother
transfer and a more coherent curriculum because
individual teachers have recognised a need and
developed their own strategies for dealing with it.
As Benyon (1984) comments:

> Where any innovation or change takes place,
> there needs to be a degree of dissatisfaction
> with an existing situation. What is happening
> has to be seen to be inefficient, unproductive
> or not very sensible. Change and development
> take place more readily and more effectively

when teachers perceive, and are convinced of,
the need for change.

It would seem, however, that curriculum continuity
is too important to be left to individual teachers
to sustain beyond initial stages. Recognising that
there are problems is but the first step.
Negotiating with colleagues in an associated school
may be within the capacity of a single enthusiastic
teacher but from this point onwards, as others are
drawn into a widening circle of involvement,
promoting continuity becomes a matter for policy
decision.
    The case for local authorities to develop a
continuity policy has been asserted by Stillman and
Maychell (1984). Based on their involvement with
teacher liaison groups in the Isle of Wight, they
concluded that for sustained activity to take place,
the LEA must both develop and implement a policy of
liaison and continuity:

> At local authority level this policy needs to
> be both overt and consistent. Ideally, an LEA
> officer or adviser would have overall respons-
> ibility for co-ordinating a unified approach to
> liaison both at school and LEA level. However,
> where this is not possible, greater attention
> will be necessary on the part of all officers
> and advisers to ensure that a common approach
> is achieved and maintained.

A further point made by these researchers is that
policies need to be sustained. They became aware of
previous initiatives that had lapsed. The considerable effort needed for imparting momentum to a
strategy for improving continuity can so easily be
wasted resulting in frustration for those originally
concerned. Not only is continuity important but it
needs to be so recognised not merely by a few
enthusiasts but by all who can contribute to its
maintenance. The more widely commitment to a
continuity policy is achieved, the more likely it is
to be sustained even when key individuals move to
other schools or other local authorities.

Conclusion

Since the turn of the century, documents
emanating from government have affirmed that the
process of education from school entry at five to
leaving at the end of the secondary stage 'should be

envisaged as a coherent whole'. Researchers have
suggested that the sharp division between primary
and secondary schooling imposes a strain on some
pupils. Incidence of pupils having to repeat in
secondary school work already completed before
transfer is well documented. There is even evidence
of fast-working pupils being slowed down in order to
fit into secondary modes of teaching. (Delamont,
1983) Schools for younger pupils 'operate as
islands' seeing their task solely in terms of
dealing with children at that stage of their
development having no regard for what went before or
will follow. Manifestly, despite many decades of
exhortation, there is more 'rhetoric than reality'
about continuity. Few dispute the importance of
continuity but its promotion is elusive.

As Youngman (1980) observes, all educational
experience involves pupils in some kind of
adjustment to new situations or demands but the
strength and variety of influences encountered
during transfer make this a particularly important
stage in education. Like most other researchers
working in this field, Youngman has attempted to
assess the influence of various characteristics on
early secondary-school performance. His major
finding provides little surprise: that performance
is strongly associated with intellectual measures.
But significant correlations with several other
characteristics prompted him to make the following
statement:

> Principally the main conclusion of this study
> serves to remind that it is rarely satisfactory
> to isolate single determinants of success or
> failure during this period. It also confirms
> that apart from certain well-established factors
> such as prior achievement or intellectual
> ability most characteristics operate in
> association with others. This recalls the
> earlier finding (Youngman, 1978) which
> identified distinct and different profiles for
> pupils of similar ability. Indeed the network
> of interactions can be extremely complex.

Because of the number and variety of interacting factors involved, experience of transfer
varies considerably from pupil to pupil. The
complexity of matters related to transfer and
continuity persuades some teachers that there is
little point in expending much effort for so little
result. Establishing a curriculum policy within one

school can be an enervating, time-consuming task. Continuity, the precursor of successful transfer, demands a working liaison between teachers from different schools. There is an understandable unwillingness to become involved in an exercise so likely to expose tensions. Yet it cannot be sufficiently professional merely to teach pupils for whom one is currently responsible, even when undertaken to the best of one's ability. The fact that there are difficulties cannot excuse lack of attention. We must try to find ways of putting into practice precepts that have been reiterated for many years.

The chapters that follow are concerned with practice. In the main, they discuss strategies that impinge on arrangements for transfer and curriculum continuity. There is a deliberately eclectic approach in an attempt to present an overview of this issue for I am persuaded it would be unrealistic to suggest definitive good practice. What works well under one set of circumstances may fail elsewhere because conditions are so different. Awareness of practice elsewhere may promote some discussion and suggest ways in which schools may collaborate to make children's learning experiences a continuous process.

Chapter Six

THE ALLEVIATION OF CONTINUITY PROBLEMS:
NATIONAL AND REGIONAL STRATEGIES

In recent years mention of the need for continuity
has been almost obligatory within reports and
surveys emanating from central government. HMI
reports on primary, middle and secondary education
have all exhorted teachers to improve continuity
within and between schools. As we have seen, the
essence of continuity problems lies in the
nineteenth century origins of primary and secondary
schools 'conceived of as giving qualitatively
different kinds of education, with different aims,
different curricula, different teaching methods, and
a different spirit'. (Parkyn, 1962) Despite the fact
that all pupils now move from one stage of education
to another, curriculum has developed within but not
across the phases. Sheila Browne (1977) at that
time senior chief HMI had to admit to a local
education authorities' conference: 'It is not
possible to talk about the curriculum as a vertical
whole, with the secondary part firmly linked to the
primary and continuing it. I shall therefore treat
the phases separately.' This admittedly pragmatic
viewpoint permeates the notion, typical of the
central authority, that 'primary' should be
fundamentally different from 'secondary'. Despite
the plea for breaking down barriers, it seems
government cannot get out of the 1944 mould of
'progressive stages'. Indeed, one of the main
reasons for caution about the introduction of middle
schools was that such a development would 'drive a
coach and horses through the traditional distinction
between primary and secondary education enshrined in
the 1944 Act'. (Taylor and Garson, 1982) A DES as
intent upon promoting continuity as advisory reports
suggest would surely have taken more positive steps
to promote middle schools, for the development of a
national three-tier system would have been an

effective means of requiring the education service
to see schooling as a continuum. Of course, the
decentralised educational system in the United
Kingdom militates against decisive expressions of
government opinion. There is, indeed, little to
suggest that the central authority recognised the
opportunity for improved continuity by radical
proposals for changes in the age of transfer in the
1960s.

Middle Schools

Middle schools have been suggested as an administrative solution to problems of continuity. This
opinion needs to be examined closely for some of the
claimed advantages have become part of middle-school
rhetoric more by reiteration of theory than by
proven practice. Sir Alec Clegg, the founding
father of English middle schools, suggested the
three-tier pattern of reorganisation in the Hemworth
division of the West Riding of Yorkshire as a
solution to the problem of abolishing selection for
secondary education whilst avoiding over-large
comprehensive schools. (Blyth and Derricott, 1977)
The fuller implications of a move away from transfer
at the age of eleven evolved only as discussions
proceeded although Clegg had never been convinced of
the unity of the 11 to 18 school. It is doubtful
whether the West Riding middle school can be
considered to have been planned to promote
continuity; it was seen originally more as an
extension of primary education. To the security and
flexibility of the primary school was to be grafted
the enrichment of opportunity made available by a
wider range of teachers and extended facilities.
Children would move out of the class unit only as
need arose, either to gain help when it was required
from the person best able to provide it, or to share
'in the enthusiasms and interests of a teacher other
than their own'. (Clegg, 1969) A pupil would thus
be more mature when he transferred to secondary
school and possibly better able to cope with traumas
caused by transition. Clegg suggested that the work
of the primary school would be continued but the
child would gradually be 'weaned' to a programme of
'limited specialisation' in preparation for full
specialisation in the secondary school. The obvious
opportunities here for effecting continuity of
learning were reiterated in the 1967 Plowden Report,
which suggested that 'a school with semi-specialist
accommodation shared between cognate subjects, and

teachers skilled in certain areas of the curriculum
rather than in single subjects, could provide a
bridge from class teaching to specialisation, and
from investigation of general problems to subject
disciplines (para. 381). But the Plowden Committee
was somewhat inconsistent in its conception of the
middle school:

> If the middle school is to be a new and
> progressive force it must develop further the
> curriculum, methods and attitudes which exist
> at present in junior schools. It must move
> forward into what is now regarded as secondary
> school work, but it must not move so far away
> that it loses the best of primary education as
> we know it now (para. 383).

Understandably, with such ambiguous origins, middle
schools developed without that unity which would
have established them as bridges between schools of
childhood and adolescence. They had the potential
to circumscribe the polarization of viewpoints
between primary and secondary education that had
intensified since the demise of eleven-plus
selection but too close an alignment with one phase
would negate their role as agents of continuity.
    Ambiguous educational arguments underlying the
origin of middle schools hindered the development of
an identity for these new institutions. A further
obstacle to their establishing a distinctive
character has been their lack of status within the
administrative machine. To comply with the
provisions of the 1944 and subsequent acts, middle
schools are deemed to be either primary or secondary
schools. Schools for the 8-12 age-range, deemed
primary, have been impelled more and more to assert
their primary affiliation. (Blyth, 1984b) As
'primary' schools, those for the 8-12 age-range have
a lower capitation allowance for equipment and a
less-favourable staffing allocation than schools for
9-13 year-olds. Taylor and Garson's survey (1982)
revealed that many 8-12 middle schools do not have
'the modest additional buildings to make them
distinctive from a traditional 7-11 primary school'.
If lack of resources reduces a middle school's
ability to offer any specialist or semi-specialist
teaching then its function becomes one of prolonging
the primary stage rather than effecting a
transition.

Middle School Autonomy

The English approach to education is to let each school have the fullest measure of responsibility for its own curriculum, teaching methods and ways of working. Of course, society applies controls: young children have to be taught basic reading and number skills; examinations exert an influence on the teaching of older pupils. With fewer external constraints, middle schools are able to exploit their autonomy. Some have refused to acknowledge their transitional role but insist, with Popper (1967) that 'middle school children need something that will be theirs and theirs alone, not something which will correct that which has not been taught properly, nor something towards which children are preparing'. Given such an approach, it would be by chance rather than design if there was correspondence between children's experiences in the different stages of education through which they moved. It is a feature of the literature on middle schools that these institutions are categorised as places in which 'much innovation and educational rethinking takes place'. (Culling, 1973) By implication, if radical rethinking is necessary then what emerges as an appropriate education for middle-school pupils will deviate somewhat from what was previously acceptable. That is it will deviate from the kind of education presented in primary or secondary schools for they were the schools in which children of middle-years age range received an education before the development of middle schools. Radical change within one stage of education will put it out of step with other stages. If radical rethinking is required, it should be exercised through the whole period of compulsory education, a task beyond the operability of a single school and one which would be undertaken by the central authority in most other countries.

When middle-school teachers cling to their autonomy and promote innovation, they tend to inhibit continuity. Clearly, there is a contradiction within middle-school ideology for institutions which insist on independence cannot claim to be agents of transition. (Hargreaves, 1980) Further, some of the statements by middle school advocates seem likely to alienate colleagues in other sectors rather than persuade them to enter into consultation. Typically, the report of a middle-school working party in Brighton stated:

> The middle school has its own tasks to perform;
> it will be child-centred and the curriculum
> will be developed to meet the burgeoning needs
> of children at this intermediate stage . . . To
> some extent it will be for secondary schools to
> adapt their curriculum and methods in the first
> year to the needs of the middle-school child.

The notion that it is up to secondary schools to
accept middle-school pupils as they are and not to
seek to influence their education at an earlier
stage has occurred frequently in the literature on
middle schools. At times one can detect an almost
arrogant tone, as for example in the report of the
Assistant Masters' Association conference on the
middle school in 1975:

> Members from the middle school insisted that
> the schools have the right to develop an ethos
> of their own and the teachers in them have the
> right to decide how to teach their subjects in
> a way which is appropriate to the age-range of
> their pupils. They claimed that any dictation
> on curriculum matters and on teaching method
> from the staffs of senior schools would be
> unacceptable, indeed intolerable, and would be
> a denial of one of the main advantages claimed
> for the middle school system that children gain
> from having a clear transitional stage before
> transfer to a large comprehensive school.

Manifestly, the 'transitional stage' this conference
had in mind was one which could exist without
reference to the other stages. It is doubtful
whether teachers in those other stages would wish to
liaise with colleagues who could make such
inflammatory statements. The language used –
'insisted', 'rights', 'unacceptable', 'intolerable'
– is typical of those taking up an entrenched
position in a conflict; it seems particularly
inappropriate in a discussion of the relationship
between middle and upper schools. Understandably,
conference delegates from secondary schools, whilst
conceding that the middle-school system had much in
its favour, argued forcibly that there must be co-
operation upon curriculum and syllabus matters
between teachers from the two sectors. It was
pointed out that lack of continuity would inevitably
occur if some middle schools taught German when
French was the only language taught after transfer,
if science in some middle schools meant, in fact,

only biology or if some middle schools insisted upon
teaching mathematics in the traditional style when
the senior school adopted the 'modern' approach. Of
course, there would be a similar lack of
co-operation if a department of a senior school
changed its syllabus radically and expected its
feeder schools to make corresponding changes.
Manifestly, schools concerned with successive
educational stages cannot work independently and
claim at the same time to be promoting continuity.
Middle schools are ideally situated, as their
originators suggested, to moderate extreme changes
of educational experience of pupils moving from
schooling appropriate to childhood to that of
adolescence. Their effectiveness as transition
agents, however, depends on their willingness to
relinquish some freedom of choice, and the extent to
which they can collaborate with colleagues in other
sectors.

Middle School Teachers

Clearly, the extent to which curriculum
continuity can be achieved is going to depend upon
collaborative efforts of teachers in successive
stages but the differential status of teachers can
obstruct this process. Ginsburg's (1977) research
in Hereford and Worcester suggests that teachers
find it difficult to enter into open discussion if
they feel themselves to be subordinate to colleagues
in other sectors. There is a tendency to resent
evaluative comments of teachers in the succeeding
stage who, by their position in a larger, more-
generously resourced school, seem insulated from
practical circumstances which impinge on curriculum
continuity. Middle-school teachers found high-school
staff intransigent but exerted a powerful influence
on practice in first schools. Thus, within the
schools surveyed in this study, a grudging
continuity seems to have been achieved more by the
downward influence of the more dominant institution
than by any collaborative effort. Whatever the
cause of dissension over matters of curriculum
between teachers in the schools Ginsburg surveyed,
there was agreement that children transferring were
caused unnecessary problems.

It is not merely status and remuneration that
cause problems. Middle-school teachers have wide,
crucial responsibilities and too many demands on
their time. As Jennifer Nias (1980) points out,
'because there are more adult functions to be

91

fulfilled in most middle schools than there are available adults, staff face the challenge of changing their roles many times during the school day'. Taylor and Garson's (1982) survey revealed 'a burden of overwork, lack of facilities and shortage of ancillary non-teaching staff' which posed a threat to maintenance of a full curriculum in some middle schools. The DES 9-13 Middle Schools Survey (1983) concluded 'the present overall level of staffing leaves little margin of teacher-time for purposes other than the teaching of a class'. Clearly, many middle-school teachers are fully occupied in their own schools; effective links with other sectors are difficult to maintain because their schools lack the flexibility to allow them to be released from teaching duties in order to attend meetings.

Primary or Secondary Orientation

The extent of continuity achievement on transfer to the upper school will vary according to the middle school's particular emphasis. Any continuity advantage obtaining to middle schools is surely forfeited if the school's policy is to extend primary methods to an older age-range without any injection of secondary work. A National Union of Teachers discussion document on middle schools comments: 'Once there is a possibility that specialist teaching is at a minimum the accusation that the middle school is simply a prolongation of the primary stage cannot be contradicted.' (NUT, 1979)

Of course the converse, secondary orientation for middle schools, is just as impracticable from a continuity point of view for it merely brings forward the age at which pupils are plunged into a subject-based curriculum. As with some primary-based middle schools, secondary orientation has sometimes been the result of expedient retention of procedures related to the school's previous designation. In the early years of middle-school development, for example, an ex-secondary headmaster justified his authority's change to a middle-school system by stating that though there had been no change at all in the syllabus, his pupils were coping adequately. He claimed: 'They are being given a secondary-school curriculum at the age of nine and are thriving on it.' (Gorwood, 1978)

What seems to be needed, then, is an amalgam of primary and secondary work but this too can present problems. A school which adopts primary methods for the first two years and secondary methods thereafter - categorised by Burrows (1978) as the 'pantomime horse middle school' - negates the weaning concept by perpetuating the original division. Hargreaves and Warwick (1978) have noted an organisational split rather than a gradual change in middle schools in which ex-secondary teachers have been 'expected to use their specialisms with upper-age pupils' while ex-primary teachers continued to teach younger ones. If such an approach is related to past experience of teachers rather than to deliberate balancing strategy it may merely be a temporary phenomenon. This approach, anyhow, does have advantages over the traditional primary-secondary system for pupils have to cope only with a change of regime and not with change of schools and unfamilar teachers. Brenda Cohen (1976) has suggested a further complication: when both primary and secondary processes are built into a middle-school design, 'benevolently-intended compromise may very easily become a battleground for competing ideologies'. As she has pointed out it is very difficult for the progressive, 'at his most vehement when attacking examinations and the pursuit of purely academic goals' to compromise with the defender of academic standards so often associated with the secondary-school examination system.

The shortcomings of too close an identification with either primary or secondary influences suggest that middle schools should not base curriculum on a blend of existing traditions but the education of pupils of middle-years age-range should be looked at anew. This, according to Burrows (1978), is what has happened in the 'pacemaker' schools. If, however, such schools develop distinctive characteristics without reference to associated first and upper schools they can cause continuity difficulties of the kind already noted in discussing autonomy. When dialogue between schools is reasonable enough for them to act as moderating influences on each other then problems of this kind can be overcome. Arthur Razzell (1975) approached the headship of Ravenscote Middle School in Surrey with the clear intention of being innovative. 'An extremely flexible type of school organisation' in which it was possible to 'provide a variable set of approaches to children's learning' was seen as being particularly appropriate. 'Specialist teaching, within the normal secondary-school meaning of the term' was kept to a minimum. He sought to create a school with a distinctive character of its own untrammelled by secondary influences. Yet according to the headmaster of the secondary school to which Ravenscote pupils transferred at the age of twelve, there had to be a very close liaison with middle schools in order to work out a common curriculum. (BBC, 1975) As an example of the informal but positive initiative taken by the secondary school to promote continuity, he commented: 'We went over to the middle school and said, "We're going to do SMP maths; we think it's advisable that you do SMP, certainly in your fourth year - what you do before that is entirely up to you - but might we suggest that you do SMP in your fourth year".' According to Razzell, the two schools had undertaken 'a bit of horse-trading over various aspects of the curriculum' and exchanged books. Whilst there was no pretence of a close relationship between these two schools, when they felt it important to work to a common pattern then this was feasible. The achievement of continuity depends less on school ethos and more on the ability of associated schools to enter into negotiation.

Middle School Size

A crucial factor in a middle school's ability to arrange for the kind of flexible organisation advocated by Razzell is that of size. Within a relatively small institution it is not possible to treat each subject separately and have it taught by a specialist teacher even if that is what the head would wish. In Towards the Middle School, the DES suggested that school curriculum might well be biased by such factors as 'the balance of skills on the staff and the facilities available'. (DES, 1970) Official support for such a contingency policy has led to anomolies. Particularly in those small middle schools anxious to extend beyond the primary class-teacher mode, the lack of a full range of expertise has led to the temporary inclusion of some subject dependent upon the duration of a particular member of staff's appointment. French can appear in the curriculum not as a part of a generally-approved scheme but because of the unpredictable presence of a French teacher on the staff. Science can be biased towards biology at one time, chemistry at another, when teacher changes are allowed to determine curriculum. Consistency can sometimes be achieved when a versatile head can supplement the skills of staff by filling in

whenever there is a lack of expertise or when upper-
school colleagues can be persuaded to help out.

The importance of school size in determining
curriculum was not appreciated in the early days of
middle-school development. In its earliest major
middle-school publication, Building Bulletin No 35
the DES (1966) provided plans for schools of two-
and three-form entry with between 280 and 480 pupils
on roll. On a basis of per capita allocation of
space, smaller schools could not provide facilities
and equipment for more advanced work in all
curricular areas. Even within a larger three-form-
entry school for pupils in the 9-13 age-range, after
the basic work space per pupil had been allotted,
options on the use of additional teaching area were
limited. If the remaining space was used for some
major feature such as a library, gymnasium or crafts
centre, then it would not be available to make
provision for more advanced work in, for example,
science or modern languages. Limitations on space
affected the initial selection of specialist
teaching facilities with inevitable implications for
future staffing.

Official acceptance of diversity of middle-
school curricular provision was implicit in early
DES literature but perhaps the most overt expression
of the attitude came from Burrows, at that time one
of HM Inspectorate, speaking at the Joint Four
Conference in 1969: 'Facilities do of course
exercise a powerful influence upon curriculum and
teaching methods in any school, and in middle
schools no uniformity need be expected.' In order
to provide some degree of specialist expertise in
every branch of the curriculum, Burrows estimated
there would need to be at least twelve staff, which
at the 1:25 staffing ratio assumed by the DES at the
time, would result in a minimum viable middle-school
size of 300 pupils. In 1970, while cautioning that
a school of 600 children would be a very large
community for eight-year-olds to enter, the DES
suggested a four-form-entry of 560 pupils would be
acceptable for a nine-year old 'especially since
this size would be likely to lead to a staff
numerous and varied enough to meet the growing
curricular needs of children over 13'. This would
seem to suggest official acceptance of a significant
difference in the needs of middle schools for the
9-13 as opposed to the 8-12 age range. Burrows had
commented that 'the ablest children by the age of
thirteen are out-distancing their fellows in
knowledge and attainment at ever-increasing speed'.

In order to satisfy the needs of such older children, a middle school would need to be of sufficient size to attract intellectually-gifted and well-informed teachers who could extend pupils' attainments over the whole curriculum.

Like the administrators, the teaching profession has based its recommendation for a middle-school optimum size of approximately 500 pupils on the needs of the curriculum. A group of Bedfordshire teachers, in 1971, suggested a middle school of 500-600 pupils because 'only with larger numbers could the use of specialists be economically justified'. The result of a small survey carried out by the NUT (1975) was that middle schools with enrolments of over 500 pupils 'have a better change of providing more specialist teaching' while schools with fewer than 400 pupils could well face problems as far as specialist teaching was concerned. Particularly interesting is the example of the implications of schools size for mathematics teaching: 'four out of six schools with enrolments of 501 and over could offer specialist teaching in mathematics compared with only one out of six with 500 pupils or less'. The 1983 DES survey of 9-13 middle schools took the argument one stage further by relating size of school to standards of work: 'large schools which had over 480 pupils on roll achieved higher standards generally than schools with fewer pupils'. Moreover, the ability of larger schools to employ senior teachers and two deputy heads who could be released from teaching duties for longer periods in the week gave them a distinct advantage over smaller schools. One of the factors influencing arrangements made for continuity and liaison was stated as the time heads were able to give to the task. The overall conclusion was that unless small schools were 'disproportionately staffed' the quality of education they had to offer would suffer.

Size of school constitutes a major source of disparity as far as middle-school curriculum is concerned. As will be seen from Table 6.1, schools vary in size markedly, not only when the middle school system is considered in toto but within a single age-range. Schools 'deemed primary' are generally smaller than those 'deemed secondary' but even within the latter group some schools are very small: over 30 with fewer than 200 pupils on roll. Burrows, in 1969, suggested a minimum middle-school size of 300 pupils. In 1983, 43.7 per cent of all middle schools were below this minimum recommendation. If one accepts the NUT optimum size of 500

Table 6.1: Size of Middle Schools in England - January 1983

i. Mean size of schools

	Type of School					Total
	Deemed Primary		Deemed Secondary			
	8-12	9-12/13	9-13	10-13	10-14	
Number of schools	746	11	605	37	6	1,405
Number of pupils	21,051	2,736	242,474	17,399	3,864	476,524
Mean number of pupils on roll	282	249	401	470	644	339
Maximum number of pupils on roll	654	412	847	763	863	863
Minimum number of pupils on roll	38	134	72	246	400	38

Compiled from DES List of Schools, DES Statistics Branch, December 1983

Table 6.1: Size of Middle Schools in England - January 1983

ii. Analysis of size

Pupils on Roll	Deemed Primary		Deemed Secondary		Total	
	No. schools	%	No. schools	%	No. schools	%
under 100	12	1.58	3	0.46	15	1.07
101-200	143	18.89	29	4.47	172	12.24
201-300	312	41.22	116	17.90	428	30.46
301-400	215	28.40	170	26.23	385	27.40
401-500	55	7.27	171	26.38	226	16.09
501-600	17	2.25	112	17.28	129	9.18
601-700	3	0.39	40	6.17	43	3.06
701-800	-	-	4	0.62	4	0.28
801-900	-	-	3	0.46	3	0.21
Total	757		648		1,405	

Compiled from DES List of Schools, DES Statistics Branch, December 1983

pupils, very close to the 480-pupil 'higher standard schools' of the DES 9-13 Survey, 87.2 per cent of middle schools fall below this figure. According to Burrows (1978) a school with fewer than 300 pupils 'will probably have to offer a restricted curriculum' whereas a school of 600 pupils 'could be very fortunately placed over staffing, for it could, for instance, appoint two or three science teachers, each strong in a different branch of science'. In 1983, only 3.55 per cent where in this 'fortunately placed' category. In summary, then, small schools, unless expensively staffed, will be unable to offer a fully-differentiated curriculum. This has obvious implications for continuity when contributory schools to the same upper school are of vastly different size.

Middle School Curriculum

A consideration of middle schools within the context of continuity must address itself to what is distinctive about middle-school curricula. Of course, middle schools are so diverse that any notion of a middle-school curriculum is untenable but some issues have been reiterated so often that they can be said to constitute generalisations about middle-school curricula.

One of the essential features of the middle school has been its recognition of the need to encourage individualised learning. The promotion of individualised approaches reflects theoretical tenets such as those of Gagné (1967) who insists that ultimately the learner is responsible for his own learning: 'The student needs to learn that learning takes place within his own head as a result of his own "thinking" activity.' It reflects, too, a recognition that whilst each individual is different no matter what his age, at no time are differences more pronounced than during the middle years of schooling. On transfer to upper school, it is unlikely that a pupil will find an emphasis on individual work. Despite the sporadic development of Mode 3 syllabuses in which there is the possibility of individual projects, the majority of the teaching in a secondary school is likely to be in the form of class teaching. This change of mode of working should not be too disturbing to children, who, in any case, have been anticipating a change and will have been prepared for it by middle-school teachers. A greater cause for concern relates to the major differences on entry to upper schools that

99

can occur not only in pupils' achievements but in
the range of their learning when individualised
approaches have predominated in the middle school.
Much will depend upon the kind of learning involved.
Curricular strategies in the middle school are
generally considered to be more concerned with the
learning process - with 'learning how to learn' -
than with the acquisition of particular content.
There can be problems for the secondary class
teacher, however, if some pupils have studied a
particular topic in depth while others have little
or no knowledge of it. Middle school advocates
claim that upper schools should not be perturbed by
individual variety if pupils have learned to acquire
and apply knowledge; indeed, their independence will
have made middle-school pupils more assiduous,
adaptable and better able to concentrate. Attitudes
to learning are obviously important but so is
curriculum content. Middle schools must provide
opportunities for pupils not only to develop
learning powers but also to encompass basic learning
necessary for later disciplined study. Themes and
projects may have the merits of relevance and
interest for pupils but they can justifiably be
criticised by upper-school specialists if they
provide no foundation in the methods, skills and
approaches of their particular disciplines.

Linear Subjects

In subjects of a 'linear' nature - that is
those in which learning of new skills and concepts
needs to be based on what has been learned at
earlier stages - a sequential approach is essential.
Mathematics, as such a subject, calls for a
systematically-planned course to be presented to
children as they progress through their education.
Manifestly, this does not always happen. In recent
years, changes have been introduced into both
content and method of teaching this subject so that
children can pass from one stage of education to
another with very different mathematical backgrounds. In the past, fairly standard textbooks and
the eleven-plus examination tended to ensure that
all young children received a similar preparation in
mathematics but the newer approaches demanded
experimentation. As institutions innovatory in
themselves, middle schools provided fertile ground
for such experimentation. As new ways were tried,
schemes of work were adapted and sometimes abandoned
altogether. (Biggs, 1973) Without adequate guide-

lines it is difficult to prevent repetition and to
ensure that vital learning stages are not being
missed; it is, of course, almost impossible to
maintain continuity when individual schools experiment without consulting associated schools. It would
be misleading, however, to attribute discontinuity
entirely to independent action by middle schools. A
middle school responding to the NUT survey (1979)
complained that it served three high schools 'each
with disparate approaches to the teaching of
mathematics'. The author's own research similarly
revealed that middle schools found it impossible to
prepare pupils for transfer to any of several upper
schools which had not agreed a mathematics policy
between themselves. (Gorwood, 1981) Self-contained
independence in any curricular matters is difficult
to justify but in sequential subjects it is vital
that decisions should involve all associated
schools.
    Burrows (1978) has illustrated from another
curriculum area the difficulties that arise when
agreement between schools has not been reached:

> The first foreign language in this country is
> traditionally French, and all first and second
> year upper school pupils are likely to learn
> it. But what is their starting point to be?
> If there are six contributory middle schools
> and there has been no co-ordination, there may
> well be two which have already given their
> pupils a four-year course, one a two-year
> course, one through exigencies of staff an
> erratic now-we-have-it-now-we-don't provision,
> one no Fench at all, and one originally-minded
> school which instead has provided German. What
> is the languages department of the upper school
> to do? One can hardly blame its members if
> they decide to ignore the preceding chaos and
> start everyone at the beginning - which is
> quite unfair to the pupils, some of whom will
> be happily whisked along, some bored at
> covering again ground they have covered
> already, some rebellious at losing their
> German, and some confused because their group
> is so heterogeneous that orderly teaching
> rapidly becomes impossible.

While there are now doubts about the value of
teaching French to young children, most authorities
feel that some start must be made before transfer
from the middle school if the subject is to be

developed sufficiently for it to become coherent.
Yet there are vast differences in middle-school
provision for French. Some headteachers have been
deterred from introducing French because they lack a
competent teacher of the subject or conditions are
otherwise unfavourable. Others feel that since it
is no longer demonstrable that there are clear
advantages to making an early start to learning a
foreign language, it would be sensible to delay
French until the upper middle-school age-range and
then give it concentrated attention. (Burstall,
1974) Others find difficulty in reconciling the
needs of teaching a highly-structured subject within
the organisational framework they see as being right
for the middle school. Gannon (1975) for example,
stated that within his prescribed year-group system
he tried to ensure a curricular balance between
members of staff and preferred to use non-specialist
teachers with supporting audio-visual material
rather than 'import' a special French teacher into
the group from another year. Single-subject
specialists dispersed through a school would
fragment the time-table and preclude the setting
aside of long, uninterrupted periods for thematic
work or integrated studies.

As with mathematics, so with French, it is
essential that middle and upper-school staff collaborate to promote continuity. There are many
examples of liaison groups working amicably to
produce recommended courses for there are seldom
major difficulties concerning methodology and
content. The major problem seems to relate to
variations in qualifications and competence of
teachers in the middle school. Understandably, some
secondary-school teachers would rather have the
introduction of French teaching delayed than receive
pupils who have already acquired an inaccurate
accent or intonation. The key to achieving
continuity in learning French would seem to rest in
improving teacher competence at the middle-school
level but even at times of teacher redundancy this
has been a 'teacher-shortage' subject. Manifestly,
when expertise is at a premium, it should be used as
effectively as possible. It is difficult to justify
the approach outlined above of using French
specialists within one year-group for they
presumably will spend much of their time teaching
other subjects whilst less competent teachers
struggle to teach French in other years. An experiment at the other extreme involves the appointment

of one French teacher to two or three small middle-schools, a strategy which fully utilises expertise but is somewhat alien to the middle-school philosophy of satisfying a pupil's need for close teacher-contact.

Another area of the curriculum which can cause problems of continuity between middle and upper schools is that of science. One commentator submits: 'teachers of science subjects in secondary schools are justified in criticising middle-school curricula that have left science to the tender mercies of 'themes' where it has sunk without trace or subsumed it under 'environmental studies' where the methods and approaches of the scientist have been neglected or ignored'. (Brown, 1983) Whether science is a 'linear' subject or not is open to question but the secondary scientist's claim that there is a vast content within science curriculum is difficult to counter. Some maintain but others deny that a start must be made to external examination courses before transfer at the age of thirteen. There is less contention that science is qualitat-ively different in the upper school from that in the middle school where discovery approaches predominate (Ross, 1975) A major Schools Council science project for the middle years age-range is discovery-based. Richards (1973) suggests that 'discovery science' is not 'science' in the generally-accepted sense of the word: it is concerned with children's accumulation of experience rather than the logical development of observation, classification, hypothesis and experiment. It has been claimed that Science 5-13 does not prepare children adequately for the secondary science curriculum (Pearce, 1974) and that it is 'too primary' in its orientation.

The polarization of primary and secondary methods in science has engaged the attention of several local authority middle-school working parties. In Brighton, for example, whilst Science 5-13 was commended as offering the most satisfactory course for their developing schools for the 8-12 age-range, it was felt that in the fourth year a more formal and rigorous approach to experi-mental science was needed. The Chester working party concerned with the same age-range was unanimous in seeing exploration of the environment under the guidance of the class teacher as the most appropriate form of scientific study for the first two year-groups. They could not decide, however, whether specialisation or integrated studies would be applicable to older middle-school pupils.

It would depend, they felt, on whether or not a science consultant was available in which case it would be his option to determine the approach. If no science specialist was available it was thought schools would have no choice but to organise an integrated science course. Yet again we find a subject for which middle schools have difficulty in recruiting staff. Transition in science, then, can create acute problems because of the need to move from a general, experience-based approach to one more directly related to specific subject content.

Evidence from some local authorities with middle schools suggests that problems of continuity in science are not insuperable. The most successful solution seems to be in general agreement being reached not merely in associated schools but within a wide catchment area. A response to the NUT (1979) survey, typically, states: 'Science teachers rapidly recognised the sequential nature of their subject and considered that a town-wide common course was most appropriate. A course was adopted and the group spends most of its energies now on assessing the effectiveness of science teaching.' The production of agreed schemes for large numbers of schools tends to be the responsibility of liaison committees which will be discussed more appropriately in the following chapter on local authority strategies for improving continuity.

Liaison between Middle and Upper Schools

An upper school within a three-tier system accepts pupils from more than one middle school; usually it is fed by several schools. It will be evident from the foregoing paragraphs that such schools may have radically different approaches to curriculum depending upon the philosophies of their headteachers and staffs, the available facilities and the number of pupils on roll. Differences are inevitable but they can be minimised if all teachers concerned are able to take part in discussions. Relationships involved, of course, will not only be 'horizontal', concerning middle-school teachers responsible for a particular area of the curriculum, but also 'vertical', including subject specialists in the upper school. Difficulties may arise at this stage if responsibility for teaching a particular subject is equally shared between class teachers, or if it is only taught within a thematic approach in one or more of the middle schools. Identifying teachers concerned presents no problems in senior

school where curricular responsibility is vested in
heads of departments. Arrangements for the discussion of matters involving curriculum continuity vary
both in organisation and degree of formality. Ad
hoc meetings may be called to discuss particular
problems as they arise or there may be standing
committees for the regular and detailed review of
curriculum in groups of related schools. The more
complex the three-tier system, the larger will be the
group of teachers involved in discussions, which
tend to become prolonged. Additionally, it is more
difficult to achieve consensus on specific matters
so such meetings can sometimes result in the
production of guidelines so general that significant
curricular differences between schools remain. When
middle and upper schools are enmeshed in a network
of interrelationships, curricular change in one
school can have repercussions in many. Yet to
allow freedom of parental choice and to avoid the
formation of neighbourhood schools it is inevitable
that there will be many affiliated schools.

Some comprehensive-school head teachers
maintain that in order to achieve a balanced social
and intellectual intake they must draw pupils from a
wide catchment area; they wish to avoid a 'ghetto
school' development. (Rowe, 1971) Whether it can
ever be justified to try to solve neighbourhood
school problems by dispersing children throughout a
city is doubtful. Such an approach is really an
avoidance of what is essentially a social problem.
(Walton, 1971) The promotion of a truly comprehensive system would seem to be no more facilitated
within complex urban schemes involving wide parental
choice than in pyramidal organisations in which
choice is limited. (Fiske, 1978) Of course, there
can be no absolute direction in any pyramidal scheme
for parents have rights of appeal under provisions
of the Education Act of 1980. Exercise of parental
choice, in any case, results in a system in which
the majority of pupils are drawn from a school's
immediate locality for most parents do not wish to
send their children far from home. It is difficult
to discern the advantages of any three-tier system
other than one in which all the children in one
sector eventually arrive at one upper school from a
small number of middle schools each fed by one or
two first schools. If such pyramidal structures had
been established as the norm for three-tier organisation many of the more extreme continuity difficulties would have been avoided. In this context,
there is merit in Walton's suggestion that a

structural alteration should be made to organisation
to make the whole age-range 5-18 the basic unit. An
'atomised structure' allowing institutions freedom
to make decisions in isolation works against the
important objective of promoting consultation and
continuity. The core of Walton's restructured
organisation would be an academic board with real
power to administer a neighbourhood unit of some
4,000 pupils in related first, middle and upper
schools. This takes the pyramidal structure one
stage further by reducing the autonomy of individual
schools. It is questionable whether such an
approach would find favour with headteachers,
accustomed to a large measure of freedom but as
experience in Devon has shown it can certainly
result in improved liaison possibilities.

On the surface, the establishment of middle
schools seems to have generated more problems of
curriculum continuity than it has solved. When set
up under optimal conditions of size, resources and
type of three-tier structure, however, middle
schools can be effective in bridging the gap between
primary and secondary approaches to curriculum. Yet
this, I contend, is not their major contribution to
improving continuity. It is rather that middle
schools, by their very existence, have placed
continuity problems in sharper focus.

Reducing the Trauma of Transfer

One of Plowden's arguments for the establishment of middle schools was that comprehensive schools
were likely to become such large institutions that
the move from a small primary schools would present
major problems for young children. A secondary-
school teacher with special responsibility for
liaison supplies illustrative detail:

> They fear the unknown. There are, of course,
> the usual neighbourhood rumours of initiation
> ceremonies - mostly untrue. In our particular
> case the sheer size of the building is in
> itself daunting: two wings separated by an
> administrative block; each wing three storeys
> high, three separate craft blocks, fourteen
> mobile classrooms, and enormous playing fields.
> They are afraid of getting lost, of not
> knowing where the cloakrooms and toilets are,
> of arriving late for lessons, of having to get
> to know numerous new teachers and worst of all
> of making mistakes. (Mahoney, 1981)

The extent of the increase in size of secondary schools in comparison with primaries over the last thirty years was detailed in chapter three, as was the relationship between size of school and social environment. Small schools, it was argued, are better able to give the average pupil a sense of security. Middle schools, of moderate size, can shield pupils for at least a year and possibly two from the harsher pressures likely to be experienced by those transferring at the age of eleven. Further, pupils will be more mature at the time of transfer so the resulting upper school will serve a more homogeneous community. Upper schools are likely to be smaller in three-tier systems than traditional comprehensives and so less forbidding to new pupils. Middle schools can take extremes out of the system. If transfer from primary to secondary schools is like taking a cold plunge after a warm bath, middle schools provide tepid water to temper the shock. That they succeed in creating a secure environment for pupils was recognised by HMI in the survey of 9-13 middle schools:

> The general picture which emerged from the survey was of relaxed and orderly communities in which teachers were friendly and consistent in their dealings with pupils and where children responded with friendliness and respect towards their fellow pupils, members of staff and other adults. (DES, 1983)

The favourable social climate in middle schools is now generally accepted and Plowden's plea that pupils in such schools should be protected from secondary influences has been fulfilled. But some critics maintain that by delaying entry to external examination courses middle schools have purchased improvements in social adjustment at the expense of academic achievement.

Attainment in Middle Schools

Research prior to the establishment of middle schools into 'transition units' is relevant to a discussion of the relationship between social adjustment and academic attainment. Ancillary to their main study into suitable age for transfer, an experiment conducted in one of Nisbet and Entwistle's (1969) research schools introduced a 'transitional phase' involving a modification of timetable and curriculum of first-year classes to

mitigate some of the effects of the traditional
'sharp break'. The number of teachers pupils
encountered was limited whilst project and
individual work retained the more generalised
primary approach to curriculum. It was found that
children who transferred under the modified system
had significantly more favourable attitudes towards
secondary education than those of a matched group
for whom there had been no transitional phase.
Better attitudes, it was thought, would lead to
higher academic attainment especially among young,
immature, working-class children, who suffered most
from the traditional sharp break. Dutch and McCall
(1974) also compared a group of pupils who spent a
period in a transition unit with those who had
transferred direct to secondary school and concluded
that as a result of passing through the transitional
system pupils had shown 'a small but sometimes
significant improvement in the social/emotional area
without loss of academic attainment'. Nash (1973)
on the other hand, in a study of transfer from five
primary schools to a Scottish comprehensive, found
that staying in a transition unit had a harmful
effect on some pupils. Those who had entered the
transition unit from primary schools where there had
been a conscious preparation for the supposedly
strict regime of the secondary school were not
accustomed to the freedom deliberately introduced in
an attempt to smooth transition from primary to
secondary. Taking advantage of less rigorous
control, which they saw as a sign of 'softness',
they were badly-behaved and made little effort.
Youngman and Lunzer (1977) similarly found that
pupils in their Nottinghamshire study who had passed
through 'lower school units' showed poor motivation
after entry into the main secondary school; they
suggested that the 'cushioning effect' of the
intermediate stage produced a reaction against
academic work.

Manifestly, the relative effectiveness of
different forms of schooling is difficult to
estimate but this should present no surprise for, as
was suggested in the previous chapter, evaluation of
school effectiveness is beset with problems. Of the
sparse evidence on middle schools, that of Bryan and
Digby (19839 is significant in its suggestion that,
in terms of external examination results, pupils
suffer no serious handicap because of later transfer
into secondary education. Within the local
authority in which their research was conducted,
transfer was effected at different ages depending

upon area. They were able, therefore, to compare attainment of pupils who had transferred at eleven-plus in a selective system, and at twelve and thirteen-plus from middle schools. They concluded that when non-school factors were taken into account, there was no statistically-significant difference in pupils' average 'O' level performance by age of transfer to secondary school.

One aspect of research by the author in Humberside was a consideration of the relationship between attainment in upper schools and factors in middle schools from which pupils had transferred. (Gorwood 1981 and 1983) After considering the attainment in all academic subjects of over 400 pupils transferring from ten middle to two upper schools, I was able to conclude that pupils adjusted quickly to the new institution. As in the Bryan and Digby study, the Humberside research showed the major determinants of long-term attainment to be found in factors outside schools. Eighteen months after transfer, with one exception, there was no significant variation in attainment between pupils from different contributory schools; in several areas of the curriculum, it took less than six months for measurable contributory school influence to fade. One may deduce from this that in terms of achievement, the influence of the institution through which pupils are currently passing overrides circumstances in their school prior to transfer.

Since pupils' long-term attainment in a receiving school seems so little related to contri-butory school experience, it is tempting to suggest that the need for continuity is not as crucial as most critics claim. But this notion overlooks several important factors. Tests and examinations providing evidence for research into this issue are mainly related to courses which are not started until pupils arrive in upper schools; it is not surprising therefore that they reflect little of what pupils learned prior to transfer. External examinations, whose results are favoured by researchers for providing readily comparable data, are taken several years after transfer; the further away from an event an observation is made, the more its effects become obscured. Even when attainment is tested earlier, the measuring instrument may be inappropriate or not sufficiently finely-tuned to expose pre-transfer learning. Above all it would be meretricious to deny the need for continuity on the basis of existing attainment evidence because data is not available to compare systems where continuity

pertains with those in which there is a lack of
continuity. It is difficult to envisage how such a
comparative study could be conducted and doubtful
whether it could ever be demonstrated unequivocally
that continuity or lack of it was unrelated to
pupils' attainments. Manifestly it cannot be
claimed that continuity does not matter nor does it
follow that lack of continuity has a disastrous
effect on attainment. There is no evidence to
support those who criticise middle schools for
purchasing improvements in social adjustment by
discontinuities in learning.

If middle schools had been established under
optimum conditions they could have been a most
effective means of achieving continuity. They are
still the best institutional agency for bridging the
gap between primary and secondary education.
Particularly when, as a high priority, consideration
has been given to conditions needed for the
promotion of continuity, middle schools have
achieved the kind of liaison their originators
envisaged for them.

Middle Years of Schooling

Before the establishment of middle schools,
curricular discussion was contained within fairly
tight 'primary' or 'secondary' contexts. Most
writers assumed there was a great divide to be
crossed at about the age of eleven. It may be that
attention would have been given to the middle years
of schooling whether middle schools had been developed or not but the focusing of interest on the
curricular needs of children between the ages of
eight and thirteen must surely have been sustained
by the existence of an institution committed to
finding appropriate ways of providing for pupils
during this vital transitional phase. If, as some
predict, the middle school will fade away, middle-
years curriculum will remain as its legacy.

In its programme of following up the Plowden
Report, the Schools Council organised a conference
in 1967, not with the specific middle school as its
theme but on the broader issue of the kind of
curriculum most suited to the needs of pupils
between the ages of eight and thirteen irrespective
of institutional context. Alec Ross suggests this
was done advisedly for there was no wish to prejudge
a question of policy. (Ross, 1969) One can detect,
too, in early writing on the middle years understandable reluctance to deviate from the

conventional phases. Some followed Plowden in
seeing the middle years as an extension of primary
schooling; reference to earlier specialisation
suggests that others were working from a secondary
model.

What was needed was 'not an amalgam of existing
traditions for younger and for older children but .
. . fresh thinking about how children in this age
range might best be educated'. The Middle Years of
Schooling Project team went on to suggest: 'The terms
"primary" and "secondary" may, in this context, be
barriers to understanding; they should not be used
as touchstones, threats, or evaluative judgements
when discussing the curriculum of the middle years
of schooling.' (Schools Council, 1972) The task,
then, was to provide materials, resources, guides
and reports with no particular institution in mind.
For project teams concerned with specific areas of
the curriculum this proved to be a difficult
assignment. Indeed, the designated age-range of
some Schools Council projects, although encompassing
the middle years, placed emphasis on younger and
older rather than middle years pupils.
Environmental Studies 5-13, for example, based on
'discovery' and 'child-centred' philosophies and
mainly concerned with the development of skills had
a decidedly primary orientation while Project
Environment 8-18, enquiry-based in the Humanities
Project mould, was aimed at secondary pupils.
Though many provided relevant material, few projects
were narrowly concerned with the specific middle
years age-range.

Middle Years of Schooling - The Whole Curriculum

Most projects dealt with branches of the
curriculum but the Middle Years of Schooling team
tackled the total curriculum for this age-range and
brought to it the 'fresh thinking' its director,
Professor Ross, had advocated. The team's approach
to curriculum planning was based on the importance
of considering education as a continuous process:

> The task of working out a curriculum for the
> middle years must be done bearing in mind the
> single sweep; of a total education bringing a
> child from infancy through childhood and
> adolescence to adulthood. It is to be hoped
> that the attention now being given to the
> middle years will result not in the intro-
> duction of further unnecessary breaks in the
> child's education but in the creation of a

transition period that will smooth rather than
interrupt the change from work that is
distinctly 'primary' to work that is distinctly
'secondary'.

So a middle years curriculum was to be rooted in
neither primary nor secondary practice but the move
towards differentiated learning posed a problem of
extent: there was too much to include, particularly
if, in addition to factual learning, there was to be
development of learning skills, cultivation of
values, interests and awarenesses, concept learning
and practice in reaching sound conclusions.
Curriculum planning could not be left to specialist
teachers concerned with their separate subject areas
for it would then probably lean too heavily on the
learning of facts and skills to the neglect of the
wider range of objectives that had been revealed by
the curriculum development movement. Yet the
project team recognised the need for a basis for
specialised knowledge within middle years
curriculum. The challenge, it was thought, was to
provide a sequence of experiences rewarding in
themselves but which encompassed alternative future
possibilities. Ross (1973) outlined the problem in
practical terms:

> One child in the class will one day read
> physics, another will become an agricultural
> worker and a third will become a seaman. If we
> are not to segregate we have to provide for the
> future physicist that network of ideas which by
> 8, by 10, by 13, he must have if he is to fulfil
> his potential and at the same time make sure
> that others, even though in due course they
> will 'drop' the subject, are left with an
> understanding of and interest in an area of
> knowledge of importance to us all.

The suggested approach involved an initial stipula-
tion by specialists of the essential features of
their subject which they would wish pupils to
acquire at this early stage in learning. They would
list facts, skills and concepts essential at the
middle years stage to an eventual sound understanding of their disciplines. They would outline
the kinds of interests, skills, awarenesses,
attitudes and values to be fostered. They would
suggest ways in which the learning and teaching of
what they had listed could be tackled. Specialists
having completed this first stage, the curriculum

112

team would compare the various lists to identify
overlaps and ensure a balance of learning
experiences. At this stage decisions would be made
about the organisation of the working day and
deployment of staff. The essential point of this
project team's argument was that in the middle
years, all subjects were to be seen as vehicles for
the general development of all children as well as
the specialist development of some. The resulting
curriculum involved a four-fold division of the
field of knowledge and skills into: basic learning
skills, empirical studies, aesthetics and morality.
It was felt that a curriculum for the middle years
which did not provide for significant experience in
each of these four categories could not be said to
be balanced. This was not a prescription for an
integrated approach to curriculum but rather a check
list for the curriculum deviser to consider whether
pupils had had sufficient opportunities for
rewarding experiences in each category. Indeed, the
team was anxious to reject the notion that one could
prescribe **the** middle years curriculum; a curriculum had to relate to a particular middle years
school. But some overriding principles were
postulated: curriculum should achieve balance
between aims, types of learning activity and
content; and curricular options should be open to
pupils until age 13 at least. It was further
strongly suggested that curriculum planning should
be a team effort, for consensus of informed opinion
rather than unilateral directive would be more
likely to result in sound decisions being made and
successfully implemented. A main cause of
continuity problems, it was felt, was 'the somewhat
isolated or fragmented planning of the whole
curriculum frequently within the class structure at
primary level and within the subject structures at
the secondary level'. In their visits to some
schools, the project team had found little
co-operation between classes or co-ordination of
work throughout the school. Before continuity could
be achieved between institutions it would have to be
established within them. No longer could curriculum
be planned on an informal, <u>ad hoc</u> basis no matter
how wise were the decisions made. Team planning and
organisation would be likely to promote
co-ordination of work within a school but there
could be a further advantage. Team teaching, being
introduced into schools irrespective of type,
effectively increased the number of teachers
normally involved with upper primary, class-taught

pupils but reduced the number of teachers working with lower-age secondary pupils, customarily taught by many specialists. If team teaching became general 'then one of the major organisational differences between the two institutions would cease to exist at the middle-years level, and a more gradual transition would replace the present abrupt change'.

By advocating 'fresh thinking' the project team proclaimed the inadequacy of either of the traditional approaches as models for middle years curriculum. The Plowden precept for extension of primary methods was not to apply; neither was Plowden's fear to be realised that secondary-school attitudes would percolate down to the younger age range. But a reappraisal exercise of the kind advocated by the team presented schools with problems. Where were they to find the time for curriculum planning? Much time and effort were already being expended in assimilating changes within subjects and areas of the curriculum; a major reconsideration of the entire curriculum was beyond the resources of many schools. Such a review demanded wide-ranging expertise which was not always available, particularly in small schools.

Variety of Approaches to Curriculum

Brian Simon (1981) has criticised the Schools Council approach for reflecting 'a pluralism run wild - a mass of disparate projects'. The lack of a systematic policy has impaired efforts to establish a distinctive middle-years curriculum. Since there was no planned interrelationship between the various middle-years projects, confusions and dichotomies were inevitable. In fact there has been a proliferation of conflicting curricular possibilities which can be well illustrated by reference to the humanities area. While one school may retain a differentiated subject approach, another may favour interdisciplinary enquiry, topics, or projects. Pupils in one school may have studied geography, history and religious education whilst their coevals in neighbouring establishments have followed environmental studies courses or worked thematically. Far from improving continuity, Schools Council projects, because of the permissive nature, have added to the problem. Fortuitous transfer to the next phase of schooling may effect an inversion on the learning mode; for example, pupils already familar with specialisation may be

taught predominantly through an integrated
curriculum, presumably to return later to a differentiated subject approach in anticipation of
external examinations. As Simon comments, 'we can
no longer afford to go on in the old way, muddling
through on a largely pragmatic or historically
institutionalised basis, tinkering with this and
that'.

The social studies field is a particularly
testing one for those concerned with continuity. The
sequential nature of subjects such as mathematics
and French can provide a structure to cross
institutional boundaries but sequencing principles
are difficult to specify in social subjects. At the
Schools Council's first conference on the middle
years of schooling, Lawton (1969) commented on the
'haphazard and patchy' nature of social studies
teaching in England. He advocated some kind of
sequential curriculum to avoid undue repetition or
gaps in learning. The need to establish sequence in
social studies learning may be open to question but
few would disagree with Lawton's comment that 'we
should try to be more specific about what we want at
various stages and how these stages link with one
another.' At the conclusion of the Schools Council
project which he directed, Lawton (1971) reiterated
that discontinuity between primary and secondary
work was very great indeed. His recommendation that
there was need to co-ordinate development work in
history, geography and social studies in the middle
years resulted in a further project directed by
Professor Alan Blyth. In the basic publication from
this project, yet again, the consequences of breaks
in schooling during the middle years were stressed:
'Lack of liaison within schools and between schools
can lead to children's experiences in history,
geography and (where it applies) social science,
being random and repetitive.' (Blyth, 1976) Despite
many years of effort by theoreticians and
practitioners alike, continuity in social studies
teaching remained elusive. The problem was
explicitly posed in yet another Schools Council
project, the local study in the London Borough of
Merton of continuity and development in social
subjects. (Harries, 1978) The major need, it
claimed, was to determine what had to be continued
and developed. It was less important for agreement
to be reached between schools or curriculum content
than that the nature of the disciplines concerned
should be clarified. Teachers should engage in
philosophical discussion of the concepts, procedures

and inherent attitudes and values of the disciplines for unless there was agreement on these issues curricular continuity would be seriously impaired. And so we arrive at a classical problem in curriculum design: the extent to which content should be subdued in favour of other objectives. (Taba, 1962) Manifestly, attempts to achieve continuity by detailed specification of content are unlikely to succeed; it would be so time-consuming for associated schools to try to arrive at consensus about the selection of items for inclusion in a course. But some general agreement is needed to avoid the kind of repetition reported in chapter four. It may be, as the Merton group maintains, that liaison on content is the least of our worries but they also point to the difficulties that ensue when schools have not arrived at some broad under-standing. 'High schools have the right to expect that all pupils they receive will have covered similar ground in the previous two years and the right to suggest that certain topics might best be left for them to tackle.' If contributory schools can give no concerted indication of what their pupils are likely to cover then the receiving school is 'absolved from taking account of what children have done previously'. The necessity of accepting such absolution would seem unfortunate from the child's point of view.

Development projects for the middle years of schooling have not in themselves led towards curriculum continuity. Though they have addressed themselves to problems of liaison, understandably they have been unable to provide ready solutions. Many, however, have suggested where practice could be improved. General adoption of the kind of planning advocated in <u>History, Georgraphy and Social Science 8-13</u>, for example, would have helped bridge the gap between the young child's projects and the adolescent's need to approach more differen-tiated learning. But the possibility of projects having serious impact on the work of schools has been impaired by the inability of the Schools Council to make them known to the ordinary, busy teacher. When the Council checked on the impact of its projects on the teaching profession, over 90 per cent of primary-school teachers stated they did not know of <u>History, Geography and Social Science 8-13</u>; only two teachers in every thousand used the project extensively. (Steadman, 1978) It would be unjust on the basis of this evidence to dismiss the School Council's effect on curriculum. The take-up of projects was higher in science, languages and mathematics.

The adoption of projects across institutional boundaries has to be preceded by a vital preliminary stage: teachers concerned within their separate institutions have to determine that continuity is sufficiently important for them to curb their partisan interest in 'specialism' or 'generalism'. Once such agreement has been reached, a national middle-years project may well provide a more acceptable approach to curriculum than one which is devised from existing practice. Middle-years developmental projects are valuable tools to be used in forging continuity if only the craftsmen can be persuaded to use them.

Core Curriculum

Overseas observers of British schools often fail to recognise any underlying similarities. Teachers in this country would probably claim that they do not have as much autonomy as is usually suggested; parental pressure and the external examination system exert a powerful influence on the content of education. Yet it has to be accepted that in comparison with most other educational systems, ours has been relatively free from central directive. Even after taking account of reforms in French education, it could be stated: 'If you look for a particular item in any part of the system, you will find identical items in the corresponding position in the whole of France. That goes for curriculum as well as structure.' (King, 1979) Visiting observers from overseas are understandably surprised by the variety both between and within our schools if they are accustomed to such centralisation. They do not understand how we could have allowed a situation to develop whereby a schools inspector could remark that if a visitor from Mars spent one day in a typical English primary school and the next in a typical secondary school, he would be tempted to believe that he was on two different planets. (Burrows, 1978) Some commentators claim there is little consistency even between schools in the same phase. (Richards, 1982) How our schools came to be so different from each other is beyond discussion here. Sinister political motives of Ministers of Education have been suggested as the main reason for reluctance to allow control from the centre to shape our school. (White, 1975) Perhaps administrative inefficiency has been the main cause. (Raison, 1976) Whatever the reasons, marked differences between schools hinder curriculum continuity.

Dennis Lawton (1980) has identified the period from 1944 to the beginning of the 1960s as 'the Golden Age of teacher control (or non-control) of the curriculum'. From the 1960s onwards can be traced a growing desire at the centre to gain more control over the school curriculum. Criticisms of 'progressive' methods and standards in schools grew. There was increasing dissatisfaction because of a proliferation of curricular alternatives from the Schools Council. As employers and the media continued to comment adversely on schooling, politicians began to realise they would have to turn their attention to what was happening **inside** schools; no longer could they confine Parliamentary debate to 'bricks and mortar and matters of organis- ation'. Mr. Callaghan's Ruskin College speech inaugurating the 'Great Debate' on education had been preceded by a DES discussion document, The Yellow Book, illustrative of the department's attitude at that time. 'It was to be an exercise in persuasion and the construction of consent. The required object, an increased centralization of control over the actual practices of schooling, would be sought through a political campaign rather than through administrative dictates.' (CCCS, 1981) The Callaghan speech was less extreme than some commentators had predicted. There were to be no drastic measures to end teacher autonomy but the shift in government stance was clearly signalled by the issues presented for study, of which one was: 'The strong case for so-called core curriculum of basic knowledge.'

Discussion now turned to clarification of what core curriculum might entail. The 1977 Green Paper acknowledged that the creation of a suitable core curriculum would not be easy. (DES, 1977) To assuage teachers, and in particular the NUT, who strongly resisted the notion of a common core, the consultative document had been so diluted that little more than a restatement of the problem was attempted:

> The Secretaries of State will therefore seek to establish a broad agreement with their partners in the education service on a framework for the curriculum, and, particularly on whether, because there are aims common to all schools and to all pupils at certain stages, there should be a 'core' or 'protected' part.

A Framework for the School Curriculum (DES, 1980)
advanced the argument a little further: the
respective responsibilities for curriculum of
central and local authorities were explored; certain
key elements of the curriculum were identified;
there was even a tentative bid to specify minimum
time-allocations for primary English and
mathematics. The Secretaries of State had been
moved to prepare guidance of this kind, it was
stated, because of the diversity of practice that
had emerged in previous years as shown particularly
in HMI surveys.

To influence such diversity, the proposals in
this document would seem somewhat modest. Yet they
have to be seen in the context of the many pronoun-
cements on curriculum from HM Inspectorate and the
DES since James Callaghan's Ruskin College speech.
There may, as Lawton (1981) suggests, have been
differences of attitude to curriculum in the
respective department and inspectorate documents but
there was unanimity of view that school curriculum
was the proper concern of government. But it was
broad policies on the structure of the curriculum
that were seen as of national concern. Local
authorities and schools would still have a large
measure of freedom to interpret a national agreement to take account of particular circumstances.
The School Curriculum, published in 1980 as the
culmination of the process begun in the Great
Debate, lacked the kind of thrust anticipated in
early forebodings. After several years of pronoun-
cements on the content of schooling, the central
authority's policy of non-interference in such
matters could be seen to have changed but schools
themselves seemed little affected. What was the
influence, for example, of discussion of the
curriculum framework proposed for primary schools?
Throughout primary schooling, pupils were to have
access to English, mathematics, religious education,
physical education and science. Apart from science,
which the Primary Survey (DES, 1978) found was
lacking in 80 per cent of classes observed, the core
elements proposed were those existing in practice.
At least six project teams in Britain had been
actively developing curricular materials for
teachers to stimulate scientific work with young
children during the ten years leading up to the
Great Debate, yet little scientific activity was
taking place in classrooms. (Kerr and Engel, 1980)
If such intense efforts to spread primary science
teaching had been so ineffective, what were the

chances of success for a mere statement of preferred curricular policy? Affirming the importance of science in the primary curriculum could do nothing to improve the level of scientific training of primary teachers or increase a school's science resources.

Pressure for the establishment of core curriculum may have encouraged local authorities and schools to examine existing practices but it is doubtful whether the diversity that occasioned the debate has been modified to any great extent. Continuity between schools is unlikely to be improved by this influence alone but the cumulative effect of several initiatives taken by a central authority much more active in matters of curriculum than heretofore could have an impect on this issue in time. There will be need, however, to move beyond mere discussion and into redistribution of resources for core curriculum to be effective in maintaining continuity, and then only in broad outline, for specific content, it seems, is to remain the preserve of schools. Lawton (1981) sees core curriculum as being concerned with 'minimum competency, output rather than input, and testing'. In The Politics of the School Curriculum (1980) he suggests 'having moved away from the Scylla of laissez-faire the DES shows no sign of possessing an adequate theoretical base for curriculum change and is in danger of getting too close to the Charybdis of behaviouristic, mechanistic approaches to curriculum and evaluation'. Such approaches can be seen as a response to recognition of the need for the education service to demonstrate its accountability to society.

Accountability

Moves towards greater accountability are probably prompted by concern about standards and the need to be cost-efficient at a time when money is short. (Pring, 1978) Though the accountability movement is not a direct response to calls for curriculum continuity, making schools more accountable would make them more homogeneous and so reduce a main cause of discontinuity, extreme school diversity. The central authority's instrument for monitoring accountability, the Assessment of Performance Unit (APU) has, over a decade, gradually encroached on the work of schools. Despite educational objections and technical difficulties, the APU's work has been influential not only within

its own terms of reference but indirectly on local
education authorities and schools in their review of
testing procedures. Of course, the standard
criticisms directed at external examinations apply
as well to the work of the APU. During the time it
was practised eleven-plus testing, for example, is
generally considered to have restricted and
distorted the primary curriculum. 'Teaching to the
test', with consequential effects on curriculum, is
almost inevitable in any large-scale examining
technique. The APU's means of countering any 'wash-
back' effect of its procedures is to rely on 'light
sampling which will involve individual pupils and
schools relatively infrequently, say once every five
to ten years'. (Selby, 1977) Teachers, it is
assumed, will not adjust curriculum to suit a test
they are likely to meet so seldom. Yet there is an
acceptance of the inevitability of effect on
curriculum, claimed as an advantage by HMI Selby:
'Monitoring can have a beneficial effect long-term
in the sense that if we monitor things regarded by a
large number of people as important this will help
to ensure that society's priorities are reflected
appropriately in school curricula.' Lawton (1980)
accuses APU officers of practising 'double-think' on
the issue of influencing curriculum:

> On the one hand it is said that the tests will
> not influence the curriculum to any great
> extent; on the other hand, it is also said that
> aesthetic development should be tested (despite
> the enormous difficulties) because if it were
> not tested then the curriculum would be in
> danger of being unbalanced or impoverished

The Assessment of Performance Unit is one of
very few national organisations with power to
influence school curricula. Unlike GCE examining
boards, APU stands in splendid isolation so schools
have no opportunity of 'shopping around' to find a
test to suit curriculum. Whereas other external
testing bodies can be seen to influence the work of
upper-secondary pupils, APU spans primary and
secondary schooling. It could therefore be a
powerful force for promoting continuity.
Particularly in a subject like mathematics with its
alternative traditional and modern approaches, the
establishment of national norms related to
monitoring both primary and secondary schools could
help reduce confusing disparities. It would seem
sensible to accept that the work of the APU is going

to have an effect on curriculum. Despite many
misgivings about APU, would it not be wise to take
the consequences of monitoring into account and plan
accordingly? One of the positive effects of the use
of these procedures could be some narrowing of the
gap between schools, with a consequent benefit to
pupils at time of transfer.

Conclusion

Though curricula were centrally determined in
the early years of state schooling in Great Britain
- indeed until 1926 - thereafter, a largely autonomous system developed, without a public debate.
(Gordon, 1978) Increasing liberalization of the
curriculum reached a point at which some questioned
whether the curricular chaos which they claimed
had resulted could continue to be tolerated.
(Fowler, 1977) But teachers had gained so large a
measure of control, even at national and regional
level within the Schools Council and on subject
panels of CSE boards, that the task of shifting the
power base was formidable. Lawton (1980) probably
overstates the case in suggesting a conspiracy at
the centre to wrest control by stealth but by
several, sometimes subtle means there has been a
gradual reassertion of the central authority's role.
Nevertheless, the legal position of the Secretaries
of State virtually prohibits the kind of control
that other countries can exercise in ensuring a
curriculum continuum as pupils pass from school to
school. As Shipman (1984) points out: 'When MPs ask
questions in the House of Commons about curricula,
teaching methods or the way individual schools are
run, they are told this is not the business of the
Secretary of State.'
Responsibilities within the education service
are defined in the 1977 Green Paper, <u>Education in
Schools: A Consultative Document</u>. Schools, local
and national authorities are said to be in partnership with responsibility for education shared
between them. The Secretaries of State 'need to
know what is being done by the local educational
authorities and, through them, what is happening in
the schools. They must draw attention to national
needs if they believe the education system is not
adequately meeting them.' The task of dealing with
practical difficulties, then, is not one for the
central authority, as is made explicit in the
section on transition between schools. There are
said to be 'substantial problems' at the point of

transition between primary and secondary schools, particular mention being made of sequential subjects and the needs of pupils moving from one part of the country to another. But the central authority, having drawn attention to the problem has fulfilled its task, with a clear indication of which partner in the triangle of responsibility should take action:

> This whole problem needs the urgent attention of local education authorities, not least to ensure that parents whose jobs demand mobility should not be deterred by fear of disruption in the children's schooling.

Chapter Seven

LOCAL AUTHORITY STRATEGIES TO IMPROVE CONTINUITY

Following the publication of Circular 10/65,
central government was criticised for having
'abdicated its management function in permitting,
even encouraging a bewildering variety of local
systems in a small, heavily-populated country and
within a society becoming increasingly mobile'.
(Taylor, 1970) By the mid-1970's, public debate had
revealed the extent to which pupils' educational
experiences could be so diverse. Even the teaching
profession itself began to question whether freedom
had been taken too far; a letter to Times
Educational Supplement (21.6.74) attributed the
problem to 'unopposable dictators, called headmasters, some of whom are prepared to sacrifice
their pupils' good on the altar of their own
autonomy'. The anonymous teacher went on to suggest
a solution: 'Continuity of courses can only be
achieved by curtailing the right of schools freely
and unilaterally to decide their own curricula.'
Mention of the DES having encouraged schools to
innovate during the previous decade was avoided
during the Great Debate following the Prime
Minister's 1976 Ruskin College speech. Clearly,
central government was concerned over the diversity
of practice at school level and would have liked to
curtail school autonomy but the necessary powerful
corrective was elusive. Articles of government
promulgated following the 1944 Education Act had not
given the central authority responsibility for what
happens in schools: 'The Local Education Authority
shall determine the general educational character of
the school and its place in the local educational
system. Subject thereto, the governors shall have
the general direction of the conduct and curriculum
of the school.' (Administrative Memorandum 25,
1945). Though definition of boundaries between

124

'general educational character' and 'curriculum' may
make precise attribution of responsibility
difficult, it clearly rests at local rather than
national level. That schools have the ability
'freely and unilaterally to decide their own
curricula' is something of a myth. Their freedom is
circumscribed by the requirements of examining
bodies, parental pressure, public opinion and by the
resources provided by local authorities. But within
such limits, teachers have been free to plan what
shall be taught. Local authorities have preferred
to 'stimulate and support, not prescribe or control
what is taught in the schools they maintain.'
(Brooksbank, 1980)

Clearly, there are difficulties in ascribing
responsibility for what happens within schools;
there are even greater problems when decisions
impinging on internal school matters relate to
several schools as is the case with organisational
transfer. Continuity of educational experience at
times of transfer cannot be a 'within school'
responsibility for it can only be effected between
schools. As Bryan (1984) comments, 'if curricular
continuity is to be realistic as well as a desirable
goal then who is to be responsible for supervising
"the spaces between schools" must be decided
quickly'. Stillman and Maychell (1982) suggest who
that should be: 'Liaison and continuity need to be
considered as a whole, and only those working at LEA
level have the authority which transcends the
boundaries between schools.' That the DES sees
continuity as a local authority concern is manifest
in two of the main questions posed in Circular
14/77, a document issued to collect information
from LEAs about their policies and practices in
curricular matters:

What steps have the authority taken to promote
smooth transition from school to school as
pupils get older? Replies should refer
specifically to:

(i)   Arrangements for curriculum continuity;
(ii)   Action to encourage contact between the
       teachers in the school from and to which
       pupils normally move;
(iii) Action to encourage or require the
       transfer of records of individual
       children's educational progress as
       children move from school to school.

125

What steps have the authority taken to promote
smooth transition from one school to another in
the authority's area when parents move house?
Replies should refer specifically to action
related to records of individual children's
educational progress.

Response to Circular 14/77

The detailed information sought by this
circular presented something of a surprise. Underlying the questions posed were assumptions that
specific knowledge of internal school matters was
readily accessible to local authority officials.
Further, it implied that LEAs have explicit policies
relating to curricular matters. When Auld (1976)
reporting on the William Tyndale School commented
that the Inner London Education Authority had no
policy on aims and objectives, standards of
attainment or methods of teaching in primary
schools, he emphasised that he was not being
critical of ILEA, whose approach, he suggested, was
typical of most local authorities. As a lawyer,
Auld was very conscious of limitations on the
intervention of LEA officials in internal school
matters. Indeed, in their responses to Circular
14/77, some authorities reported inability to
impose uniform policy on autonomous schools.
Typically, one stated: 'the problems arising from
transfer from school to school as pupils get older
are inevitable whilst schools have their current
degree of autonomy over syllabuses, teaching methods
and indeed general curriculum'. (DES, 1979)
Circular 14/77 can be seen not merely as a
fact-gathering instrument but as a means of
prompting local authorities to take more initiative
in curricular matters. Responses to the circular -
almost all related to primary-secondary transfer -
revealed a wide diversity of emphasis in practical
arrangements for transition between schools.
Several strategies were given specific mention as
promoting curriculum continuity. In some
authorities, working parties or discussion groups
had been established to consider particular areas of
the curriculum. The modus operandi and degree of
formality of such organisations varied but all
shared the same objective of bringing together
teachers from primary and secondary schools to
consider the treatment of particular subjects in
both phases of education, and to improve the
co-ordination of their curricula. Advisers were

considered to be influential in encouraging
continuity, particularly by promoting in-service
training courses. A further feature of advisory
provision seen as making it easier to deal with
problems of transition was that of giving advisers a
pastoral responsibility for schools across the whole
age-range in a given catchment area. To encourage a
common general approach throughout the schools in an
area, some authorities had published guidelines to
support particular aspects of the primary
curriculum; assessment procedures were considered by
some LEAs to have a similar effect of promoting
consistency. The exchange of schemes of work and
the appointment to secondary posts of teachers with
primary experience were cited as further methods of
cross-fertilization between the two stages.

In seeking information about contacts established between teachers in the different phases of
schooling, we can assume the DES implied contacts to
promote curriculum continuity, yet some authorities
responded in more general terms giving the
impression that their focus was on smoothing the
passage of children from one institution to another.
As Lois Benyon (1984) has pointed out:

> Liaison between schools and curriculum
> continuity between schools are not one and the
> same thing. It is easier to talk about and to
> effect smoother transition from primary school
> to secondary school than it is to establish
> what is meant by, and implement real curriculum
> continuity.

Typically, teachers met 'to discuss transfer
arrangements and problems in general'. Given the
acknowledged difficulties in negotiating curriculum
continuity, it is open to question what proportion
of meeting time was allocated to this topic as
opposed to more straightforward discussions about
processing pupils for transfer. The one contact
predominantly concerned with curriculum matters was
that between primary class teachers and heads of
first years in secondary schools who met 'with the
object of discussing the curriculum in each school
as well as the strengths and weaknesses of
individual pupils'. Other meetings, between head
teachers in a locality, between individual teachers,
and between groups of teachers, involved wide-
ranging discussions about transfer within which
continuity might be considered.

LOCAL AUTHORITY STRATEGIES

The transfer of records of pupils' educational progress when children moved to a new school was required or expected by nine-tenths of local authorities. Standard record cards were sometimes produced by groups of schools, sometimes by the authority itself. Basic information contained in record cards was often supplemented by other material such as samples of pupils' work and the results of standardized tests. Transfer records were cited as the principal means of dealing with the transition of pupils required to change school because of parental movement of home. Ensuring the transmission of information between schools could present difficulties when local authority boundaries were crossed and when the new school was not known at the time of a pupil's leaving. Some LEAs involved education welfare officers to trace the whereabouts of children and put schools in touch; others required the receiving school to take the initiative in seeking information from the feeder school.

The questions in Circular 14/77 asked specifically what steps local authorities had taken to promote smooth transition. Some answers merely described school practice with an obvious implication that in this field, many of the initiatives to be taken are properly the concern of schools rather than LEAs. Local authorities undoubtedly have a difficult task in reconciling concession of school autonomy with fulfilment of responsibilities stipulated by central government. Encroachment on territory traditionally the preserve of individual schools would likely be resented but some aspects of transfer have long been accepted as matters for the proper attention of LEAs.

Transfer Documents

The need for cumulative records concerning a child's total experience of schooling rather than progress within one institution was implicit in the 1944 Education Act's requirement that LEAs should make provision for different ages, aptitudes and abilities of pupils. By 1961, keeping of records became a specific requirement. Statutory Instrument 1743 states: 'Whenever a pupil ceases to attend the school and becomes a pupil at another school or place of education or training . . adequate medical and educational information concerning him shall be supplied to persons conducting that other school or place.' It was

intended that such record keeping should relate to
individual children but a concomitant effect, it was
thought, would be that continuity could be
maintained as groups of pupils moved from one school
to another.

In the period immediately following the passing
of the 1944 Education Act, when fee-paying grammar-
school places were abolished and pressure for
success at eleven-plus correspondingly increased,
there was an understandable emphasis in transfer
documents on factors relating to allocation
decisions. Local authorities expected their records
to be useful also in other circumstances. In her
1955 survey of the nature and use of cumulative
school records, Alice Walker noted that the
documents were seen as constituting, among other
purposes 'help to teachers in taking over a fresh
class', 'a diagnostic test', and 'effective
continuity in guiding the development of children.'
Indeed, there was a tendency for LEAs to demand such
records to be kept without establishing a clear
purpose for them. Miss Walker's verdict on record
cards, then being used by 74 per cent of all LEAs
was that the emphasis was on the collecting rather
then use of the material. Many teachers had been
led to feel that compiling full, detailed records
was a waste of time if neither they nor the
administrators had any clear-cut purpose for them
nor sufficient opportunity for acting upon
information made available. Rather than attempt to
encapsulate the various aspects of a pupil's
development within one cumulative record, Walker
recommended that only 'significant' matters should
be included. The record card should not be regarded
as a substitute for consultation between teachers
but rather a source of reference to supplement more
subjective assessment of pupils. This 1955
appraisal of cumulative record keeping was that it
was little more than a useful aid; yet LEAs
continued to use such records as a major means of
contact between schools.

As selection of children at eleven-plus for
grammar-school education decreased with the
corresponding growth of comprehensive schools, one
of the uses of record cards diminished. But local
authorities, with advice from the NFER, simply
adapted their records cards rather than abandon
them. As a consequence of greater emphasis on
counselling in the comprehensive school, information about specific difficulties, health problems
and general home background of pupils was given

prominence. Some local authorities devised transfer documents which forwarded assessments of personality and confidential matters about a child's home background but others considered this to be too contentious an issue. Records continued to include information about a pupil's academic ability, but increasingly, as the need for eleven-plus objective testing declined, scholastic achievement was expressed in terms of teachers' ratings. Standardized tests existed only in basic subjects: inevitably schools had to resort to subjective assessment if they were to pass on information relating to all areas of the curriculum. Many LEAs recommended the grading of pupils' work on a five-point scale but as each teacher's idea of standard was coloured by specific experience, it was impossible to find a common basis for ratings. The inadequacies of transfer records became apparent not only because of discrepancies in standards and problems of comparability but from curricular differences too. Teachers of some subjects in receiving schools were not always able to find direct reference to pertinent pre-transfer experience in their area of the curriculum. Even when the results of standardized tests were included there could be problems if contributory schools had not used the same test. The scepticism of secondary-school teachers about assessments sent on by primary schools is understandable given their many limitations.

Recent Developments in Transfer Documentation

Local authorities differ widely in their approach to record-keeping. In some areas, schools are required to forward highly detailed information whereas in others, so sparse is the advice available to receiving schools that the practice is dismissed as inadequate or even unreliable. A 'ticks in boxes' technique is favoured by several authorities in an attempt to meet teacher criticism that record keeping is too time-consuming but the information conveyed by this method can be so rudimentary that little impression is gained of the pupil being transferred. There is general agreement that transfer documentation is an essential feature of changing schools but the ideal approach to record keeping is elusive. A recent survey of teachers in primary schools revealed that though most of them 'agreed that school records should be relevant, systematic and unambiguous, there were widely

different interpretations as to the main constit-
uents of relevance, clarity and system'. (Weiner,
1978) What is surely significant at a time when the
theme of continuity in education is dominant is that
LEAs are encouraging a revision of record keeping in
their schools. Typically, at the Birmingham
Education Development Centre, a group of teachers
working within the Continuity in Education Project,
spent several years standardizing a transfer document to be used in the authority's consortia-based
schools. (Neal, 1975) It was, however, the stimulus
provided by the DES 1977 Green Paper, Education in
Schools, that prompted many local authorities to
overhaul record-keeping practices. 'The keeping and
transmission of records', it stated, 'should be
systematic and understandable'. There was need for
a 'reasonable consistency of practice between
different areas of the country' particularly because
of the greater number of transfers between schools
taking place as a result of increased parental
mobility. Local authorities were asked to review
existing practices with regard to records
themselves, arrangements for parents to see records,
and the currency the records should have. The extra
dimension of parental access presents a further
complication because of the tendency for open
records to be more restrained than those protected
by confidentiality. An interesting side-light on
this issue is presented in guidelines on continuity
produced by one local authority: because transfer
records are generally accessible, it suggests,
'points of strict confidentiality should be kept
elsewhere',
      The response of several local authorities to
DES pressure for curricular review was to establish
working parties to consider various 'areas of
concern'. In the late 1970s and early 1980s, school
records were subjected to scrutiny by many such
working groups. Understandably, changes made in the
content of transfer documents were somewhat superficial for their basic purpose remained the same: to
transmit explicit information about the pupil as
succinctly as possible. Yet, as Clift, Weiner and
Wilson (1981) discovered, when they analysed
transfer records from 66 LEAs, a wide variety of
forms existed. The number of items included in
record cards varied a great deal: some had over 70
categories whilst others had as few as ten.
Overall, the researchers were able to identify 120
possible items of information within the records
analysed. They identified, in order of priority,

the more important items required by a pupil's new
teacher:

(a) pupil's name, date of birth, home address;

(b) vital information required for a child's
     well being;

(c) person(s) to contact in emergency;

(d) details of any handicaps, physical or
     socio-emotional, which may affect progress
     in school;

(e) details of any learning disabilities,
     including spoken language;

(f) details of referrals to psychologists,
     reports from social workers, educational
     welfare officers, school medical officers,
     etc;

(g) details of prescribed remedial treatment;

(h) stages reached on reading, language and
     mathematics schemes;

(i) details of any screening or other tests
     carried out;

(j) other medical, academic and personal
     information.

It does not follow, of course, that all features
listed need appear within one transfer document.
The procedure followed by the Service Children's
Education Authority allows for confidential material
to be passed through official channels, while
transitory information about current academic
attainment is contained in a transfer report taken
by the pupil to his new school. This strategy has
advantages for educational continuity of individual
pupils involved in migratory transfer for it places
information where it is needed - in the hands of the
receiving teacher. Organisational transfer of large
groups of pupils, however, requires advance
planning; information about pupils needs to be
available sufficiently far ahead for teaching groups
to be arranged.
     The SCEA procedure also highlights the need for
different information to be available to several

recipients: general information may be filed in the
school office; medical details are required by the
school nurse; pastoral tutors and subject teachers
seek different kinds of information from transfer
documents. Local circumstances must be taken into
account when decisions are made about the ideal
format for transfer documents. An anecdote reported
to the author serves to illustrate the need to
ensure that information should be not only put
together but made available to those who need it.
A first-year teacher in a very large, dispersed
comprehensive school explained that he had not
consulted transfer information for any of the 360
incoming pupils because in order to do so he would
need to move to the central administration building
across a public road, consult house lists to
determine the location of files, obtain filing
cabinet keys from a deputy head, locate the relevant
file and wade through an eight-page document to find
the one item of concern to him. Stillman and
Maychell (1984) found that although transfer forms
arrived at Isle of Wight high schools, the
information they carried often failed to reach
subject departments and classrooms. Working parties
have rightly given much attention to the collection
of relevant information but little consideration to
the machinery for disseminating it.

Complementing working party activity, several
LEAs have issued guidelines on the use of transfer
records. The concern expressed by Alice Walker in
1955 that there was an emphasis on the collection
rather than use of information in record cards is
still distinctly voiced by LEAs in the 1980s.
Another dominant theme, but one of fairly recent
introduction is that of confidentiality. It seems
that the difficulties there have always been of
access to reports are exacerbated by an excessive
concern for confidentiality. 'Ought there to be
some members of staff with more access to private
information than others?' asks one local authority
document. It is obvious from LEA guidelines that
there are no simple solutions to difficulties
involved in the transfer of information. The issue
is explored fully in Leeds Education Authority s
Continuity in Education:

> What information should be collected within a
> school, how it should be recorded, by what
> means it should be transferred to another
> school and under what degree of confident-
> iality are questions of endless concern.

The existence of a standard proforma for the
transfer of information will not preclude the
examination by groups of teachers and of
schools of how movement may be made smoother.
Teachers seek to improve the organisation of
the wealth of fine detail which goes to compile
accurate profiles of the academic and
intellectual competences and potential of
individual pupils. Equally, they concern
themselves with the collation of the data
involved in a detailed pastoral record,
attempting to sift the relevant from the
irrelevant and establishing what is of permanent rather than transitory importance.
Different schools inevitably establish
different needs and different priorities.

It is in the pastoral field that problems
of liaison are most sensitive and complex. Not
only are two schools involved in access to
information which is of the utmost confidentiality but the problems ramify into the areas
of operation of many other agencies. Social
welfare, medical, police, housing and even
prison authorities may be involved. The
complex dialogue between school, home and such
external agencies often reveals information
which, though relevant to the educational
progress of a child, is of such delicacy that
careful thought must be given as to whether it
should ever be permanently recorded. Much
valuable information is transferred orally
rather than in written form because teachers
realise the damage which may be done if
information is misused by irresponsible
persons.

Interesting work in the field of information transfer is currently being conducted by
a group of Headteachers in one area of Leeds.
Their work has included a complete review of
the Authority's standard record-card and the
agreement of a new mode of information
transfer. Headteachers in Middle and High
Schools have met regularly to examine the
requirements of their schools in respect of
testing procedures, the balance between
academic and pastoral information, and the
weight which must be attached to personal
contact between teachers from linked schools.
Headteachers from Primary Schools are now
involving themselves in the process of agreeing
a commonly acceptable information transfer

card. Pilot tests of the cards are being
arranged in the area and schools in another
area are acting as a control group by testing
the cards, not having been involved in their
compilation. Dialogues such as this and
experiments in other areas emphasise the value
of regular meetings aimed at solving particular
problems. That a variety of answers is found
need not be confusing, for they present the
chance of testing solutions in practical
situations, and of finding local solutions to
local problems.

Liaison and its effectiveness will often
depend on written records and schools linked
with eacher other are well advised to work
together to produce as effective a system of
recording as their ingenuity and awareness of
local needs can devise, taking into account
that no system is perfect and there will always
be clashes between the needs for speedily
compiled yet explicit records and between the
needs of confidentiality, ease of access and
consistency and simplicity in the terms used.

The Leeds guidelines rightly draw attention to
limitations of transfer records; some information
can be more appropriately transmitted by personal
contact between teachers from linked schools.
Transfer documents can be properly effective in
providing a vehicle for passing on factual statements and objective measures of abilities and
attainments.

In the period of tri-partite secondary
education, wher allocation decisions had to be made,
objective measures of verbal reasoning and
mathematics ability tended to be recorded in such
documents. The demise of eleven-plus selection
procedures, however, resulted in a reduction in
information being passed on from primary school and
an increase in testing by secondary schools of new
entrants. Such testing often involves the placing
of pupils in temporary groupings, delaying the
commencement of the next stage of education and
intensifying the break in continuity. (Neal, 1975)
Youngman and Lunzer's (1977) recommendation for
close vigilance during the early days of secondary
school envisages that the monitoring of pupils in
order to detect crucial changes in their behaviour
should involve a comparison of secondary-school with
primary-school attainment. It would seem that some
assessment of a pupil's attainment at the completion

of one stage of education should be available for passing on to the next. Yet, as we have seen, there are many limitations to the passing of records from one school to another.

Modular Assessment

The NFER (originally the foundation for Educational Research) has been in the forefront of work on record-keeping since the 1940s. Recently, they have been involved in the development of 'modular assessment materials' to be applied before transfer and used to improve the quality of information available to a receiving school. Assessment materials were developed initially for English and mathematics, and tested on samples of Hillingdon pupils who transferred in summer 1975. Utilization of the information by receiving schools was guided and monitored during the late summer and early autumn. The researchers, Sumner and Bradley, published their report, Assessment for Transition, in 1977.

Two working parties of teachers were set up with a view to specifying various areas or aspects of basic subjects where assessment could be made. Worksheets were prepared for each of nine areas chosen for assessment in English and mathematics. The modular structure used in the majority of the worksheets was devised to simplify grading of pupils according to level of achievement for the item being assessed so that, for example, pupils could be tested at 'basic', 'intermediate' or 'advanced' levels in 'ratio, proportion and percentage'. Whereas a test involving graded items was appropriate in all nine areas being assessed in mathematics, it suited only four of the English worksheets, the remaining five, involving, for example, essay-writing, could not be objectively marked but were rated by three experienced teachers.

Both primary and secondary teachers involved in the study approved of the gathering of information on pupils' performance in the period before transfer and the sending of condensed summaries to the receiving school. There were reservations, however, about the modular assessment scheme, particularly among primary-school teachers. Some were worried that information which had taken great effort to assemble would not be used by the receiving school or would be used for the purpose of streaming rather than for improving learning opportunities of pupils at the outset of secondary careers. There was some

136

worry that secondary schools might begin to exert pressure for changes that primary schools might not desire or that choice of worksheets concerned with 'basics' might place undue emphasis on a narrow segment of primary-school learning. Another source of anxiety among primary-school staff was that high, all-round performance on worksheets would become important to schools because prestige and competitiveness could be associated with the results. But the major problem which the researchers identified centred on the demands for more information conflicting with lack of procedures for rendering it both intelligible and useful.

The basic premise on which the Hillingdon modular assessment materials were developed was that a child's learning up to a given point in time would influence his future learning. If a receiving teacher could know with confidence the stage reached by incoming pupils, course planning could be more effective with a consequent improvement in educational experience for the individual pupil.

The transmission of fuller information about pupils will become much more feasible as computer-aided profiling techniques develop. (Maxfield, 1983) The quality of that information can be improved by increasing use of modular assessment methods but to complete the process, receiving schools must make use of the knowledge others have taken care to assemble. In the past, local authority concern has been directed to the collection and recording of information in contributory schools but these efforts have been frustrated because teachers for whom information is prepared seem unable to use it effectively. Though they must obviously be vigilant to continue improving the content of transfer documentation, LEAs should turn their attention to persuading secondary schools of the advantages of using transfer information to allow incoming pupils to continue their education rather than start afresh. There would seem to be a need for a change of emphasis in in-service courses from compilation to use of records.

Clearly, the use of transfer documents is still seen as an important means of improving continuity but there are dissenting voices. Caroline Moorhead (1971) commenting on an investigation into transition in Bristol suggested that the record form 'which would seem to provide a way of bridging the gap, may in fact merely blur the problem. Since the goals of the secondary teachers are usually different from those of the primary teachers its

usefulness is perhaps limited.' Orsborn (1977) a
London primary-school headmaster, discovered, when
lecturing about comprehensive reorganisation to a
group of secondary teachers, that many had never
seen the transfer documents that were passed on from
primary schools. The attitude of many secondary
teachers is probably reflected in the comment of one
of Orsborn's disputants who argued in favour of a
tabula rasa policy for new entrants. 'He
contended that his objectives were academically more
specific than those of the primary-school teachers
and that he could more efficiently ascertain a
child's ability in his subject without reference to
primary records, which were often vague and sometimes misleading.' Similar criticisms were
presented by local authorities themselves in
response to DES Circular 14/77. One LEA had
carried out a survey in which two-thirds of the
secondary-school headteachers had expressed 'some
degree of reservation about the effectiveness of
what was passed on to them'; lack of standardized
information, well-intentioned but inaccurate
subjective information and lack of subject coverage
were some of the complaints. A tendency was noted,
also, to include detail of a transitory nature and
to pass on a school's unedited, cumulative records.
    In the second stage of the Isle of Wight School
Liaison and Transfer Procedures Project, a
reappraisal of documents was carried out to try to
improve the use of transfer data. (Stillman and
Maychell, 1984) Several specific principles were
suggested to guide the development of a new system
of information transfer. From these can be extra-
polated some general guidelines:

1. there should be uniformity in presentation
    and comparability of assessments;

2. subject information should be 'needs-related
    i.e. it should provide what the receiving
    school wants;

3. information should take as direct a route as
    possible between compiler and user;

4. there should be the possibility of different
    types of assessment for different subject
    needs;

5. information should be available when it is
    needed.

Significantly, in identifying existing successful
practice, it was noted that 'teachers annually met
in their groups to discuss the assessment instruments used, the transferring pupils, and the
progress of the previous year's cohort'. This
surely highlights the importance of teacher contact.
If transfer documentation supplants teacher contact
it may indeed 'merely blur the problem'. The use of
transfer records is but one of several strategies
for transmitting relevant information about pupils
when they transfer schools.

Committees to Discuss Curricular Continuity

Curricular continuity depends upon communication between teachers in the different stages of
education. In most walks of life, when responsibility for some activity passes from one person to
another the transition involves communication; a
nurse taking over patient-care scans a temperature
chart and exchanges a few words to note things to
watch; a new driver has the vehicle log book to give
basic details but the vehicle's idiosyncrasies are
best discovered from someone who has driver it
previously. But there the analogy with education
ceases for a teacher taking over an intake class
cannot refer back to the one previous teacher.
Administrative complexities can result in a first-
year secondary class having been taught previously
by many primary teachers; in the most extreme case
known to the author, a class of 28 pupils had
arrived from 19 primary schools. In large urban
areas where parental choice is one of the main
criteria on which decisions about allocation are
made, it is inevitable that schools become so
enmeshed in a complex web of interrelations that
conversations between individual teachers about
individual pupils can seldom take place. Problem
child apart, communication is likely to be about
groups of pupils and to involve several teachers.
Once the need for such arrangements has passed
beyond contact between pairs of related schools,
there is an important role for the local authority
advisory service to act as agent for the promotion
of discussions.
Fred Ward, Wiltshire's organiser for primary
in-service has outlined the approach developed in
his county over recent years in response to requests
from teachers for a more organised programme of
contacts:

A neutral person, such as an adviser or education officer (neutral in the sense of not being from the locality) has sounded out opinion in an area and then, in conjunction with the secondary and primary heads, convened a meeting that included the senior management team from the secondary school. The main purpose of the meeting has been to clarify the aims of primary/secondary liaison and to accept the principle that more contact would be beneficial. Soon after, an open forum has been held for primary and secondary teachers and has attracted large numbers, over 100 in one case. Under these circumstances all the meeting can hope to achieve, once the aims have been explained, is to throw out a wide range of activities that could be undertaken and to appoint a small working party to organise a programme.

The results have varied in ambition but some of the most successful have centred on the establishment of a permanent classroom-base in the secondary school for use by visiting primary children and their teacher. A surplus room has been time-tabled out and then fitted with all the accessories of a junior classroom, including reference and fiction books, equipment and consumables. The LEA has helped with a small initial pump-priming grant but the feeder schools and the comprehensive have covered running costs from their capitation and school fund.

The primary fourth-year children visit the secondary school on three or four occasions during the year, beginning with a day in the autumn and ending up with four consecutive days in the summer. To get the most from the exercise, the primary teachers have found it essential to liaise with their secondary colleagues to discuss the curriculum content of the visits. Secondary teachers have been able to prepare and take specialist lessons, using the more sophisticated resources available to them, with the primary children.

The initial impetus for teacher contact is often concern for smoother transfer. A laudable outcome of the Wiltshire case-study was a noticeable fall in both parent and child anxieties and a smoother start to the new school year. But a significant development from this essentially pastoral concern is

usually some reference to curriculum continuity.
Ward comments, 'the real spin-off has been the
growth of in-service sessions on different subject
areas across the middle years of schooling'.
Approaching curriculum continuity by circuitous
means can be effective; indeed it may be more
successful than the direct route. Discussion about
transfer arrangements is seldom contentious so
groups can become well-established before any clash
of curricular philosophies.

Arrangements for the discussion of matters
specifically involving curriculum continuity vary
both in organisation and degree of formality. Ad
hoc meetings may be called to discuss particular
problems as they arise, or there may be standing
committees for the regular and detailed review of
curriculum in groups of related schools. In recent
times, secondary reorganisation provided the first
impetus for the formation of working groups to
discuss curriculum across stages of education.
Later, there was a further development of such
groups when the Great Debate and accountability
movement led to LEAs producing policy documents and
curriculum guidelines. Discussion of deeply-held
convictions by teachers of different philosophical
view is likely to involve heated debate and
exasperation. Indeed the very establishment of
working groups can present problems. Usually they
are constituted on a subject basis and are often
under the leadership of a local authority adviser
with subject responsibility. In many primary and
middle schools an integrated curriculum is class
taught with no individual teacher clearly accountable for a specific area of the curriculum.
Identifying teachers concerned presents no problems,
of course, in secondary schools where curricular
responsibility is vested in heads of departments. So
the very constitution of such groups is sometimes
criticised as having a secondary bias. It seems the
exposure of polarized opinions is an inevitable
first step in discussions concerned with continuity.

Committees established to promote liaison
between schools have had varying degrees of success.
Some have progressed to the promulgation of agreed
syllabuses; others have found it difficult to
establish general principles. A frequent complaint
has been that unnecessarily large working parties
have been formed, but when vital decisions are to be
made it is likely that most of the teachers affected
will want to participate. Committees with a one-
year mandate to recommend whatever action would

seem to be necessary to ensure continuity at transfer have sometimes been at work for several years. Drawn together by a general agreement on the need for close links between the work of schools across a divide, they have come to realise that it is no mean task to work out detail.

From the comments of representative groups of teachers and advisers who have participated in liaison committees, it would seem there are two major areas of difficulty: the first pertains to an inability to arrive at consensus about curriculum objectives; the second, paradoxically, relates to a seeming desire to prescribe syllabuses for contributory schools. Groups of English teachers have argued at length about the need to insist on correct grammar and spelling as opposed to an increased emphasis upon spoken language work. Upper-school geographers and historians have found it difficult to accept primary or middle school environmental, social and thematic approaches as providing adequate preparation for later work in their subjects while teachers in contributory schools have been reluctant to lay much stess on factual learning - 'the content curriculum' is a term frequently used - seeing their task rather as being to concentrate on developing skills and concepts in their pupils. Lois Benyon (1984) commenting on research by the North West Educational Management Centre, suggests that in cross-phase discussions about the humanities curriculum, autonomy not only of schools but of individual primary class teachers becomes readily apparent. Primary topic work and secondary differentiated subject approaches are so disparate that common ground is often difficult to find. Of course, individual attitudes of secondary teachers can impinge on continuity too. Subject specialists with no direct responsibility for language work may see the promotion of oracy as of no concern to them, in contrast with the previous stage of education when all areas of the curriculum were seen as vehicles for language development.

The tendency at the time of secondary reorganisation was for LEAs to establish subject panels to discuss curricular matters across and between phases. As the Leeds guideline document comments:

> The history of such groups is chequered. Some
> subjects have maintained unbroken a chain of
> regular meetings and even point to a detailed
> understanding of teaching problems (and some
> solutions) across a wide front. In other

subject areas there is little evidence of a willingness of teachers to undertake the often demanding task of setting up and maintaining such groups.

Speculation on reasons for success or failure of subject committees focuses on the size of groups, the personality of chairpersons and the nature of subjects concerned.

Criteria for Success of Discussion Groups

The larger the group of teachers involved in discussions, the wider is likely to be acceptance of recommendations proposed. Within large groups, however, there is likely to be more dissension, attendance at meetings tends to be variable and it takes longer to reach general agreement. Optimum size is difficult to determine and seldom capable of achievement for a controlling factor is the number of schools involved. When there are city-wide implications of decisions, working groups tend to be large. Humberside Education Authority provides an example of the influence of size on the extent of curriculum continuity achievement. Following comprehensive reorganisation there were two areas with middle schools for pupils in the 9-13 age-range: Hull and Goole. Even though the city was divided into zones, 17 upper schools and just over 50 middle schools in Hull were so inter-related that curricular change in one could have repercussions throughout the system. Subject continuity discussion groups were therefore constituted on a city-wide basis. In Goole, four middle schools fed one upper school; discussion was contained within a small group of related schools. Discussion groups were soon at work in Hull to explore the possibility of determining an agreed policy for mathematics, science and technical subjects but it took three years for the publication of documents. In other areas of the curriculum progress was even slower. One year after reorganisation in Goole, there were agreed syllabuses in English, French, mathematics science and the creative arts, whilst humanities were covered by a study skills matrix. Indeed, copies of some of the agreed schemes of work had been in the possession of heads-designate of upper and middle schools in the term before reorganisation took place. Clearly, curriculum study groups had been able to reach agreement quite rapidly. A local adviser's influence was partly

responsible for Goole's success but it was mainly
attributable to the existence of the pyramid
organisation. Small working parties were not only
able to reach agreement quickly but could produce
detailed schemes of work. The mathematics syllabus
itemised by year 230 topics to be covered during the
middle-school phase and specified associated books.
The mathematics common-core syllabus for middle
schools in Hull consisted of some 80 items mainly
stated as concepts to be covered at some stage
during the four years; recommendation of course
books was not attempted mainly because of lack of
consistency between upper schools. (Gorwood, 1981)
    An LEA exercises an indirect influence on size
of working parties by the administrative system it
establishes. It can be more directly involved in
promoting continuity if its advisers take a
significant role in the work of discussion groups.
The extent to which advisers become involved in
discussions varies: some chair meetings; others
prefer to stay on the sidelines ready to provide any
solicited advice and expertise. Someone has to
convene meetings and circulate papers; the necessary
support services to smooth the running of discussion
and working groups can often best be supplied by the
adviser's office. One local authority, commenting
on its practice of encouraging chairmanship of
groups to be taken by members of the advisory staff,
suggested this as one way of avoiding positions of
influence always being taken by teachers from large
schools. Limited clerical help and very little free
time put primary teachers at a considerable disadvantage if they sought responsibility in
competition with colleagues from larger secondary
schools. Another LEA attributed success in some
subjects rather than others to the 'energetic
leadership of advisers with both administrative
expertise and an intimate knowledge of the
essentials of the discipline concerned'. It is
interesting to note that discussion groups in Hull
earliest to arrive at some continuity agreement were
those concerned with subjects spanned by the city's
advisory team. The chairperson's influence can be
exemplified as well by failure as by success. The
elected chairman of one discussion group was the
head of science at a large comprehensive school.
At the first meeting, he alienated middle-school
members by stating that he had been driven to take
an active part in establishing continuity because of
the inadequacy of pupils' preparation before
transfer for secondary science. He could not be

144

disabused of the idealised notion that it would be possible to work out quite detailed syllabuses to satisfy the needs of the many different schools involved. There could be no possibility of individual interpretation, he claimed, because 'O' level syllabuses were prescribed. The committee was disbanded after several sessions during which there had been very little discussion of ways to improve curricular continuity in science but a far-ranging debate on the merits of the three-tier structure of educational provision. As the Leeds document comments, 'There is certainly a correlation between the effectiveness of a group and the energy and initiative of the chairperson of that group.'

Another factor influencing the level of continuity agreement reached by discussion groups has been the nature of the subjects of the school curriculum. The vast differences between primary and secondary approaches to the social subjects are not as evident in mathematics, for example. It may be easier to achieve consensus about the teaching of subjects of a linear nature because progression follows fairly well-defined paths. Lois Benyon (1984) noted that the schools involved in the NWEMC study readily perceived the need for close continuity in mathematics. Speculating on the reason for this, she asked: 'Was this because the structure of the subject where teaching and learning progresses in small, logical, sequential steps, lends itself naturally to agreement on procedure?' In subjects where objective criteria apply, statements of curriculum objectives tend to be more direct, more explicit and more susceptible to wider acceptance. This does not apply to English, in which emphasis has moved away from the structure of the subject towards the development of the individual learner. Following recommendations in the Bullock Report (DES, 1975) discussion groups were set up in many local authorities to consider continuity in language. Bullock saw this as being achieved mainly by transmission of information about individual children. A 'profile' would be sent on to secondary school together with actual examples of pupils' written work so that staff there would have access to the experience of the child that had been accumulated by other teachers over the years. Discussion was concerned less with English as a subject in its own right and more with the complicated logistics involved in arranging transfer of pupils' work. Understandably then, the disciplines with which discussion groups were concerned exercised considerable influence on the outcome of deliberations.

Local Authority Documents

Local education authorities over many years have published documents in which mention has been made of curriculum continuity. Often such documents have been prepared because of the enthusiasm or the initiative of a group of teachers or an adviser in a particular curricular area. The approach tended to be piecemeal; in one LEA, for example, pamphlets were published on mathematics, handicraft, French and science but there was nothing on English, the social subjects or the arts. Understandably in view of traditional attitudes, in the era following secondary reorganisation, subject structure was the basis for curricular planning but unease began to be expressed from the mid-1970s onwards. A school's responsibility to provide not only an academic education but one which took account of the needs of a comprehensive population was expressed in several publications but most forcibly in the Secretary of State's consultative document, Education in Schools (DES, 1977). The pressure which continued to be exerted culminated in Circular 6/81 being issued, urging the preparation of policy statements on curriculum. Local authorities were to review policies for the school curriculum in their areas and arrangements for making that policy known to all concerned; they were to review the extent to which current provision in schools was consistent with policy and plan future developments accordingly, within available resources. Policy documents published thereafter have tended to take a wide view of the whole curriculum. Typically, Northumberland Education Authority calls on its teachers 'to view the child from a wider perspective than, say, that of the specialist subject teacher within the restrictions of that subject. Any lesson is only one element in the pattern of the pupil's day and the experiences of the day are only one stage of the progress made through school'. In most documents, reference is made to continuity, teachers being enjoined to consider the total span of schooling in their planning. In Cumbria's statement of policy 'it is argued that the curriculum 4-19 is the concern of all teachers, and that they will wish to examine their contribution to each child's develop-ment within that time span, in full awareness of what has already been achieved and what is to

146

follow'. The tone of most local authority statements is, however, hortatory rather than determinant:
teachers are given plenty of advice but there is
little indication of positive intervention by LEAs.
Indeed, there is frequent reiteration of the
intractability of continuity problems and allocation
of cause - teacher autonomy. 'The Authority
(Northumerland) recognises that institutional and
individual teacher sovereignty may, on occasion,
prove difficult to reconcile with the requirements
of the best education interests of the children of a
locality.' And the solution is seen in
'professional determination to achieve agreement and
dynamic progress'.

Documents stating LEA policy on curriculum
seem, at first glance, to have advanced the cause of
continuity very little. Yet, more careful study
reveals a shift towards LEAs trying to assert a
greater influence. In apportioning curricular
responsibilities, for example, Humberside Authority
gives to itself rather than schools 'policy
decisions on arrangements for coherence and
continuity across schools for various age groups'.
Cumbria suggests that in discussions between phases,
all schools in a catchment area will be involved
'with the advisers/inspectors available to assist in
achieving a greater degree of co-operation'.
Northumberland LEA states that first and middle
schools 'should work towards establishing common
detailed sets of objectives in each of the main
curriculum areas'. Further, receiving schools have
a right to be consulted before such common policies
and objectives are finalised. In the context of
suggesting a policy for evaluation in primary
schools, Walsall Education Authority suggests that
headteachers of 'partner schools' should meet every
term under the chairmanship of inspectors to report
on their work as it relates to the partnership. The
Inspectorate provides 'the essential context in
which a school can relate its own endeavours and
opinions to those of other partner schools'. There
is, then, a suggestion of greater involvement of the
inspectorate in trying to co-ordinate the work of
schools, but the secondary sector is generally left
inviolate, emphasis being on the achievement of
consistency within feeder primary and middle
schools.

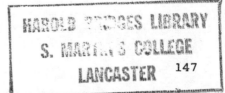
HAROLD BRIDGES LIBRARY
S. MARTIN'S COLLEGE
LANCASTER

Academic Boards and Councils

An interesting organisational development pioneered by Devon Education Authority is that of Academic Boards or Councils. It is over ten years since the first board was established and since then many schemes have evolved, different in detail but with the same basic characteristic, a federation of schools to maintain overall collaboration in a particular geographical area. Membership of boards is usually confined to heads of associated schools and advisers; it is considered the presence of school staff members would inhibit discussion. There are opportunities, however, for general teachers to become involved in working parties to consider particular issues. The establishment of another administrative level between school and LEA can present problems mostly revolving around the autonomy of individual institutions and the relationship of the middle tier to the authority itself. Unity, however, can bring greater strength and help to articulate the major concerns of a given area.

Each of the academic councils or boards seems at some time to have addressed the problem of the extent of its powers. Exmouth Academic Council, for example, has produced a policy document in which it asks how it can guide or direct teachers in schools. '"Guidance" is acceptable', it says; '"direction" may send shivers down the spine. Nevertheless there is a nettle to be grasped.' The solution proposed is for statements by the Academic Council to be categorised 'mandatory', 'suggestions for action', 'suggestions for consideration' or 'optional'. Arrangements for primary-secondary transfer would be mandatory. The terms of reference of academic councils are not laid down by the local authority, which has been careful not to impose these structures on heads of schools. Ideally, heads and staff request the opportunity of establishing a council and there is negotiation and full agreement before proceeding. The process seems to be one of infection: Exeter drew on the experience of Barnstaple; Dawlish and Exmouth developed their own councils with their own constitutions but took into account practice already established elsewhere.

Understandably, 'inter-phase liaison' occurs as a theme in most of the discussion papers emanating from these councils. Typically, stated as aims for the Dawlish Council are:

- to ensure that the local education system (the catchment area of Dawlish School) will provide a single, coherent and continuous educational process rather than two separate phases;

- to promote and maintain federal agreement on the curriculum, whilst at the same time recognising the need for each school to preserve a sufficient measure of autonomy to develop its own way.

Though these groups are not a complete solution to problems of liaison and continuity, they are potentially very influential.

Similar schemes are developing elsewhere with differences of nomenclature and detail: Birmingham has its 'consortia and there are 'pyramidal' systems in several middle-school areas. Their effectiveness has yet to be evaluated but there is a growing appreciation of the greatly enhanced possibilities of improvement in liaison and continuity by these new administrative structures between school and LEA.

Evaluation

Recent emphasis on evaluation is evident in several LEA curricular documents. By presenting checklists against which schools measure their own performance, LEAs can make quite telling proposals whilst avoiding authoritative attitudes. Some authorities contain reference to continuity within general documents whilst others produce material concerned specifically with this topic. For example, within one LEA's Instrument for in-school evaluation in the primary school some 150 questions are posed of which three are pertinent to continuity:

- Is the recording system successful in assembling information that is relevant to another school or to parents?

- Are there any serious obstacles to achieving continuity of record-keeping from class to class or from school to school? If obstacles exist, how are they being tackled? What further steps might be taken?

- How do I ensure continuity of progress

between years groups and between schools
from which and to which children transfer?

In contrast, Essex County Council's Continuity
between primary and secondary schools is a check-
list of approximately 70 items, each expanded by
comprehensive commentary. Specific observations are
made. On curriculum content, for example, schools
are asked to take the following into account when
planning their practices and procedures:

Whilst some familiar content is useful during
the first few days, curriculum should be
approached with awareness of what children have
done before:

(i)   overlaps lead to boredom - they are
        expecting something new;

(ii)   check that use is not being made of
        material identical to that which they had
        in primary school;

(iii)   check primary-school library to ensure
        that the choice of books available to
        them is at least as wide as they had in
        their primary school.

Clearly, there are characteristic differences
between seeking specific assurance based on factual
appraisal and merely asking whether procedures are
successful. Which of these strategies is the more
effective is open to question. Unless there is some
auditing of self-evaluation schemes it could be
argued that to present a school with a long check-
list is to invite non-observance. The position of
local authorities is extremely difficult for though
they may accept the promotion of continuity as their
responsibility, curriculum, the agent through which
continuity is maintained, remains the preserve of
schools. Some LEAs, however, require a school to
undertake a curriculum review and produce a report
on it. (McCormick and James, 1983) Within that
review, schools can be obliged to comment on the
links they have established with associated schools.
It is generally considered, however, that more is
achieved by encouragement than by coercion. Schools
need the help of guidelines which suggest specific
things to do. The ideal to be pursued should be a
compromise between detailed prescription and random
generalization. Humberside's policy statement

provides an example of this stance: curriculum
planning is assigned to schools but the LEA stipu-
lates terms of reference:

> However a school plans its curriculum, each area
> of study or subject offers its own blend of
> opportunities for the acquisition of attitudes,
> concepts (forms of understanding with the
> crucial related language development),
> knowledge (content) and skills. Each school
> should prepare and regularly review schemes of
> work for each of the areas of study or subjects
> in its curriculum with clear statements of
> intent under the above four headings.

Somewhat more contentious is Humberside's categoris-
ation of areas of experience, owing much to Hirst's
(1969) 'forms of knowledge', to be used by schools
as a check list against which to assess how
curriculum contributes to development of 'aesthetic
and creative, ethical, linguistic, mathematical,
physical, scientific, social and political, and
spiritual' experience. Irrespective of the phase of
education in which schools are located, they are to
use the same check-list of skills and areas of
experience; clearly, within this authority it is
intended that curriculum should have unity throughout
the school age-range. By requiring schools to think
of curriculum in the same terms, the local authority
is taking a small but positive step towards
promoting continuity. In contrast, some authorities
contain reference to curriculum within secondary and
primary contexts. Croydon's statement of policy on
curriculum is typical of several LEAs in noting the
need for better liaison but perpetuating the notion
of differences between the stages: 'Although
education is a continuous process all children are
affected by the transfer from primary to secondary
education. In spite of the growth of closer links
between the two sectors in recent years both still
represent significant differences of approach.'
Within curricular areas, aims in English and
mathematics are considered throughout the 5-16 age-
range but in other fields discussion is of primary
and secondary approaches with no indication of
bridges between the two. Other LEAs go even further
in accentuating the divide by producing separate
documents for the two stages, seemingly produced by
different working parties. Ironically, within one
such document there is a plea for teachers in the
two sectors to liaise more closely but there is no

indication of any communication with the working
party concerned with the other stage. It is
understandable if a group set up to consider post-
primary education does just that; within a hundred-
page document produced by one working party there is
nothing to suggest pupils receive any schooling
before the age of eleven. In constituting
curricular discussion groups LEAs would be well
advised to ensure representation from both primary
and secondary stages as one simple but effective way
of ensuring that the transfer issue is not
neglected.

Continuity in Specific Subjects

Though in recent years emphasis in LEA documents has been on the whole curriculum, in one
subject, mathematics, there have been several local
initiatives intended to promote continuity both
within and between schools. By producing a document related to the middle years, Humberside
concentrates on the transitional stage and sees
continuity as the responsibility of a mathematics
co-ordinator, the primary or middle-school teacher
responsible for planning and oversight of
mathematics throughout the school but also charged
with paying special attention to maintaining
continuity when pupils transfer school. Bradford's
mathematics guidelines are contained in a collection
of papers written by a group of teachers from first,
middle and upper schools, reflecting 'a continuity
of thought' throughout the period of compulsory
schooling. A series of checklists covering
mathematical skills, facts and concepts concludes in
two lists of objectives for pupils aged 8-10 and
12-14 years 'to indicate that the work in the first/
middle schools and middle/upper schools must be seen
as a continuum'. Some local authorities have
progressed beyond guidelines to the provision of
mathematics courses. As they often serve the same
purpose as commercially-produced, nationally-
distributed materials, it could be argued that the
considerable effort expended in developing them
could have been better spent. Yet locally-devised
courses tend to be widely used in the authority in
which they were produced. If, as in the Kent
Mathematics Project, they are devised for primary
through to secondary age-ranges, they obviously have
value in promoting continuity. The Kent Mathematics
Project provides a course unique for each individual
child, using material suitable for all abilities of

children between nine and sixteen. In the guide to
the project, particular mention is made of the
advantages the project offers for school transfer:

> One hurdle in mathematical education is often
> created by change of school. Unless all
> schools use the same syllabus, much of what has
> been learned in one school is wasted and it
> often happens that gaps are created in concept
> development, frequently so vast that they are
> never filled properly. This would never happen
> in any transfer between any two KMP schools.

This seemingly extravagant claim warrants consideration. By placing mathematical concept development
in a hierarchy and arranging work so that pupils
progress at their own pace through a learning
sequence, KMP seems an ideal vehicle for continuity
in mathematics. But is it not the nature of the
subject rather than the particular approach which is
significant? So often, continuity difficulties
arise because there is no unanimity about sequencing
principles. Determining sequence in the social
disciplines, for example, is a major problem; lack
of agreement about ordering pupils' learning is a
main cause of repetitions and lacunae, symptomatic
of discontinuity.

Despite considerable expenditure of finance and
effort, local authorities have not been as
successful in other areas of the curriculum in
producing guidelines and materials as they have in
mathematics. Where national schemes, such as the
Schools Mathematics Project, exist there would seem
to be little need for local initiatives. One LEA's
strategy in this connection is to offer SMP books on
long-term loan. The bonus of materials not charge-
able against capitation allowance has persuaded many
schools to adopt this course. The same authority
gives a 75 per cent grant towards the purchase of
En Avant materials for French teaching. Given
such financial incentives, the active interest of
local advisers and in-service courses directly
related to the teaching materials, there has been a
considerable achievement of compatability of
curricula in mathematics and French. As the chief
education officer for Somerset has commented: 'The
most direct impact which the LEA can make upon the
curriculum is by deciding how to spend its money.'
(Taylor, 1984) He suggests, 'the LEA has a seminal
role in relation to the curriculum, particularly in
bringing teachers together, providing thinking time

and the means to implement their plans'. If schools are to engage in joint curricular decisions, which Taylor advocates, teachers must be released from classroom duties in order to attend meetings. Curriculum continuity warrants the attention of all teachers, not merely those enthusiasts who attend course after course in their own time. Several LEA documents on curriculum continuity acknowledge the dedication of teachers 'who have spent many out-of-school hours in drawing up guidelines to promote smoother transition'. LEAs could demonstrate their resolve to promote liaison and curriculum continuity by a more generous investment to enable teachers to engage in inter-school discussions during normal working hours.

Teacher Visits and Exchanges

It is now many years since Caroline Moorhead (1971), commenting on the lack of contact between primary and secondary teachers, cited the case of teachers in associated schools a mere hundred yards apart who had made no attempt to communicate with each other. Though their headteachers were close friends, differences of attitude to education were so strong that they could see no purpose in visits, meetings or exchanges of staff. One would hope things had changed. Yet the same reluctance to take anything more than a superficial interest in the work of related contributory or receiving schools can still be discerned. A minority of responses to the author's invitation for comment on continuity resembled those Moorhead received:

- Staff here are busy enough; I don't want them getting involved in other schools.

- We have our own way of doing things - not like the primary school. The sooner pupils get used to us the better.

- Secondary teachers are the ones with time to spare for making school contact. We couldn't do it.

The barriers between teachers in the different stages of education may not be so well-defined but they are still there. There is an understandable reluctance to approach an associated school with suggestions for improving transition when there is a chance of rebuff because of sensitivity to

criticism. Yet when an initiative is taken by a
local authority, usually through its advisory
service, the possibility of fruitful co-operation
increases. Seemingly, chance incidents can forge
permanent links. An adviser visiting a secondary
school commented favourably on a science wall
display in a neighbouring primary school. On her
next visit to collect transfer information, the
first-year liaison teacher made a point of viewing
the display but was told of the problems science
presented because of lack of apparatus and limited
expertise. She talked to the head of science, who,
after consultation with the adviser and his own
headmaster, was able to loan equipment and help with
planning a science programme. From this there
developed a system of teacher visits and exchanges,
firstly in science but later in several other areas
of the curriculum. On the face of it, the local
authority's role in this exercise seems minimal, yet
by keeping a watchful eye on developments, the
adviser was able to forestall potential difficulties.
The first hint of criticism came from a deputy head
in the second school, who complained of the 'one-way
process': help was being given to the primary school
but nothing was received in return. The adviser
suggested that the primary staff's considerable
experience with teaching reading could benefit the
secondary remedial department. By this and other
sometimes subtle means the adviser was able to
safeguard the continuity link.

  Essex local authority's <u>Continuity between
primary and secondary schools</u> provides a useful
check-list to assist schools in planning transfer
and liaison procedures. One of the key areas
identified in the pamphlet is 'contact and understanding amongst teachers', within which visits and
exchanges of staff are given particular mention.
Visits to related schools give teachers opportunities not only to view pupils' work but also to
observe methods used by colleagues and to pick up
new techniques. Staff who are to receive pupils can
gain useful indications of children's commitment to
work, responses to tasks set and usual behaviour.
Administrative difficulties in exchange teaching in
an associated school make this a somewhat rare
practice but the Essex pamphlet points out that
early summer leaving by some secondary-school pupils
provides a time when staff could be released for
such an exchange; it further recommends that at
least a week should be spent on this exercise.
Suitability of the final weeks of the summer term

for exchange visits is also mentioned in Leeds
authority's continuity document, which cautions that
progress in teacher exchanges may be slow; 'other
elements of liaison work' may need to precede it.
Nevertheless, successful teacher exchanges are
effected in Leeds. 'Teachers involved discuss how to
work with pupils they have taught or will teach and
become aware of the constraints and advantages of
working in a school with curriculum, apparatus and
classrooms unfamiliar to them.' The strategy of
exchanging teaching posts is less concerned with
directly improving pupil transfer but more with
widening the experience and expertise of staff.
The rationale for staff exchanges is outlined in the
Leeds pamphlet:

> Different experiences of initial training may
> result in many teachers being unaware of even
> the basic aims and objectives of schools
> outside their own stage. Different philoso-
> phies as much as different buildings, equipment
> or methodologies, can best be understood and
> appreciated by working directly with colleagues
> outside the usual framework of day to day
> teaching, and possible misunderstandings
> between colleagues are best eliminated by
> practical experience in each other's schools.

Teacher exchanges are usually of a temporary
nature and arranged on an ad hoc basis. A more
extensive exchange scheme has been developed in the
Wandsworth division of ILEA. (Benyon, 1984)
Teachers of the top forms in three of its feeder
primary schools move with their classes to Hydeburn
School, a comprehensive for 1,000 pupils. There,
they serve as class teachers in basic subjects for
the first year. At the end of the year, they return
to their primary schools while another three
teachers move up with their pupils to continue the
cycle. The link scheme began in 1977 when the first
group of primary teachers visited the secondary
school for several periods each week to get to know
the staff, discuss with heads of departments
curriculum content, teaching styles, subject
materials and their expectations of new pupils.
The project was not accepted by everybody: some
secondary staff originally felt that pupils would
merely have their primary education extended taking
up a valuable year needed for the secondary-school
curriculum and style of teaching. (Harthill, 1977)
The link teachers learned to be tactful in order to

nurture a scheme with such potential for easing primary-secondary transfer. Though several local authorities have expressed interest in developing schemes on the 'link teacher' model, their efforts seem to have been thwarted by difficulties in recruiting staff with both general expertise for primary work and the ability to teach as semi-specialists in the secondary school.

Clearly, there are many initiatives to improve continuity that can be taken at individual school level but problems are so formidable that it is doubtful whether independent institutions can be sufficiently effective. As Stillman and Maychell (1984) comment:

> Although it may seem most appropriate for teachers themselves to initiate liaison activities, since they are the ones who will ultimately be involved in altering syllabuses or teaching new ones, in practice it appears that without the LEA playing an initial role in co-ordinating inter-sector discussions and coaxing staff at various levels to gradually take over responsibility, very little will occur.

Recent pressure from central authority to persuade LEAs of their responsibility for involvement in matters of school transfer and curriculum continuity has had some effect but the response seems to have been sporadic. In an attempt to find out more about LEA engagement in continuity and transfer, a survey of all local authorities was conducted.

Survey of Local Authorities

Early in 1984, all local authorities in England and Wales were sent a brief questionnaire seeking information about ways in which they attempted to promote school liaison and curriculum continuity. Replies were received from 75 local authorities, a 72 per cent response. The main concern of this limited survey was to discern trends in the attitude of local authorities towards continuity. The DES has been inviting attention to this issue for several years; it was considered timely to check on LEA response.

Three questions were asked to gain an impression of measures taken by the authority to promote liaison and continuity; responses to these questions are tabulated in Table 7.1:

157

1. Is there within the authority an adviser/
    inspector with specific responsibility for
    promoting school liaison and/or curriculum
    continuity?

2. Has the authority organised courses/
    conferences on the theme of school liaison/
    curriculum continuity?

3. Has the authority produced a document on
    school liaison/curriculum continuity?

**Table 7.1: Practical steps taken by LEAs to promote
liaison/continuity**

	Response	Yes		No	
	N	N	%	N	%
Adviser with specific responsibility for liaison/continuity	75	18	24	57*	76
Courses/conferences organised on theme of liaison/continuity	74	63	85	11	15
Document produced on liaison/continuity	72	30	42	42	58

*21 qualified response to indicate that this was
taken care of

Though few LEAs assigned continuity and liaison as a
specific responsibility, most were anxious to affirm
that it was taken care of by someone. Several
authorities with a middle years adviser saw
continuity as being one facet of his or her role.
In some authorities it was considered to fall within
the orbit of all primary advisers. It was pointed
out by one respondent that liaison was implicit in
the responsibilities of all advisers in his LEA
since they were all concerned with pupils across the
age range 4-19. A most revealing comment was that
of a chief adviser who observed that continuity was
the responsibility of every member of the advisory
team - 'which probably means that no one is
particularly concerned and so we don't tackle it as
well as we should'. Obviously, as was pointed out
by several respondents, more pressing issues can

take precedence; advisers concerned with reorganisation, school amalgamations or changes in catchment
zones may find themselves so committed to immediate
practicalities that they have no time for less
urgent matters such as continuity, particularly if
they are not explicitly part of their brief. The
impression gained from responses was of general
acceptance of responsibility but with continuity
being seen as merely one of many tasks for a hard-
pressed advisory service.

As Table 7.1 shows, the majority of LEAs have
organised courses or conferences on the theme of
liaison and continuity. These range from one-day
events to protracted courses often involving working
groups of teachers over many months. Although fewer
than half responding authorities had produced a
pamphlet specifically on continuity and liaison,
many included some reference to these concerns in a
more general document, frequently a review of
curriculum policy. Documents concerned solely with
continuity were very general in approach presenting
the collected wisdom of interested groups, working
parties, headteachers and advisers rather than LEA
policy. Even in the central matter of transfer
documentation local authorities seemed loath to
extend beyond guidance. LEA responses to <u>Circular
14/77</u> indicated that almost nine-tenths of
authorities 'required or expected schools to
transfer records' (DES, 1979); this gives an
impression of directive that is difficult to discern
in the relevant documents. Though many LEAs produce
a standard proforma for the transfer of information,
few 'require' its use, relying rather on strong
persuasion and self-evaluation.

The survey sought opinion on the extent to
which curriculum continuity posed a problem for
local authorities. Several respondents considered
the question too negative, suggesting that 'problem'
was inappropriate; 'challenge' would be better. One
response was annotated: 'This is the wrong question.
We are concerned: some areas do reasonably well,
others less so.' Despite its inadequacies, the
question did yield an indication of local
authorities' impressions of the scale of continuity
difficulties.

Table 7.2:   LEA estimate of curriculum continuity
             problems

	N	%
No difficulties	4	5
Minor difficulties	15	21
Some difficulties	40	56
Major difficulties	13	18

Manifestly, the majority of LEAs acknowledged
continuity as a problem. Asked to identify the
major cause of difficulties, local authorities
mentioned most frequently:

1.   lack of time (stated by 18 LEAs as the main
     cause)

2.   teacher attitudes (11)

3.   the larger number of feeder schools (10)

4.   scattered rural schools (9) and

5.   communication problems (7)

'Quite simply', one chief education officer replied,
'there is too much for inspectors to do and they
need to make considerable effort to overcome the
natural inertia of schools.' Lack of time was also
considered to be at the root of problems. There is
not enough time for teachers to make contact with
colleagues in other sectors, it was thought, and so
misgivings and misconceptions about the kind of
education at the other side of a transfer barrier
persist. Authorities acknowledging major continuity
difficulties cited the large number of contributory
schools to each upper school as the main problem.
In urban areas, this tendency was the result of free
parental choice of many secondary schools within
commutable distance; in scattered rural communities,
secondary schools received pupils from very many
small primary schools. Communication problems were
illustrated by one adviser, who pointed out that the
large number of teachers who should be consulted
before any policy was implemented made it impossible
to effect any change in sometimes unsatisfactory

procedures 'unless the notion of school autonomy is
abandoned'. 'Productive inertia', according to this
respondent was 'better than stirring up a hornet's
nest.'
      Problems cited tended to be interrelated and
resolved in the main to lack of communication
between teachers. As several respondents commented,
the extent to which local authorities can influence
fundamental differences in philosophy is limited.
Indeed, one reply suggested that curriculum
continuity was entirely a matter for schools to
settle between themselves. Another response
identified the main difficulty as inability to
develop a reliable but flexible structure for
maintaining continuity between different educational
phases. A point touched upon by several respondents
but considered the main problem by one LEA was that
there were always other priorities on advisers'
time; despite accepting the need to promote liaison
and continuity, they could never give it enough
attention. The frankest response to this question
was that which stated 'lack of LEA initiative'.
      It was, perhaps, unrealistic to expect local
authorities to be able to specify areas of the
curriculum in which they had achieved most and least
success in promoting continuity. Several declined
to respond; some suggested that the situation varied
according to locality; others stated that they did
not know. Though incomplete, responses yielded an
interesting indication of local authority notions of
subject fields in relation to curriculum continuity.

Table 7.3: LEA estimates of achievement in
            promoting continuity by areas of the
            curriculum

Most successful	N	Least successful	N
Mathematics	43	Humanities	23
Language	25	Science	9
Science	16	Mathematics	4
French	11	Language	3
Humanities	3		

N = Number of LEAs designating this subject area.
    Subject areas mentioned only once are not
    included

161

As can be seen from Table 7.3, local authority representatives considered the greatest success in promoting curriculum continuity to have been achieved in mathematics and language. Under the impetus of Bullock and Cockcroft Reports, many courses and conferences had pondered the problem of discontinuity in the basic subjects but a more telling reason for success, according to several LEA responses, was that in language and mathematics, primary and secondary schools tended to have similar objectives. The same could not be said for the humanities. There were several comments indicating inability of LEAs to bring primary and secondary teachers together: in-service courses in differen-tiated subjects were attended mainly by secondary teachers whilst integrated approaches such as environmental studies attracted primary and middle-school teachers but few from the secondary sector.

Finally, the questionnaire offered the opportunity for general comment. One clear message emerged: local authorities consider their power to influence continuity to be extremely limited. 'Individual schools work well'; 'where bridging groups have been established continuity is achieved'; 'very patchy but there are local initiatives' - the impression is of LEAs seeing schools playing the major role. One adviser commented, 'Schools provide the machinery - all the LEA can do is see that the machinery is well-oiled.' The few responses indicating LEA acceptance of an obligation to promote continuity were qualified by statements of inadequacy. One respondent acknow-ledged that continuity was poor in areas of the curriculum not covered by a member of the advisory team. Another commented, 'So much depends on advisory staff acting as neutral and unbiased agents but advisory time is limited and there are many demands on it.'

Conclusion

Of those responsible for school education, local authorities would seem to be best placed to influence school liaison and curriculum continuity. Their attitude is likely to be less parochial than that of individual schools yet they are not so far from practicalities to make unrealistic recommend-ations. The basic responsibility to maintain continuity across breaks in schooling, postulated by the central authority, has been accepted by many leading LEA administrators. (Taylor, 1984)

162

LOCAL AUTHORITY STRATEGIES

Some local authorities have been very effective in developing continuity strategies and supporting school initiatives but, considered nationally, the picture is very uneven. At least two major factors inhibit LEAs in this matter. Firstly, there are many calls on an authority's limited resources. The advisory service tends to be fully occupied responding to other needs; there always seem to be more pressing concerns to take precedence over continuity. Secondly, LEAs lack actual power to influence matters on which effective continuity depends. A chief education officer of many years experience has outlined the problem local administrators now face:

> It is clear that many of the most crucial decisions affecting the nature of service offered by a local education authority lie beyond its control. The dispersal of power is an important principle in the running of the education service and one that many involved would defend to the death. Yet dispersal of power may now have gone too far for the well-being of the service and the time may be at hand that we should seek to define more clearly who is responsible for what in the hope that firm decisions can be taken and progress made. Only with clarification of responsibility is it possible to pin-point accountability. (Fiske, 1980)

Fiske would prefer power at the centre to be strengthened rather than a continuance of the current local authority situation of 'responsibility without power'. Yet despite recent strong initiatives, central government has not been successful in gaining control over curriculum. Schools insist on determining curriculum but successful continuity is so dependent upon the release by schools of autonomy in curricular matters. Those LEAs content to leave liaison and continuity to individual schools will probably find considerable, successful effort being put into the pastoral care of pupils at time of transfer but the more thorny problem of curricular continuity will continue to defy solution. But pastoral care cannot be really effective unless there is continuity for significant change will cause pupils to become disorientated and confused. 'For any group of children progressing through the system, the parts must be seen to make a cohesive whole - and that is the LEA's responsibility.' (Taylor, 1984)

163

Chapter Eight

IMPROVING LIAISON AND CONTINUITY AT THE SCHOOL LEVEL

For many children, school transfer is more traumatic
in anticipation than realization. Worries about the
unknown are dispelled as new routines become
established. Alarming rumours of extreme bullying
are found to have been exaggerated. 'Harder work at
the big school' proves manageable. Indeed, the
change is often seen as one for the better. (Makins,
1982) Yet we have to accept transition from one
stage of education to another as presenting a crisis
point in a child's school career, albeit the period
of difficulty is of brief duration in the total span
of compulsory schooling. However carefully
organised, school transition impresses on the child
the notion of being a little fish in a big pond.
(Mahoney, 1981) After transfer, pupils are bound to
feel the weight of seniority above them,
particularly since they have previously enjoyed the
prestige of being 'in the top class'. Changed
surroundings, different teachers, new conventions -
all have to be accommodated. There will probably be
further travel, resulting in a longer school day and
- the biggest worry of all - separation from former
friends. Knowing in advance of the numerous
challenging differences a new school will present
gives no assurance of ability to cope with them.
Schools aspiring to ease transfer difficulties must
do more than merely provide information. How
persuaded were his future pupils when a secondary-
school headmaster, at the junior-school prize-giving
ceremony, assured them they would take trigonometry
and chemistry in their stride? Many schools, of
course, do more than offer enigmatic glimpses of an
ominous future.

CONTINUITY AT THE SCHOOL LEVEL

Posts of responsibility for transfer

Schools concerned to improve arrangements for transfer of pupils usually make liaison a responsibility of a key member of staff. The importance assigned to this topic can readily be gauged by the place transition occupies in this teacher's allocated tasks. A deputy headmaster in charge of discipline, the time-table and staff matters may be hard-pressed to give similar attention to transfer, which he may estimate of vital concern for but a brief period in the year, to be ousted by more urgent affairs. A member of staff with limited non-teaching responsibilities can sustain the attention transition warrants. Paul Doherty (1984), a primary-secondary liaison teacher in Greater Manchester, has outlined the range of curriculum-based liaison activities that can be developed when someone specifically charged with this task is time-tabled for a morning each week to attend to ways of smoothing transition. The larger the school, the more the likelihood of matters related to school transfer being a teacher's sole extra responsibility.

The common secondary-school practice of establishing posts combining liaison and the pastoral care of first-year pupils has much to commend it. Its main advantage is that, of many new adults to be confronted, someone familiar is there to help pupils through the potentially difficult first few weeks in upper school. This implies, of course, that the liaison teacher has met pupils in their primary schools before transfer. When there is a limited number of contributory schools, some meeting with future pupils is generally arranged but the extent of contact varies. Some liaison teachers can spare time to make only one visit to each feeder school to give information and to answer questions. Celia Allen (1977), head of lower school in an Uxbridge comprehensive, suggests it is useful to take first-year pupils to these meetings, particularly to primary schools they have previously attended. Children, she finds, 'are able to allay fears more easily than an adult'. She provides insight into the worries uppermost in the minds of prospective pupils whose questions fall into the following groups: 'new subjects, uniform, sport, school meals, discipline, how to find their way around a large building, how to cope with a large number of new teachers, bus routes, and bullying'. In another London case study, reference is made to

the way in which recently-transferred pupils can
assist in preparing those about to transfer:

> We draw from up to 44 primary schools but 10 of
> them account for the major part of our intake.
> Each year first-year pupils from about 15 of
> our feeder schools go back to talk to those
> about to transfer. Most look forward eagerly
> to this visit. Some prepare short talks on
> aspects of secondary-school life: 'The First
> Day', 'A Typical Day', 'Homework', 'Lessons',
> 'Differences between Primary and Secondary
> School'. I fill in between the talks ensuring
> that no essential information is omitted.
> Questions from the audience are important.
> Seldom are they academic in nature; school
> dinners, sanctions, bullying, 'Is the work
> hard?', 'What are the teachers like? . . . .
> The interests of pupils are personal and
> immediate. (Holly, 1977)

In a single, large-group meeting, a two-way
exchange of information is difficult. The liaison
teacher can tell pupils about their new school but
can gain little insight into future charges. A
thorough but time-consuming technique to overcome this
difficulty is to interview each future pupil before
transfer. By this means, pupils can have their
queries resolved whilst teachers gain information
about personal, social and emotional backgrounds to
complement details of academic achievement provided
in transfer documents. When transfer to secondary
school is deferred beyond eleven, it is particularly
useful to gain early information about newcomers in
order to expedite organisation of external examination groups. Consequently, pre-transfer interviewing is a strategy favoured in areas where three-tier
systems have been established. Typical of this
approach is that of an upper-school in Hull. The
head of first year, also responsible for liaison, is
assisted by two class teachers in a programme of
interviewing all 240 pupils in up to 20 feeder
middle schools. The standard local-authority
transfer document provides brief personal details
and teachers' assessments of a pupil's academic
abilities. The interviewer fills out the personal
history by asking about parents' occupations,
brothers and sisters, hobbies, interests, membership of organisations, subject preferences, career
intentions and friendship patterns. Although there
is a set structure, a deliberately informal

166

atmosphere is engendered to encourage pupils to expose reactions to impending transfer. Interviews can be lengthy. The allotted sixty hours spread over many days are seldom enough to complete the process. The start of interviewing must wait on firm decisions being made about school placement late in the spring term. Within one school term, a busy round of feeder schools to see staff as well as pupils is fitted into a slightly more generous free-time allocation. Work to be completed on transfer details, including remaining interviews, occupies most of the last two or three weeks of the school year when, after external examinations, 'moving-up' throughout the school frees first-year staff of teaching commitments. It is claimed that the laborious task of establishing comprehensive records for each child is essential at the start of an upper-school career which may last less than three years.

Pre-transfer interviewing of each pupil is not without its critics. John Sharp (1975), outlining the approach to transfer he adopted as head of a comprehensive school, argued:

> If I interviewed several hundred children for say 15 minutes each over a period of weeks in the spring, I don't believe that I should recognise many of them when I met them in school months later. For me, therefore, the interview is rather barren. More important, to the child I suspect that it is usually unproductive and sometimes rather an ordeal.

Shared responsibility for liaison

It is unfortunate if specific liaison appointments encourage other staff to avoid involvement in matters concerning transition. The successful teacher is aware of pupils' previous experiences. Concern for continuity, then, should not be left to the person responsible the liaison teacher, but should be shared by the whole staff. This has been achieved in a Chichester comprehensive school by encouraging volunteers to become 'primary link teachers'. Whilst the head of lower school and head of first year are mainly concerned with liaison, any member of staff can become associated with one of the twenty or so primary schools from which pupils are drawn. The link teacher is a channel of communication between secondary and primary school. Social events, curriculum problems and the specific

anxieties of pupils about to move school are dealt
with whenever they arise by a teacher who is, above
all, a recognisable face from the 'big school'.
Regular, informal contact can lead to exchange
visits to observe lessons and occasionally to teach,
although time-tabling problems and differences in
expertise inhibit this practice. It would be
difficult for the head of lower school to maintain
links with many feeder schools, some very small and
some rural, without the support of a large team.
Furthermore, this network of contacts is well-placed
to appreciate currently-dominant concerns which can
provide themes for exploration at the annual
conference of the local Primary Liaison Association,
a body set up in the mid 1970s at the suggestion of
Chichester's comprehensive schools. The most significant effect of this innovation, however, is
probably the understanding that develops between
primary and secondary teachers. Of course, the mere
establishment of links does not guarantee a productive outcome but it is an essential first step to
breaking down the barriers so explicitly exemplified
by Orsborn (1977) and Moorhead (1971)

Curriculum consistency

Pupils can arrive at the secondary stage of
education with different previous experiences.
Reasons for such diversity were considered in
chapter three. Given 'the astonishing degree of
autonomy' accorded to British headteachers (Peters,
1966), it is difficult to speculate how schools
might solve problems caused by differences of level
and content in their intake classes. A link teacher
comments, 'They wouldn't welcome being told what to
do by someone from the upper school - but they
should try to decide some common practice between
themselves at least for the pre-transfer year.'
Despite evidence from the primary school survey
(DES, 1978, para.6.9), many primary teachers remain
unconvinced of wide differences between their
schools. A strategy used by one secondary headmaster 'to get some uniformity between feeders' has
proved effective if contentious. Eight main feeder
schools supplied four-year time-tables which were
compared for subject time allocation and 'curricular
labels'. The analysis proved the great variation
between schools. In one school, pupils had spent
almost half their time in art or craft lessons
whilst in another, this area of the curriculum
occupied only two periods a week. Even in English

and mathematics there were big differences in time
allocation. In two schools there was an emphasis on
creativity; in another two the environment was the
focus of all curricular activity; the remainder used
traditional subject designations. A tentative
further approach to try to compare the content of
mathematics courses revealed that in one school
there were no guidelines of any kind although it was
claimed the monitoring of pupils' progress provided
a mathematics framework. Without identifying
schools, the analysis was circulated and proved a
powerful stimulus to the establishment of a
committee to review curriculum in associated primary
schools.

No attempt was made to devise agreed syllabuses
but for several subjects, lists were drawn up of
skills to be acquired before transfer. Achieving
curriculum balance was more difficult. Whilst
general class teaching predominated, primary schools
reflected the interests of their staff. In some
schools, science was taught with reluctance, in
others with enthusiasm. Even had rigid time-tabling
been acceptable, the many opportunities to bias
general work towards a favoured subject would have
resulted in pupils receiving very different
curricular backgrounds. Nevertheless, the upper-
school head declared himself well-satisfied with the
exercise. He had partially achieved what Richards
(1982) advocates if we are to move towards a more
genuinely comprehensive education: 'Primary schools
feeding common secondary schools could develop much
closer links (as have some middle schools) to ensure
that there is a definite measure of consistency in
the curriculum experienced by their oldest pupils
prior to transfer.'

Passing on pupils' work

Unless receiving schools have knowledge of
pupils' abilities, they can misjudge acceptable
levels of performance, as Newsam (1977) illustrated.
During the long vacation, youngsters do little to
maintain the standards achieved by the end of the
summer term. It is easy to understand how early
work in the new school can be unrepresentative.
Passing on to secondary school samples of pupils'
primary work could provide a realistic measure by
which to gauge future efforts. This practice was
recommended in the Bullock Report. As many as three
or four pieces of English work per year were to be
transmitted to supplement objective data.

The 'profile' of each child would be sent on to the
secondary school so that staff there would have
access to the experience that had been accumulated
by other teachers over the years. The comprehensive
picture of pupils' language attainment would, as
Bullock suggested, provide receiving schools with a
valuable 'instrument'. But an instrument is only of
service if it is used. Few schools would seem to
have taken heed of this recommendation. It is
unrealistic to expect a school to find space to
store the sheer bulk of written work involved. Even
if time was available to read through such a vast
collection, most secondary teachers feel it could be
better used. The most telling reason for dismissing
the recommendation, however, is that suggested in
the Bullock Report itself:

> The English teacher may feel that within a
> comparatively short time he will be able to
> assess his new pupils on the strength of the
> work they produce for him. He may therefore
> ask whether there is much value in his knowing
> what has happened before they reach him. (para.
> 14.9)

The extent of passing on pupils' work is difficult
to ascertain. A Barnsley (1976) Report states that
80 per cent of primary schools sampled did not
forward any written work to receiving schools but
Frances Findlay's (1983) small survey of liaison and
continuity practices in Peterborough revealed that
22 out of 40 primary schools passed on examples of
pupils' work. There are probably regional
variations in this practice. Those secondary
schools that receive primary work claim there is
value in the practice.

In one London school, the procedure has changed
over the years. The school's head of English, as a
key member of the local authority's working party on
the implementation of the Bullock Report, was keen
'to react positively to its recommendations'. In
the spirit of the report's advocacy of considering
language across the curriculum, other departmental
heads were involved in drawing up guidelines for the
consideration of the main feeder primary schools.
The secondary staff wanted to receive the same kind
of work from each pupil but it became obvious that
standardisation of the kind they had in mind was not
possible when the diversity of practice in contributory primary schools was revealed. It seemed
reasonable to ask for typical pieces of creative,

formal and project writing. Feeder school headteachers, however, raised many questions secondary
colleagues were hardly qualified to answer from
their superficial knowledge of primary practice:

- 'We don't do formal writing in our school; do
  you want us to write something special?'

- 'A project can be 40 pages long and only
  makes sense as a whole. Surely you don't
  want pupils to copy out an extract. We
  should be loath to let you have the full
  projects as pupils like to keep them.'

- 'It would be difficult to determine what is
  'typical' for some pupils. They have their
  good days and their bad days.'

- 'Creative writing: prose or poetry? Do you
  want final corrected versions or first
  stumbling efforts?'

There was little to portend success except that
dialogue had been started. Inevitably, feeder
schools were given a fair amount of freedom to
decide what they would send on. Some forwarded
several exercise books; others a few sheets of
paper. With an intake of 300 pupils, the school was
faced with the major task of chasing, receiving,
assigning to tutor groups and finally storing over a
thousand pieces of work. Volunteer older pupils
helped, a classroom was set aside, and by the first
day of the autumn term some primary school work from
95 per cent of intake pupils was available for staff
to consult. It was considered unnecessary to look
through a pupil's pre-transfer work unless some
cause presented itself so most of the material so
laboriously collected remained unseen. Nevertheless, there were advantages to the procedure.
Unexpected performance led to 20 pupils being 'case
studied' in the first month and by the end of term,
the primary work of a further 30 'problems' had been
looked at. It was useful to compare pre-transfer
with post-transfer work but the greatest benefit was
gained when it was possible to discover the standard
expected by primary teachers. Even originally
reluctant participants agreed that the exercise had
been of value but it would need to be simplified.
        Over several years of discussions, visits and
some exchange teaching, the scheme has been
modified. At times, during the final year in

primary school, pupils write four exercises which, they are told, are to let secondary school staff know more about them. The first, entitled 'self-portrait', serves as an example of formal writing. Then, a letter is written to a pupil already in the school seeking answers (which they receive) to queries about the new school. 'My favourite lesson' often provides information on pupils' attitudes to school whilst providing another piece of typical writing. Finally, pupils choose the best creative or free writing produced during the year to pass on to their future teachers, with the possible bonus of publication in the secondary-school's magazine. One pre-printed large envelope contains all four exercises and fits readily into a filing system. Primary staff pass on a few exercise books, on an informal basis, to give total perspective - a feature of the original scheme considered so valuable.

The passing on of pupils' work was originally the main purpose of setting up the scheme but now it is just one facet of a more positive liaison policy whose main benefits can be delineated as follows:

1. there is a quicker response to the needs of remedial pupils;

2. there is a greater awareness of the extent and depth of learning already achieved by the brightest pupils;

3. some curriculum integration has been introduced in the first year;

4. staff in both sectors are much more sensitised to the notion that children's learning should be seen as a continuum;

5. in pressing for more consistency between feeder primary schools, senior staff have found greater team spirit themselves and now work much more closely than in the past;

6. amongst both secondary and primary staff there is greater awareness and appreciation of the approach to learning in the other sector.

Pastoral schemes

In recent years, boundaries between primary and secondary schooling may have become less well-defined but it has to be accepted that there are fundamental differences of ethos and practice between the two sectors. Some teachers consider liaison schemes, which probably delay the true start of secondary schooling, do more harm than good, and there is evidence for this if there is lack of communication between those at either side of an interface. (Nash, 1973) Others believe there is need to develop a programme for young secondary-school pupils to help them adjust to their new situation. Some schemes are essentially pastoral in nature whilst others impinge on academic arrangements.

The development in recent years of a pastoral organisation in secondary schools has been in response to the pupil's need for the kind of security and identity provided in primary schools by the class teacher. The ubiquitous class teacher was available whenever queries arose. The tutor in the secondary school has fewer opportunities to meet his charges and so must develop more systematic techniques for dealing with pastoral matters rapidly and efficiently. Further, during set tutorial periods he must concern himself with the whole class rather than the individual problem child. (Button, 1976) In response to a growing demand for teaching materials to use in form tutorials, Lancashire Education Authority promoted the development of Active Tutorial Work. (Baldwin and Wells, 1979) This five-year programme of pastoral work starts with exercises to help new entrants settle into secondary school. But many of those concerned with the welfare of first-year pupils consider the primary school to be the right place for pupils' transfer problems to be dealt with. Sheila Sarley, head of first year at Woodside School, Newham, became convinced that she needed to meet future pupils on their home ground but something more than an informative talk was needed. The Lancashire Active Tutorial programme provided her with a model for a scheme suited to Woodside's particular needs.

Each main feeder primary school to this six-form entry comprehensive is visited by Mrs Sarley, who takes pupils through a two-hour session designed to familiarise them with Woodside School. With a copy of the school plan, in a 'game' atmosphere, they plot routes based on movements they will make

173

after transfer. Work, time-tables, new subjects, sports and games - all are discussed at length. Children are encouraged to tell 'horror stories' so that their worries about change of school are exposed. Helpful advice and information, most of it well-disguised, is woven into anecdotes about how previous transfer groups have coped with difficulties. An essential feature of the Active Tutorial approach is the stimulation of class discussion by posing a series of questions that take pupils step by step towards the resolution of difficult issues. As is shown in Figures 8.1 and 8.2, pupils start the Woodside worksheet by writing about themselves, continue on the familar topic of classmates but by the completion of the two-hour session have explored much new ground. Obviously, Woodside School gleans much information from this exercise but the greatest benefit is to pupils whose often unspoken worries have been explored. When invited to ask questions of the visitor from the big school, primary pupils may be overawed or may fear ridicule from classmates for the triviality of the matters they raise. Things which may seem of little consequence to adults can loom large to children; such matters can arise naturally and inconspicuously when a comprehensive approach of the kind developed at Woodside is used.

A project similarly concerned with the development of social skills as a preparation for transfer has been reported by Jordan (1981). As part of the University College of Swansea's Action Research Project, a six-week experiment was conducted at Plasmarl Junior School, Swansea. A programme was devised involving: practice of conversational skills; action research including conversations with strangers; an examination of personal friendships; self-description and self-assessment; examination of personal roles; exercises to facilitate the expression of personal feelings and develop self-assurance; and a specific enquiry into pupils' preparedness for the move to senior school. At the conclusion of the experiment, the team 'felt there was something here of value for those at such a transitional stage in their school careers. They saw it as offering pupils general support and the chance to develop personal and social skills which they would need. It was also valuable in highlighting the particular difficulties of individuals and creating the opportunities for them to make progress.'

Figure 8.1:   Extract from Pre-transfer Active
              Tutorial Worksheet used at Woodside
              School, Newham

ALL ABOUT ME

My name is....................................

I am usually called ....

My eyes are..........and my hair is..........

My very best friend in school is.............

I like it in school when.....................

I work hard when I sit with..................

In school I DO NOT LIKE it when..............

Sometimes I do not get on with...............

My best lesson is............................

In school, it makes me laugh when............

I find it hard to............................

In school, I should not sit with.............

      and this is because........................

I get worried when...........................

IN MY CLASS

I think that these children:

1.   are always good.........................

2.   try to be funny all the time............

3.   are really clever.......................

4.   do not know how to behave...............

5.   are very quiet and shy..................

6.   are usually late for school.............

7.   never do as they are told...............

8.   are good at P.E. and games..............

9.   are often away from school..............

10.   are kind and helpful....................

11.   always do their very best...............

Figure 8.2: Revision Questions used at the
             conclusion of the Pre-Transfer Tutorial
             - Woodside School, Newham

WHAT WILL IT BE LIKE AT WOODSIDE ?

How many will there be in my new class?

How will we be sorted out?

Will I know anyone?

How many new classes will there be?

How many children in the whole school?

How many teachers are there; will I know any of
them?

Who will be there when I arrive

Who is the headteacher?

Who is the head of Lower School and what is
Lower School?

How will I find my way about?

When does school start; at what time shall
I arrive?

What shall I do at breaktime; at what time is
break?

Where shall I go if it is raining at breaktime
or dinnertime?

What happens if I do not like school dinner?

How long is dinner time? When is afternoon
registration?

What shall I bring with me on the first day?

How will I know where to go?

What shall I do if I get lost?

How will I know where I should be?

What will happen on the first day?

What is the P.E. kit and how can I buy it?

What is a Tutor Group?

Who shall I go to see if anything is worrying me?

　　Use the space below to write any more
　　questions you would like to ask . . .

A strategy found to be effective in one school may be impracticable in another. Spending whole afternoons visiting the few primary schools supplying Woodside with over 90 per cent of its intake can clearly be seen as an economical means of dealing with transfer but the Plasmarl experiment was made possible only because of the contribution of several students on a University course. The problem becomes even more extreme when many primary schools are involved in transfer to an upper school. In 1982, Holloway School, Islington, received its intake of 175 boys from 51 primary schools, only three of which sent more than 10 pupils. Making contact with future pupils is a time-consuming task when so many individual visits result in meeting only one or two boys. The primary-school liaison teacher talks to all potential future pupils in the fourth year of primary school but she must wait until final transfer choices have been made before she interviews boys individually. They are assured that someone who knows them personally will be there to help them settle in when they arrive but the main strategy to prepare boys for a change of approach when they leave primary school is Holloway's **Gateway Scheme.** (Brice, 1984)

Most schools make special provision for their new intake. A common practice is to delay start of school for older pupils on the first day so that newcomers can receive individual attention and for a brief time accustom themselves to new surroundings unharassed by the turmoil of a large organisation. The Gateway Scheme extends this practice. At the end of the summer term, when the rest of the school has broken up for the holidays, new boys are invited to attend school for a week. In the mornings there are lessons similar to the ones they will have in the autumn term; afternoons are given over to games. Technically, pupils are free to come and go as they please, but as the exercise is treated as 'official', the drop-out rate is low. During the trial week they are given as broad a spectrum of subjects as possible depending upon the teachers participating in the scheme. In their tutor groups, a subtle monitoring of problems and personality clashes takes place but there is no formal assessment of pupils. Perhaps some of the mathematics and English that is done gives an impression of how boys will cope in September but the main purpose is not to evaluate pupils but for them to be eased into secondary schooling. The few newcomers who do not take part in the Gateway programme are given extra attention

177

at the start of the autumn term but for the
majority, a week of familiarising themselves with
the routine and values of a secondary school has
served to unravel some of the mystery.

Teaching Programmes

The assumption of fundamental differences
between primary and secondary schooling underlies
many transitional schemes. If successful transfer
is assessed by the rapidity of adjustment to a
different mode of working, continuity ceases to have
much meaning. As Daunt (1975) so cogently argues,
there is no justification for a change at time of
transfer in the principles underlying the
educational process. Yet so often, the sequence
from five to sixteen is broken at the age of eleven
or so when the dominant primary-school principles of
expanding autonomy and collaboration in learning
'are submerged beneath other contrary principles
which emphasise discipline, instruction and
competition'. In many secondary schools, of course,
efforts are made to avoid a rigid change of regime
for the new intake. Typically, an integrated
studies course is used to extend pupils' contact
with fewer teachers. At Plashet School for girls,
in the centre of a large immigrant population in
Newham, the previously separately-taught subjects of
geography, history and classical studies have been
combined so as to allow one member of staff to teach
a first-year class for eight periods a week instead
of two. The major motive for the change was the
need to continue teaching basic skills to many of
the girls who have language or learning
difficulties. But a further benefit has been the
establishment of a teaching area for first-year
pupils who now have something akin to a primary-
school base in which to work rather than moving
every 35 minutes, often between buildings. Taught
mainly by humanities staff and a member of the
remedial department, the integrated studies course
has generated a need for de-centralised classroom
libraries, another feature borrowed from primary
practice. It seems that a commitment to adjust ways
of working to respond to pupils' developmental needs
has a 'ripple' effect on many facets of school life.

At Bolsover School in Derbyshire, first-year
pupils similarly enjoy prolonged contact with one
teacher. (Bestwick, 1984) Here, the prime motive
for the particular transfer strategy was the split-
site nature of the school. Re-organisation in the

mid-1970s resulted in the amalgamation of three
schools at distances of up to a mile away from each
other. Potential travel problems and the perceived
need to ease transition for eleven-year-olds led to
the introduction of the 'core programme' and 'core
tutor'. During the first year, pupils are taken by
their form teacher, a core tutor, for 16 of the 40
periods in each week. English, mathematics, history
and geography are taught by the same member of staff
responsible also for registration and form assembly.
Extended association with one teacher who gets to
know each child very well gives the sense of
security primary pupils take for granted. Subjects
other than those in the core programme are taught by
specialists and so pupils are introduced to the
secondary mode of working.

Being a core tutor limits the extent and scope
of teaching and could adversely affect promotion
prospects. There is a further disadvantage for
teachers in their increased work load by virtue of
membership of several departments each with its own
demands, not least of which is the number of
meetings to be attended. As recompense, core tutors
have the satisfaction of knowing that their pupils
have a happy and secure beginning to life in the
secondary school.

Understandably, in a scheme designed to improve
transition, the process starts in the primary
school. Each feeder school is visited by a deputy
headteacher, who takes assembly, talks to primary-
school staff and gets to know some of the pupils.
Senior tutors and first-year core teachers also
visit their prospective pupils. By the time
children arrive at Bolsover School they should each
know at least three members of staff. Prior to
transfer, they will have spent half a day in their
future form room with their future teacher. They
may also, while still in the primary school, have
been taught by secondary teachers, for the Bolsover
scheme has also involved some exchange teaching, an
oft-recommended but rarely achieved strategy. A
revision of the mathematics scheme was negotiated to
start in primary schools so exchanges of teachers in
this area of the curriculum became possible.
Differences in expertise between general and
specialist teachers make such exchanges difficult
but Bolsover core tutors are well-qualified to
achieve a dove-tailing of mathematics.

A now well-established liaison committee
involving not only feeder junior schools but their
infant schools too provides a vehicle for both

discussion and the promotion of improvements in practice. It is considered important for feeder schools to know how their ex-pupils fare in the secondary school, so attainment details are passed back. Through the liaison committee, weekly out-of-school drama and art workshops have been arranged to give primary pupils and their teachers a chance to use upper-school facilties and to work with older pupils under the instruction of specialist staff. Established now for several years, the core programme has been the springboard for other liaison strategies and has been closely watched by county advisory staff and colleagues in neighbouring schools. As Mrs Bestwick comments, 'if imitation is any appraisement of our scheme, then it can be truly said that we have succeeded'.

At Colonel Frank Seely Comprehensive School, close to Nottingham, David Martin and Paul Buck (1982) see their study skills course as a means of bridging the gap between primary and secondary education. As in other schemes, school design influenced the development of work to integrate pupils whose previous educational experience had been diverse. An open-plan lower school unit for 420 first and second-year pupils, arranged in four self-contained work areas, provided a base for an integrated, individualised humanities course. Guided by worksheets, pupils made use of the unit's multi-media resource area. Difficulties arose, however, because children newly arrived from primary schools set about their work in different ways. Clearly, some feeder schools had taught basic learning skills whilst others had not. Pupils accomplished little unless considerably helped by teachers. 'Many topics were completely misinterpreted, many more mishandled. It was not simply a case of the able succeeding while the less-able floundered.' It had been assumed pupils would already have gained experience of working with resources by themselves. The staff at Colonel Frank Seely School were expecting a demonstration of skills which they had never specified let alone taught.

On analysing the stages needed for successful completion of the tasks they had set, the teachers realised the complexity involved. New worksheets were devised to teach pupils library and presentation skills, and to provide them with techniques for identifying significant points from their references. Above all, the study skills course supplied a basic approach to tackling any topic.

CONTINUITY AT THE SCHOOL LEVEL

Having received specific guidance and working to a formula, pupils improved but there were still problems to be dealt with at an individual level. The restructuring of courses in response to recognition of difficulties experienced became, and continued to be, a feature of the work in the lower school unit. Manifestly, this study skills course centred on the individual owes much to primary practice, but by developing sophisticated learning techniques, it provides a bridge to a secondary style of education.

Access to Expertise in Primary Schools

Schemes providing a period when pupils are presented with an amalgam of primary and secondary ways of working would seem to accord with current views on child development. A sudden change of regime presupposes a narrow time-span during which all pupils progress from concrete to abstract ways of thinking. As those who teach the middle age-range will testify, this is manifestly not so. Yet extending primary methods beyond the eleven-plus divide is but one way of achieving gradual transition. Despite Plowden's misgivings about secondary influences percolating into primary schools, some young pupils are ready to approach knowledge from a differentiated point of view. The existence of nine and ten-year-old devotees of science and mathematics is but one indication of the inadequacy of a primary programme devoid of any specialist elements. This is a plea, not for a content-based curriculum, nor for external examination dominance but for acceptance of the notion that pupils of whatever age should have access to knowledge in the form most suited to them. Even if, as Blenkin and Kelly (1983) argue, educational planning should begin 'not with statements of knowledge to be acquired but with an analysis of the processes to be promoted', some of those processes will be difficult to appreciate without reference to the distinctive nature of experience. Ideally then, older primary-school pupils should have access to expertise covering a complete curricular range. Given the laudable emphasis in primary schools on class teaching, this is not easy to achieve. At such times, secondary schools can provide a valuable service. The consequences of primary-school emphasis on organising to promote child emotional stability is that pupils work predominantly under the influence

of one teacher. The young child's needs may be well
satisfied by a teacher's general expertise but at
the approach to secondary education, increasing
specialist demands can tax the powers of the most
gifted class teacher. Though his teacher may not be
a specialist, the older primary-school pupil needs
access to specialised knowledge. Books, resources
and other teachers in the school may suffice but
when links have been established with an associated
secondary school, a further valuable source can be
tapped. There are many instances of exceptionally-
gifted primary pupils working to programmes prepared
by secondary-school teachers. Requests for help are
not always successful, however. One secondary
mathematics teacher is reported to have refused help
because his task would be the more difficult later
when pupils transferred if some had already embarked
on secondary work. A negative response to requests
for help is fortunately rare. In general, secondary
teachers recognise that they have a part to play in
preparing pupils not only for the social and
emotional upheaval of transfer but also for changes
in curriculum. Some schemes to help pupils prepare
for curricular change are co-ordinated by local
authorities but often the initiative is taken by an
individual school or enthusiastic teacher.
Inevitably there is diversity of detail but the
approach adopted at Jack Hunt School, Peterborough,
will serve to show the kind of exercise being
undertaken.
    It is not surprising that a curricular area in
which there was seen to be a need for improved
liaison by staff at Jack Hunt School was science.
Kerr and Engel (1982) suggest that despite the work
of many project teams and a mass of commercially-
produced materials, efforts to spread science
teaching in primary schools over the past decade
have been largely ineffective. They cite three
factors commonly thought to impede the improvement
of science at the primary stage:

    (i)   the poor science background of teachers,
           resulting in lack of confidence to
           attempt work in science;

    (ii)   failure of headteachers to recognise the
           potential contribution of science to the
           curriculum; and

    (iii) inadequate provision of simple apparatus
           and materials.'

In their opinion, however, it is the dominance of a child-centred philosophy with its emphasis on 'process' rather than 'content' that has limited progress in primary science.

Science staff at Jack Hunt School do not subscribe to the content-process dichotomy. They accept that their primary colleagues are preparing pupils for secondary science when they involve them in such activities as observing, recording and explaining phenomena. As they approach transfer, however, pupils need a stronger infusion of planned science activity. To give them an impression of the curricular change they face, a 'Junior Day' is arranged. For one day, Jack Hunt pupils are sent home and their place taken by top juniors who, in the words of the head of department, 'have a secondary time-table inflicted on them'.

Established for over ten years, Junior Day is the central liaison feature but other strategies have been built around it. Attempts have been made to interest junior-school staff in advance of the event and to provide them with follow-up work. David Smith, head of the science department, admits that progress has been sporadic. At times, the needs of transfer pupils have been displaced by more pressing matters; some communications may have been too academic; nevertheless, dialogue between primary and secondary schools has been maintained over a long period. This achievement probably comes of placing primacy on practical matters. Junior staff would have to be extremely churlish to reject Junior Day follow-up teaching suggestions when offered loan of equipment and books, and specific help at the end of a telephone. It would be misleading, however, to suggest that teachers in the primary sector are passive recipients of secondary wisdom. The liaison exercise involves interchange of documents between primary feeders and Jack Hunt School with some thorough analyses of science teaching within a child-centred environment. Recently revitalized, the Junior Day scheme now involves all subjects and is co-ordinated by a deputy head.

A scheme similarly originating in the need for science input into primary schools has developed in the Melbourn area of Cambridgeshire. An adviser for primary education set up a science curriculum group whose members were the nine primary-school heads, the head of lower school and members of the science department of the receiving secondary school, Melbourn Village College. Their discussions led to in-service science courses for all 65 primary-school

teachers in the catchment area; in turn, interest in
science was stimulated within the schools. As the
scheme developed, secondary teachers became more and
more involved in their feeder primary schools,
attending primary staff meetings to help organise
science projects, suggesting teaching strategies,
providing equipment and going into primary schools
to teach. When aims and objectives have been
devised after joint discussion by primary and
secondary teachers in close contact it is unlikely
there will be a wide gap to be bridged at transfer.

Success in science led to a similar initiative
in English: a language curriculum group was formed
with membership from headteachers and those in
feeder and receiving schools with responsibility for
language in the curriculum. The group has organised
in-service courses for all staff teaching within the
5-16 age-range and has promoted discussion on the
language policy in each school. When overall agreement can be reached on a particular aspect of
language teaching, a document is produced setting
out area policy. Agreement has been reached on
handwriting style, punctuation, spelling, the
testing of reading and the assessment of writing.

In other areas of the curriculum, liaison is
developing. The secondary school has allocated a
post of responsibility to a member of its remedial
staff to liaise with primary schools about
mathematics. A termly meeting is now held at the
secondary schools to discuss general matters
relating to transfer and continuity. As association
between primary and secondary sectors develops so
ad hoc arrangements become more workable.
Children from feeder primary school have joined
secondary pupils in metal and wood workshops
throughout a summer term. The prospect of handling
heavy, potentially dangerous tools can be daunting
to young children.   Those who had a foretaste,
albeit limited, of workshop practice were found to
be much more confident after transfer. Secondary PE
staff have arranged for primary pupils to use the
extensive facilities in their sports hall. Primary-
school projects in the humanities and science have
been actively supported by advice and loans of
equipment and books from secondary staff.

Sallie Dixon, one of the primary-school headteachers actively involved in the Melbourn scheme,
comments:

It seems sad that whenever children have to
transfer from school to school, whether primary

to secondary, infant to junior or middle to
upper, a gap in learning and working together
occurs. It seems much more sensible to work on
the idea of a continuum of learning from 5 to
18. This requires a trust in each other's
establishment and in each other as individuals.
A great deal of contact and confidence is
required to be able to discuss aims and
objectives, content, materials, strategies and
perhaps ask the all-important questions: 'Why
and for whom are we teaching this?' The
greatest value of our meetings is in our open
discussions; we all learn a great deal from
each other, and respect and trust is built up.

Many secondary schools arrange familiarisation
visits for their new intake but there are few
reports of pupils becoming actively involved in
learning situations as at Jack Hunt School or
Melbourn Village College. Attending the secondary
school for lessons introduces pupils not only to
their future curriculum, but to the norms pertaining
in a large institution. Sylvia Walton (1983), head
of first year at Shevington High School, Wigan,
reports, 'recently we have arranged for small groups
of J4 pupils to join first-year pupils in lessons
eg. Language lab., science, craft and modular maths.
Not only are they becoming familiar with the classroom but they become aware of the fact that when
1,000 pupils take to the corridor it is fast, it
is noisy but it is possible to move safely
about'. In addition, the school's outside
activities such as those in the music centre,
gymnasium, modern languages club and science club
are open to upper junior pupils. Aware of the
criticism that such activities attract the more
confident pupil with an interest and the initiative
to journey to the high school, Sylvia Walton still
considers it a worthwhile venture. As she points
out, children become aware 'not only of the location
of the science block but where the tripods are kept,
too'. This writer makes the further point that the
new intake should not be cushioned unduly from the
experience of starting secondary education. The
young pupil's desire to get things right inevitably
causes some degree of tension but 'makes the first
year the most productive of the secondary-school
career'. The ultimate test of the reassurance
pupils receive before transfer is the extent to
which they find they can cope on arrival in
secondary school. Involving parents of the new

intake in the transfer exercise is part of that
reassurance process. At Shevington High School
parents see the school in action on an ordinary
working day. Their guides are the most recent
transferees, first-year pupils, who are well-
qualified to present the customer's viewpoint.
Two weeks after the start of term when trivial
upsets have resolved themselves, specific residual
problems are dealt with at a cheese and wine
evening.

Primary-school Initiatives

Though most information about liaison and
continuity strategies emanates from the secondary
sector, it would be misleading to suggest that
initiatives are seldom taken by primary schools. It
has to be admitted, however, that differences of
philosophy between the two sectors pose problems of
emphasis. As Lois Benyon (1984) points out, the
statement 'Primary schools teach children: secondary
schools teach subjects' may be simplistic and
incorrect but it 'holds within itself some seeds
which may point up further why curriculum continuity
is difficult to achieve.' Primary schools aim to
smooth the passage of each individual child moving
from one institution to another; secondary schools
want to know where to start disciplined study with
pupils from diverse backgrounds. Again, this
generalisation is confounded by specific reference
and it probably holds true only in the preliminary
stages of any movement towards transition. The
catalyst for secondary action may be the need to
achieve curriculum continuity but it is soon
realised that settling pupils into a new school is a
prior condition of continuity: a confused or disorientated pupil obtains little benefit from schooling
no matter what arrangements have been made to achieve
a close curriculum match. Likewise, primary schools
come to realise that they can ease the transfer
process for pupils if there has been liaison with
secondary colleagues on matters of curriculum.
Preparation of pupils for the kind of education
they will experience after transfer benefits pupils
and their future teachers but is tinged with sadness
for primary teachers; paradoxically, satisfaction
from involvement in liaison strategies comes from
successfully thrusting pupils away from them.
Teachers of the top year at Barnehurst Junior
School, Bexleyheath, comment: 'We are allowing
children to grow away from us in order that

eventually they may prosper in a secondary school
environment without the traditional "primary-type"
support.' Barnehurst School provides an interesting
case study, for it illustrates how a now sophisticated transition procedure developed over a period
of many years. Sybil Camsey (1984) tells us that it
was in 1973 that a decision was taken to do
something to help pupils through what was seen as a
very difficult period in their lieves. A club,
started in that year for pupils and past-pupils of
10 to 14, is now flourishing. Run by a team of 25
to 30 adults, parents and staff, the club meets once
a week in the evening to provide its 150 or so
members with a wide range of activities: crafts,
pastimes and games, both indoor and outdoor.
Children have somewhere to go and interesting things
to do but the club also provides an opportunity for
top-year primary pupils to meet older children who
attend schools to which they will transfer. They
find out about their future schools over a prolonged
period, in a relaxed atmosphere from their peers.
Such an approach contrasts markedly with the
conventional single visit when teachers, under
fairly formal conditions, meet new pupils in the
term before transfer. The club also offers an
opportunity for past pupils who experience problems
to maintain contact with teachers already well-known
who can provide a listening ear and suggest ways of
resolving difficulties. Further, it allows children
to retain friendships; this feature of the club is
particularly useful for children with long distances
to travel for they need time to establish new and
secure friendship patterns outside their local
community. Of course, the club provides important
feedback for the primary-school teachers. Through
discussions with past pupils they gain an insight
into current secondary-school practice and learn of
the problems pupils experience.

An awareness of the extent of pupils' difficulties in making the transition to secondary schooling
developed as a result of increased contact and
regular discussions with past pupils. It seemed
that some of the problems could be avoided if more
specific preparation was given for changes in
organisation and teaching methods pupils would
encounter after transfer. In 1978 a 'junior-
secondary transition course' was started for pupils
in the final primary-school year. The first three
years at Barnehurst are organised in class groups
but in the fourth year, classes are combined and
'the top year' becomes the administrative unit.

There are still 'home base groups' for registration, pastoral care and to give a sense of security, but for most of their time pupils are involved with larger numbers than in the usual class. Three traditional classrooms have been made into an inter-communicating unit within which pupils are introduced, albeit on a small scale, to the idea that they move to different rooms for different lessons. 'They have to learn to be in the right place at the right time with the right books and equipment. Once lessons have started, interruptions to retrieve forgotten items are not allowed so children learn to plan ahead.' During the week they make contact with up to nine teachers, each making different demands. With fifteen subjects on the time-table, they learn to cope with changes of activity and the different thinking processes involved.

For 23 periods in the week, lessons in specific subjects are taught; the remaining 17 periods are spent in working on individual assignments. Assignments can be completed in any order during available private study time and handed in for marking as they are completed. For some part of the week, then, pupils are organising their own time and gaining experience of meeting a series of deadlines. Those who find difficulty in organising for themselves report daily to their home-base teacher who checks that work is satisfactory. There is, too, a study skills course to help pupils in library research and the making of notes.

The Barnehurst approach, then, is to simulate the curricular and organisational variety of secondary schooling while pupils are still within the security of a familiar primary school. Reports of difficulties by past pupils result in a reappraisal of the transition course in an attempt to prepare the next 'top-year' more effectively. It could be argued that by responding to circumstances of secondary practice, the school is developing a stricter regime than is normal in primary education. It could be argued that the Plowden edict that primary schools should not be dominated by secondary-school influences is being violated. Nash (1973) has illustrated the ineffectiveness of inclining primary practice towards a rigid secondary model when secondary schools are themselves becoming more liberal. Sybil Camsey accepts that the measures she and her colleagues have developed at Barnehurst Primary Schools are not endorsed by everyone:

Many primary teachers may feel we are wrong to introduce this approach to work but in doing so we have not sacrificed good primary-school practice - we have extended it. Our children thoroughly enjoy their top year. They like having more subjects and different teachers; they find self-organisation a challenge - they say it makes them feel 'grown-up'. They no longer regard the six months after transfer-test results are announced as a frustrating period of marking time but as an opportunity to acquire as many skills as possible. When they leave us, we feel they are mature and confident with a sense of eager anticipation. Certainly our secondary colleagues appreciate our efforts. They have visited, advised and encouraged us and there is now a primary-secondary discussion group to share ideas on transition on a borough-wide basis.

Barnehurst illustrates several important features of effective transfer and liaison schemes. Though it was conceived and has been nurtured by an individual, many others have been actively involved; the wider community of parents, ex-pupils and colleagues in other sectors has taken interest in its success. Communication between primary and secondary sectors has ranged beyond the formal transfer of documents; dialogue has been at a practical, workaday level. The scheme has been adapted in response to changing needs and has developed to include all aspects of the transfer process; pastoral care and curriculum continuity are seen as being inevitably inter-related. Above all, the teachers concerned have eschewed the kind of self-sufficiency sometimes seen as a virtue. Some dedicated primary-school teachers can become so involved with their pupils in very worthwhile creative activity that what happens beyond their classrooms can seem inconsequential. As is suggested in New Directions in Primary Education (Richards, 1982):

The laissez-faire approach to the primary curriculum which leaves all curriculum decisions (or non-decisions) in the hands of individual practitioners operating in comparative isolation . . . is not just an inappropriate approach to curriculum decision-making but paradoxically it devalues the professionalism of the individual practitioner

189

by assuming a degree of individual self-sufficiency which could only be sustained if the task in question was simple, uncontentious, fully understood and self-contained. Educating young children is none of these.

Teachers who see primary education as being 'self-contained' are unlikely to provide the kind of opportunities afforded pupils at Barnehurst Junior School. Success in liaison and transition demands an outward-looking attitude.

Even the most comprehensive of schemes to promote good transfer practice probably started very simply. There has to be an initial recognition of a need but other more pressing affairs are likely to take precedence. The day-to-day practical measures to be taken within one school present enough challenges without seeking further problems in other institutions. There are many occasions when colleagues can be invited to visit associated schools. Finding time to respond positively to such invitations may be difficult but it is often from such seemingly casual visits that effective transfer practice can be developed. A primary-school head-teacher (Cox, 1984) comments:

> I know that in the early stages of my first headship I gave scant attention to the problems faced by children transferring to secondary schools until one of the nearby secondary schools underwent a general inspection and HMI suggested that liaison with feeder primary schools could be improved. The immediate result was a flurry of invitations to primary heads to visit the school. During the visits I noticed that many children still had difficulty performing tasks they ought to have been proficient in by then. Many children were not using pencils, pens and rulers correctly and had little idea how to handle compasses, set-squares and protractors. Some of these children had come from my school and had been using this equipment for several years.

This head ensured that thereafter pupils transferring to secondary school were given a more thorough grounding in basic skills. Recognition of regression in proficiency in handling writing materials alerted him to other needs: more attention was given to measuring accurately and using mathematical instruments; practice was given in the

use of unfamiliar narrow-lined paper that so
affected pupils' writing style after transfer; extra
emphasis was placed on the quick and accurate use of
dictionaries and reference books. Primary teachers
in daily contact with their class can monitor
standards almost by the hour. The same continuity
of attention cannot be achieved by secondary
colleagues who see pupils perhaps only once or twice
a week. At transfer, pupils must be sufficiently
proficient in basic everyday activities to be
independent of teacher monitoring; only then can
undivided attention be given to new learning.
Further, teachers in primary and secondary sectors
find it difficult to negotiate more advanced
curriculum continuity if basic skills are not firmly
established; fruitful discussion depends upon mutual
confidence.

Adverse Effects of Preparation for Transfer

Increasing proficiency in basic learning skills
is but one way in which primary schools can help
pupils to transfer with fewer worries. Mention was
made earlier of schemes to develop social skills and
of ways in which pupils can be prepared for more
differentiation in the curriculum. There is much
for pupils to absorb; an overload of pre-transfer
information in a short period of time can be
counter-productive. Ideally, preparation for
transfer should take place over a protracted period
but there is an inevitable quickening of pace as the
time for change-over approaches. If the first
official transfer preparation is the standard
familiarisation meeting when a member of staff from
the next sector talks to pupils and answers
questions, then pupils can become abruptly aware of
the many aspects of transfer. A parent's comments
to the author on her daughter's experience of
transfer serve to illustrate this: 'She was alright
until the teacher from the senior school came to
talk to them. She came home buzzing with worries.
She didn't sleep properly for days and there was a
flurry of questions every meal time.' Most of the
child's anxieties were groundless. Within a month
of moving to the new school she had settled in
happily. Her mother felt she had been unnecessarily
sensitized to difficulties that never presented
themselves. It seems too that certain types of
visit to upper schools by pupils from contributory
schools can increase anxieties. (Stillman, 1984a)
Frances Findlay (1983) questions whether a talk

giving information about the new school, particularly when given during a visit to that school, is
very effective. In a case study of a Peterborough
school she comments:

> Although it was important for the teachers to
> show themselves as human and pleasant, these
> talks were the least satisfactory part of the
> visit from the pupils' point of view. Pupils
> could remember very little of what they had
> been told, although I spoke to them only a
> matter of a couple of hours after their return
> to their primary schools.

Pupils in the Peterborough case study enjoyed
lessons they had been involved in during a visit to
the school to which they were to be tansferred but
details about school routine, clubs and uniform were
not easily recalled. There seems little point in
presenting such information orally. When there is
much to absorb, it is far better for it to be
presented in written form. Sharp (1975) warns that
we must get the style right when writing for young
children and there are, of course, problems for poor
readers. One technique that commends itself is that
at a Wandsworth school, where a guidebook for
incoming pupils is prepared by young first-formers
who write with recent experience of transfer.

Parental Involvement in Transfer Arrangements

Some information given to pupils before
transfer seems more the concern of parents. A
school's policy on uniform and homework, its success
rate in external examinations, the range of subject
options available in the run-up to examinations -
all have been mentioned to the author as occurring
in introductory talks to pupils. Such information
is best conveyed in written form to parents. The
practice of sending a booklet to parents in advance
of a meeting at which questions can be answered
seems an appropriate means of transmitting
information of a policy nature. Stillman and
Maychell (1982) suggest that it is particularly
beneficial for parents to be in communication with
schools when transfer is imminent for they can
support children who may experience feelings of
anxiety. They quote a headteacher's letter to
parents: 'The best-motivated children and the most
successful children in their studies are those with
their parents firmly behind them and the school in

its educational objectives.' It is not merely a
matter of informing parents but of gaining their
support for what the school is trying to achieve.
Some written communication and a general meeting
before transfer bring school and parents into
contact. After transfer, concern is more specific:
the need is to discover how well individual children
have adapted to the new school. Ideally this should
involve a parent-teacher exchange of view but this
is time-consuming. Some schools offer appointments
to parents; others hold open evenings with likely
opportunities for parents to meet their children's
teachers informally. There are, however, some
headteachers who see little need for organised
meetings; one writes:

> There are too many demands on my staff as it
> is. I expect them to be available for third-
> year option meetings, for consultation with
> parents and 5th and 6th Form examination
> entries as well as the meeting for parents of
> incoming pupils. I offer an open invitation to
> parents of our first year to contact us if they
> feel there is the need and, of course, we can
> approach parents of the few - and there are
> very few - who worry us.

Scepticism of the value of early meetings for first-
year parents has been expressed even by those who
continue to arrange them. Two difficulties are
frequently mentioned. The parents of pupils about
whom the school feels concern are often the ones
least likely to accept invitations to a meeting.
A further problem is caused when parents misunder-
stand the purpose of a meeting: they wish to discuss
their child's achievement before the school has had
time to make a valid assessment. Yet the value of
establishing firm relationships as early as possible
persuades many schools to continue organising such
meetings.

Inter-school Social Activities

At time of transfer when schools are concerned
with the smooth transition of pupils, academic and
pastoral matters take precedence. But the many
opportunities for less formal contact between
related schools can contribute to improved transfer
practice. Inter-school sports and games or visits
to concerts can give primary pupils their first
glimpse of 'the big school'. Secondary-school art

displays in feeder primary schools are not merely
decorative, they are powerful indicators of expected
standards. Because the secondary school has better
facilities and more specialised expertise, it tends
to be the dominant partner in such ventures. Yet
younger pupils gain immeasurably if they can be
involved as participants rather than spectators.
Typical of many such enterprising projects is one
regularly arranged at Orchard School, Slough.
Feeder schools, first and middle, join the upper
school in music and drama performances. Early
rehearsals can take place in up to six schools under
the direction of their own teachers but pupils unite
in the later stages. Joint undertakings inevitably
require teachers as well as pupils to work together.
Team work of the kind involved in inter-school
informal activities establishes a trust which can
transfer to more general liaison discussions.

Regular Review of Procedure

'Agreements fade with time'; Stillman and
Maychell's (1982) comment is unfortunately
applicable to many transfer initiatives. In the
course of my own research, I have followed up
several reports of interesting and innovative
practice to discover they have lapsed. A scheme
warranting a full-page report in Times Educational
Supplement was, seven years later, not even
remembered by members of staff in the school
involved. Such lapses are particularly likely when
a strategy has been originated and developed by an
individual. To become established as an integral
part of a school's organisation, a feature must be
adopted by a group rather than an individual.
(Miles, 1964) Liaison strategies which, of course,
cross school boundaries must be endorsed by a group
involving teachers from more than one institution.
They are, therefore, particularly vulnerable because
of the potential for change within a complex
structure. Changes of staff, new ideas in
curriculum, movements of catchment zone - there are
many potential sources of decay. To become
established it is not enough that a group of
teachers becomes involved; there must be sufficient
commitment to survive change. Clearly, the participation of someone in a position of authority is
desirable. It is interesting to note the leading
role taken by heads or deputy heads in several
schemes of long standing.

CONTINUITY AT THE SCHOOL LEVEL

A further feature of effective transfer and liaison strategies is their ability to respond to changing circumstances and new advice. There is a tendency for initial enthusiasm, probably following an in-service course, to generate a working party with a brief to develop a school policy for transfer and liaison. A document is produced, policy is established and the working party is dissolved. Thereafter the mechanism for continued debate no longer exists. The regular review of practice is important in any aspect of school life but particularly so in matters of continuity and liaison because of their instability.

Summary

Manifestly, there is much that can be done by individual schools to ease pupils' transition from one stage of education to another. The most potent stimulus for the development of a course of action is awareness of a need. But for a need to be obvious there has to be communication across school boundaries. Any opportunity for interaction between associated schools should be grasped for ever a seemingly inconsequential event can lead to teachers at different stages of education talking to each other and getting to know each other's ways of working. Exchanges of pupils' art and written work, use of each other's facilities and expertise, invitations to exhibitions, plays and concerts, perhaps even joint productions - all can provide scope for the development of more explicit liaison initiatives.

A school's commitment to the improvement of transfer and liaison arrangements can be demonstrated by the appointment of a member of staff to take care of this aspect of organisation. The job specification of such a post will almost certainly make reference to the transmission or reception of transfer records and to arranging details for the transfer of pupils; it may also enjoin the incumbent to promote curriculum continuity. Difficulties inherent in the latter may well result in a concentration on efforts to reduce the trauma of transfer and on common administrative issues. Procedures can be devised to prepare pre-transfer pupils more thoroughly in basic and social skills; after transfer, pupils can be used to help the next novitiates by writing guide books, giving talks and eventually conducting them round their new school. To prepare comprehensive transfer records, the liaison teacher may need to arrange for individual pupils to be interviewed, a process which is likely to identify anxious children who may need particular help. More ambitious schemes may involve giving pupils a foretaste of the kind of schooling they will experience after transfer. When such a scheme involves teacher exchanges it can lead to improvements in curriculum continuity. Becoming actively involved in schools outside their accustomed sector can lead teachers to an understanding of the values and practices in such host schools. Several researchers have identified as a major obstacle to curriculum continuity 'negative attitudes founded on misjudgment of the other sector's role or simply lack of knowledge about what was being taught and the methods being used. (Stillman and Maychell, 1982) Teacher co-operation is crucial to so many aspects of transfer and liaison.

As we have seen, there are many strategies that schools can develop to ease the process of transfer for pupils but as John Sharp (1975) comments, detail matters far less than getting relationships right:

> When they actually arrive, the children need more help than most of us give. A plan of the building may not be understandable to all, but many children will like it and they can help others. An older pupil attached to a group can be an 'angel'. Shepherding from one classroom to the next; help to understand the time-table and the daily routine including where matron, head of house or counsellor can be found; writing on the board all names of teachers; careful explanation of homework; looking out for the loner who, because he doesn't go around with others, hasn't discovered where the canteen is; above all, saying daily that we don't mind being asked simple questions - all these are useful. Each school will add something peculiar to its circumstances. It's the attitude that counts.

But successful transition does not depend merely upon the minutiae of adjustment to secondary schooling. It is right that schools should take some trouble to help pupils through organisational complexities in the first few weeks but familiarity with timetable and location of classes can do little to reassure pupils if what actually happens in lessons is unintelligible. The relationship between learning in the new school and that in the previous

196

one needs to be made explicit but this can only
happen if teachers are aware of what pupils have
already done. Too often there is a dismissive
attitude to what has gone before. 'You are in my
class now and I have my own way of doing things' is
a notion which denies education as a continuum for
it contains learning within segregated compartments.
Intelligent, well-motivated pupils will make the
necessary integration; others will find great
difficulty. Improvement in continuity at the school
level could be effected if teachers would take the
trouble to see their contribution to pupils'
learning within a broader perspective. Two precepts
follow from this: teachers must enter into dialogue
with colleagues at other stages of schooling; and
there should be acceptance of the need to relinquish
some of the curricular autonomy previously enjoyed.

Chapter Nine

A SUMMARY OF GOOD LIAISON AND CONTINUITY PRACTICE

The time is right for sustained efforts to improve
curriculum continuity and transfer procedures.
Particularly since the advent of middle schools,
curricular discussion has broadened beyond the
'primary' and 'secondary' contexts within which it
used to be contained. Recent documents from both
central and local authorities have tended to deal
with the total span of compulsory schooling rather
than focusing on one phase. 'Transfer', 'liaison'
and 'continuity' appear as key issues in research
programmes. Above all, the teaching profession
seems ready to move 'from the parochialising effect
of working and thinking in terms of the immediate
school context only'. (Alexander, R, 1984) Stillman
(1984b) found teachers in his research group to have
'a strong desire to see children encounter a
continuous and planned educational experience from 5
to 16'. There was acceptance by a large majority of
teachers in contributory schools that their final
year curricula should link in with the receiving
school's first-year work. But a very small
percentage of teachers actually participated in
curriculum discussions with associated schools.
Stillman suggests that the key to this dilemma of
teachers wanting but not attempting curriculum
continuity lies in the belief that it is an
impossible goal.
     Undoubtedly, curriculum continuity and school
transfer are beset with problems but these are not
intractable. It is unlikely, however, that a
fundamental improvement can be achieved without
concerted effort. Though individual teachers and
schools can start the process, continuity must
involve other teachers in other schools. There is a
tendency for enterprises of this kind to become too
unwieldy to be managed by individual institutions.

Further, strategies developed in isolation can so
easily fade away when a key teacher moves to another
school. Because of the English inclination towards
institutional autonomy, many different strategies
for dealing with transfer and continuity have
emerged. Rich variety of practice is encouraged by
a system allowing individual enterprise but to
profit from such initiatives and ensure their
continuance, there is need for policies to be
developed. It is in those local authorities which
have established what Stillman calls 'co-ordinated
and orchestrated policies' that we are beginning to
see the practical effects of continuity. One can
understand the reluctance of some LEAs to become
involved in decisions which traditionally have been
the preserve of schools but they have to recognise
that someone has to take responsibility for supervising 'the spaces between schools'. Manifestly,
local authorities are ideally placed to take on the
task of managing continuity and transfer matters.

Curriculum Continuity and Pupils at Risk

Educational literature dealing with school
transfer places pupils at the centre of discussion;
their difficulties are explored and adjustment to
new forms of schooling is assessed. Within writing
on school curricula, however, pupils are given
little mention. Curriculum theory is the concern of
teachers: it explores philosophies and processes
that seem, on the face of it, to have little to do
with children. Of course, pupils are implicit in
any curricular discussion for curriculum is the
agent through which they learn, but scant attention
is directly given to the impact of curriculum on
pupils. Curriculum continuity - or discontinuity -
is experienced by pupils. Of course, there is
great variation in pupils' adjustment to the work to
be done after transfer. Some take readily to new
subjects, a detailed time-table and specialist
teachers: they are ready for a change and welcome
'the more grown-up atmosphere' in their secondary
school. Others become confused and disorientated.
It should surely be part of any school's transfer
policy to identify children who fail to settle in.
Indeed, it should be possible to inform receiving
schools of pupils likely to experience difficulties.
Primary-school teachers, knowing that ability,
attainment, personality and home circumstances in
combination may cause transfer insecurity, may yet
fail to inform secondary colleagues. The machinery

may not exist for such information to be transmitted
but more frequently, details contained within a
transfer document are not collated. Like temperature and blood-pressure readings on a patient's
chart, facts are recorded but no one makes a
diagnosis. Teachers in contributory schools provide
data but would see it as an encroachment on the
professional autonomy of colleagues in receiving
schools to provide an interpretation. But large
comprehensive schools can have as many as 500 new
pupils to admit. It is unrealistic to expect such a
large number of transfer documents to be scrutinized
to try to locate potential problems. The tendency
is for transfer information to be used selectively
by particular teachers; those in the remedial
department look for reading ages, for example, while
PE teachers need to know of asthmatic children.
Tracking down pupils at risk because of a combination of indicative factors is a complex, time-
consuming task to be undertaken at a period when
there are other priorities. A procedure widely
applied in one LEA has much to commend it.
Receiving schools are warned of pupils needing
particular attention by a coding system. Different
coloured dots attached to the cover-sheet of
transfer documents indicate facets of a pupil's
background to which primary teachers consider
secondary colleagues should be attentive. The
system provides a quick way of classifying, for
example, pupils with learning or personality
difficulties, those who are disruptive, and ones
with medical needs. Children particularly at risk
stand out, as several dots appear on their records.

Transmission of Information

It is difficult to encapsulate in condensed
form the accumulated wisdom of several teachers who
have known a pupil over a protracted period. It is
even more difficult for a teacher new to that pupil
to interpret information and take action to ensure
continuity of educational experience as a result of
such interpretation. Of all available strategies
for improving school transfer and curriculum
continuity, transmission of information by record
card has been in use for the longest period but
there is little evidence to suggest that such
documents are effective. Alice Walker's 1955
verdict of an emphasis on collection rather than use
of data still applies. Several LEAs have set up
committees to revise transfer documentation but

there is seldom in-service follow-up to familiarise
teachers with the new records and consider how data
can influence their work. Understandably,
subjective evaluations tend to be disregarded;
results of objective testing give a useful but very
incomplete picture of a pupil's attainment. In any
case, the cause of curriculum continuity is little
advanced by pupils' measurement expressed, as it
usually is, in numerical terms; verbal-reasoning
scores and reading ages give no indication of
specific skills acquired or level achieved in a
sequential course. Transfer documents are of use
only if they provide information which teachers in
receiving schools find useful. Modular assessment
techniques of the kind recently developed by the
NFER should give receiving teachers better knowledge
of pupils' previous learning on which to base course
planning but, as research in Hillingdon demonstrated,
there can be worries about the effect assessment
will have on curriculum and suspicion of the motives
of those promoting such techniques. (Sumner and
Bradley, 1977) One reason for teachers discounting
transfer documents is that they are seldom devised
in conjunction with curriculum design. An effective
approach to transfer documentation would surely be
one in which decisions about what should be passed
on to the next teacher were made at the same time as
courses were planned. Checklists of the kind
suggested in the Schools Council History, Geography
and Social Studies 8-13 Project (Cooper, 1976) could
provide a basis for the transmission of specific
detail of skills and concepts pupils have attained.
    Robin Alexander (1984) suggests that the debate
about school evaluation has become skewed away from
the teacher and from classroom actualities. There
is a danger that all evaluative strategies, transfer
records included, become distanced from practice by
the very process involved. Successful teaching can
never be reduced to a list of techniques that the
checklist approach seems to imply. Ideally, lists
which attempt to encompass pupils' learning should
be drawn up in relation to specific experience; very
general documents in use throughout a local
authority can only be fully effective if there has
been widespread assent about items to be recorded
and this implies prior agreement on curricular
matters. An overriding requirement of transfer
documentation is the provision of information about
what pupils have assimilated before transfer; only
with such knowledge can upper schools utilise
previous learning.

Communication Between Teachers

Transfer documents reflect rather than influence practice. If modes of working and approaches to curriculum are very different in contributory and receiving schools, transfer records can serve little purpose. Too frequently, the secondary sector finds it impossible to accommodate extreme variation in pre-transfer learning. It is not merely that pupils arriving from different schools have received different kinds of tuition but that individual pupils from the same school present diversity. The need to individualise learning is an essential part of current primary and middle-school ideology (Galton, 1983) and since pupils learn at differing rates and with differing standards of excellence, after six or seven years of schooling there is bound to be extreme diversity. Indeed, as an American commentator has reasoned: 'Education itself is a differentiating not an equalising process . . . the better the educational program the more it differentiates.' (Downey, 1965) But, as the ORACLE research showed, after transfer the mode of learning tends to change: pupils are made aware of the specialist nature of learning and schools find it much more difficult to allow individuals to progress at their own rate.

Differences in ways of working in primary and secondary schools exacerbate problems of communication between teachers. Initial training, in-service courses and educational literature reinforce the notion of difference rather than similarity. To counter the implicit assumption of division between 'primary' and 'secondary' in so many aspects of education, there is need for emphasis on matters of interest beyond sector boundaries. Schools sharing the same catchment area have a common concern for the same pupils; they could well get together to discuss joint pastoral affairs, testing and recording procedures, the sharing of expensive resources, joint visits and many similar non-controversial matters. The long process of establishing trust between schools is best tackled in easy stages. A frequent cause of breakdown in curriculum continuity discussions is the clash of philosophies that occurs when there has been no previous working relationship between contributory and receiving schools. Every opportunity needs to be taken to encourage teachers across the stages to enter into dialogue.

SUMMARY OF GOOD PRACTICE

There are several levels at which inter-school
involvement should occur. Regular meetings of headteachers in associated schools are essential for
'nothing of lasting value can be achieved without
the support and active co-operation of the headteachers operating within any liaison scheme.'
(Leeds City Council, 1983) To prevent any sense of
patronage by the secondary school despite its better
facilities, heads should host meetings in turn.
Headteachers are suitably placed to consider matters
of broad policy on curriculum and pastoral arrangements; their perspective enables them to consider
the wide range of implications incumbent upon
continuity initiatives. Inter-school meetings of
subject teachers are obviously essential if
continuity is to be pursued at a specific level but
it is necessary to establish consistency between
parallel schools before attempts are made to
articulate the different stages. Extent of liaison
may well vary in different areas of the curriculum
for agreement is notoriously difficult to achieve
in some subjects whilst others, usually those of
a linear nature, present fewer problems. The
pastoral care of pupils is the mutual concern of
class teachers, form tutors, year co-ordinators and
'link teachers'; there are several terms to
delineate those with an interest in easing the
'trauma of transfer'. This represents another level
at which teachers need to enter into discussion not
only before transfer but during the time when pupils
are settling into their new schools.
    One of the main benefits of teacher discussions
is the spreading of knowledge about ways of working
in other parts of the system. Unless genuine
attempts are made to understand how other schools
function, it is difficult to achieve the degree of
openness needed to progress towards continuity.
There will need to be changes but these should be on
a 'give and take' basis. Insight into practice
elsewhere is the surest way of assessing the
viability of any transfer or continuity proposal.
Such understanding can be reached fairly quickly if
teacher exchanges are possible. Differences of
building, facilities and methods of teaching will
make an immediate impact but beyond these a
different basic philosophy may well become apparent.
Exchanges are difficult to arrange but any
opportunity should be grasped for teachers to work
in schools outside their sector. One school may
offer another temporary help to maintain a specific

teaching programme which would otherwise be
disrupted because of unforeseen absence of a member
of staff. There may be opportunities of trying out
a new course with a different age range.
Particularly in subjects of a linear nature, it is
essential to gain general agreement before making
fundamental changes. Working out how to teach
pupils of an unfamiliar age-range in a different
working environment exposes constraints and possibly
advantages that would be difficult to appreciate by
other means. There are innumerable practical
problems to this form of liaison but the benefits in
improved understanding between teachers compensate
for the effort involved.

The fundamental obstacle to continuity caused
by lack of communication between teachers is
exhibited at its extreme when other learning is
dismissed or minimised. This can happen even within
the same school: the science teacher may complain
that his pupils lack a basic understanding of
mathematics; the history specialist blames the
English department for failing to teach essay-
writing. It is standard usage to underrate previous
learning. A pupil's first offering to a new teacher
follows the long vacation; after a two-month lapse
in practice, one would expect some regression yet
teachers accept such work as a bench-mark. A good
working relationship with the pupil's previous
teacher should allow a more realistic starting point
to be determined. British teachers may take some
comfort in the realisation that they are not alone
in belittling previous experience, as this American
epigram shows:

Which One?

    The College President -
        Such rawness in a student is a shame
        But lack of preparation is to blame.

    High School Principal -
        Good Heavens, what crudity, the boy's a
        fool!
        The fault of course is with the Grammar
        School.

    Grammar School Principal -
        Oh, that from such a dunce I might be
        spared!
        They send them up to me so unprepared.

204

SUMMARY OF GOOD PRACTICE

> Primary Principal –
>> Poor kindergarten block-head! And they call
>> that preparation! Worse than none at all.
>
> Kindergarten Teacher –
>> Never such a lack of training did I see!
>> What sort of person can the mother be?
>
> Mother –
>> You stupid child – but then you're not to
>> blame,
>> Your father's family are all the same.
>> Shall father in his own defense be heard?
>> No! Let the mother have the final word.
>
>   (Bossard, 1956)

Undoubtedly, it is difficult to get the level right
and one can appreciate the teacher's almost
impossible task in trying to relate to pre-transfer
learning. The usual strategy of retracing work done
in primary school will result in boredom for the
majority; general teaching pitched at a higher level
may mean that some pupils become bewildered.
'Boredom or bewilderment' should not be the only
available alternatives, but there are no easy
solutions if the receiving school's approach is to
teach as one group pupils of mixed achievement
levels from a variety of feeder schools. Individualised learning – about which there are many
misgivings (Boydell, 1978) – does not accord with
secondary modes of working but without some
concession towards the range of previous experience,
receiving schools cannot avoid transfer presenting
some pupils with major difficulties.

Pupil Transfer

Better communication between teachers should
lead to improved transfer experiences for pupils.
Many problems encountered at change of school can
only be mitigated by teachers at either side of an
interface agreeing on matters of curriculum and
methodology. Some strategies for making transfer
less traumatic are, however, fairly straightforward.
Impending change of school causes many anxieties but
it is the new relationships that have to be
established that are most worrying to pupils.
Meeting one's future form tutor or year co-ordinator
before transfer at least provides a familiar face
when school starts in September. It is preferable

for first meetings to take place on the pupil's home ground, so secondary teachers should try to visit feeder primaries. Such visits need careful planning. Little is achieved by the 'cosy chat' in which the teacher from the big school tries to assure pupils they will soon adjust to the new routine and will not be bullied. Indeed, such talks can create anxieties where none existed. The most successful visits have been ones with a clear practical purpose in which pupils have been able to recognise what they understood by 'teacher'. Some interaction between pupils and a teacher who is businesslike but sympathetic produces a reassuring familiarity.

Pre-transfer visits by pupils to schools they will join later in the year can be invaluable but again, careful preparation is essential. The new school should be presented as a stimulating place in which to work but if pupils are overwhelmed by a dispersed site, complex organisation and the number of staff they encounter, the purpose of the visit is defeated. There are advantages to protracted or repeated visits in which acquaintance with the new environment and mode of working can be approached gradually. Many secondary schools have been able to arrange special programmes for their next term's intake after the completion of external examinations in the summer. If a single exploratory visit is all that can be undertaken, it should be focused not on extensive buildings and facilities but on the essentials needed to proceed in the first few days. Phased admission at the beginning of the autumn term can allow teachers to concentrate on the needs of new pupils without hindrance from older ones but this is a poor substitute to pre-transfer visiting. Though many schools are aware that pupils need to be reassured about seemingly trivial detail, others overload them with information concerning academic matters whose import cannot be appreciated in brief intimation. Involving pupils recently established in a senior school in the process of introducing new entrants to ways of working has been used to good effect in some areas. First-formers who remember their own experience of transfer, can prove to be useful guides to newcomers on exploratory visits. Other strategies have included the exchange of letters between pupils and the production of magazines and other material to inform younger children about life in the secondary school.

SUMMARY OF GOOD PRACTICE

Curriculum Guidelines

Unless a child's experiences throughout the
stages of education lead to a recognition of
continuity in the curriculum, it is unlikely that
transfer from school to school will be effected
without problems. Induction programmes merely guide
pupils across the frontier; once over, the ground
must be familiar enough to allow them to proceed.
Recent emphasis on curriculum and evaluation in
local and central authority documents has brought
the majority of schools to awareness of the need for
guidelines in all areas of the curriculum. There
are now probably few schools that would be unable to
produce curriculum documents on demand. But realistic guidelines covering the total span of
schooling are not as evident. Many local authorities have produced excellent statements of curricular
policy but they generally lack the specificity
needed to make continuity meaningful. Once school
guidelines have been drawn up in the light of broad
LEA policy, there is need for further documentation
outlining the curriculum concordat between related
schools. Such a seemingly ponderous approach to
curriculum planning offers a compromise between
prescription by an outside authority and total
autonomy by an individual institution. Of course,
there has to be agreement between teachers in
related schools - agreement to achieve consistency
within a phase of education as well as continuity
between phases. It is difficult to reach such
agreement across a wide area but it should be
attempted within the catchment zone of an upper
school and its feeders. The daunting task of
amalgamating primary and secondary curricula seems
more feasible if effort is concentrated on the age-
ranges immediately before and after transfer. This
argues for a 'middle years' conception of
curriculum. National suggestions for middle years
curricula already exist. Local authorities anxious
to promote continuity should take account of such
suggestions in forming their guidelines. Thereafter, schools should agree between themselves a
common policy for children across the transfer years
and produce appropriate documentation to guide
practice.

SUMMARY OF GOOD PRACTICE

Local Authority Responsibilities

In the context of curriculum continuity and
school transfer, the word 'responsibilities' is used
advisedly for DES Circular 6/81 required local
authorities to have a curriculum policy. Since the
mid-1970s there has been a continuous flood of
documents on curricular themes from government
sources. Though curricular responsibility still
rests mainly with schools, the purpose of recent
advice has been gradually to change attitudes within
the profession towards shared responsibility for
curriculum. Teachers are no longer surprised to
receive LEA counsel that 'all first schools in a
pyramid, and all middle schools, should work towards
establishing common detailed sets of objectives in
each of the main curriculum areas'. Yet 'no school
has the right to dictate the curriculum of another'
although recipient schools are entitled 'to expect
common curriculum policies and objectives in their
group of feeder schools'. (Northumberland Education
Committee, 1982) LEAs have no mandate to determine
curriculum content; they are, however, accountable
for the principles on which curriculum decisions are
made in schools. In addition to the documents it
produces, both general and related to specific
subjects, a local authority has an advisory service
to communicate its policies to schools. The current
relationship between that advisory service and
schools has been aptly outlined by Daniels (1984):
'There is no way in which the adviser would be
accepted as curriculum overlord; his best hope is to
act as curriculum ombudsman.' A more appropriate
role would seem to rest somewhere between mere
arbiter and unchallengeable authority. Early
adviser intervention in curriculum discussions can
prevent individual schools from developing policies
too disparate to permit continuity being promoted
later. A more positive stance taken by a local
authority, such as the setting-up of working parties
across primary and secondary stages, offers better
opportunities for continuity to become a recognised
feature of school policy.
    The main way in which a local authority can
promote curriculum continuity is by providing
resources. The need for in-service education
throughout a teacher's career has been stressed in
many recent reports and LEAs have generally accepted
that such staff development demands a considerable
share of the budget. There are, however, severe
financial constraints and many essential calls on

208

limited available funds. It is therefore vital that
allocation of resources should be carefully
considered. There is an understandable desire to
update subject expertise and to offer courses which
can readily influence classroom practice. It would
be a pity if the promotion of continuity, an
admittedly long-term undertaking, were to be
relegated in favour of projects with more immediate
impact. One can agree with the LEA document which
states 'effective continuity depends upon sympathetic relationships and close understanding between
associated schools', but such relationships can be
given a fillip by injection of LEA financial
support. Regular attendance at working parties - an
essential feature in establishing inter-school
procedures - is a source of stress, which could be
relieved by LEAs granting temporary staff replacements. More generous staffing would allow teachers
involved in the transition years to visit and
possibly teach in associated schools. Without
substantial teacher commitment of time and energy
outside school hours, many of the initiatives
discussed earlier would have collapsed prematurely.
But there is a limit to what can be done without
financial support. Reassurance at finding
curriculum continuity discussed as an important
issue in recent LEA documents is tempered by such
comments as: 'Until such time as levels of
resourcing are improved, schools should work to
implement this policy to the greatest degree
possible with the resources currently available.'
     The Chief Education Officer of Somerset has
suggested that LEAs should adopt 'positive
discriminatory policies' to enhance curricular
provision in schools needing extra attention: 'those
struggling with growing and worsening inner-city
problems and those so small as to attract only two
or even one teacher to provide for as many as seven
age groups'. (Taylor, 1984) Certainly in the first
of these types of school, and possibly the other
too, there are many children at particular risk of
losing their tenuous grasp on education at the time
of transfer. Identification of schools for extra
financial support is one way of ensuring that help
is given where it is most needed. If, additionally,
specific schemes to improve transition were given
priority then we may start to solve the major
problem of disenchantment with education soon after
transfer to secondary schooling.
     School transfer and curriculum continuity are
matters for the attention of all involved in

educational provision but local authorities are in
the best position to mediate between the various
factions and to ensure that resources are provided
to give strategies a good chance of success. That
such strategies are needed is sometimes denied by
those who argue that the majority of pupils settle
into a new school fairly soon. But the very notion
of adjustment to a new school suggests a major
change is involved. By contrast, seeing education
as a continuum implies that there are gradual,
almost imperceptible changes which take the infant
through adolescence - and beyond. There is no place
for 'rites of passage' or major leaps when pupils
change school. We have some way to go to achieve a
natural progression throughout the span of
compulsory schooling but there should be no doubt of
the need to go on striving. What is needed to
promote curriculum continuity, and therefore more
effective school transfer, can be stated simply but
is far from simple to accomplish: collective
decisions need to be made on the basis of a common
purpose being determined by groups of teachers.
There is a price to be paid for improved continuity:
teachers will lose some of their autonomy. Those
who question the need for such a sacrifice should
look again at the views expressed by White and
Brockington's (1983) 'consumers' of British
education. Let the comments of one of them, Andrew
Seal of Birmingham, summarize the opinion of that
sizeable minority whose experience of transfer was
one of failure:

> I still don't understand it. I was enjoying
> myself in the juniors and then I went to senior
> school and everything stopped. I suddenly
> didn't want to go to school.

BIBLIOGRAPHY

Alexander, R.J. (1984) Primary Teaching, Holt,
Rinehart and Winston

Alexander, W.M. (1984) 'Middle level schools in the
United States' in Gorwood, B. (ed.),
Intermediate Schooling, Aspects of Education No.
32, Institute of Education, University of Hull

Allen, C. (1977) 'Liaison with primaries', Times
Educational Supplement, 22.4.77

Assistant Masters' Association (1976) The Middle
School System - an AMA Survey

Auld, R. (1976) William Tyndale Junior and Infants
School Public Inquiry, Inner London Education
Authority

Ausubel, D.P. (1963) The psychology of meaningful
verbal learning, Grune and Stratton, New York,
USA

Averch, H.A. et al (1972) How Effective is
Schooling? Rard, Santa Monica, USA

Ayerst, D. (1969) Understanding Schools, Penguin

Badcock, E.H., Daniels, D.B., Islip, J., Razzell, A.G.
and Ross, A.M. (1972) Education in the middle
years, Schools Council Working Paper 42, Evans-
Methuen

Baldwin, J. and Wells, H. (1979) Active Tutorial
Work, Blackwell

Bantock, G.H. (1975) 'Progressivism and the Content of
Education' in Cox, C.B. and Boyson, R. (eds.),
Black Papers 1975, Dent

Barnard, G. and McCreath, M. (1970) 'Subject commit-
ment and the demand for higher education',
Journal of the Royal Statistical Society, 133,
Part 3

Barnes, D. (1982) Practical Curriculum Study,
Routledge and Kegan Paul

Barnsley Education Committee (1976) Developments
from the Bullock Report - Continuity of
Language Policy at Transfer Stages

211

BIBLIOGRAPHY

Baron, G. (1965) <u>Society, Schools and Progress in England</u>, Pergamon

Bassett, G.W. (1970) <u>Innovation in Primary Education</u> Wiley

Bates, P.J. (1978) 'The Transition of Children at Eleven-Plus', <u>Journal of Applied Educational Studies</u>, vol. 7, no. 2

Becher, T., Eraut, M. and Knight, J. (1981) <u>Policies for Educational Accountability</u>, Heinemann

Bedfordshire County Council (1971) <u>Report of a Second Conference on Aspects of the Middle School</u>

Bellaby, P. (1977) <u>The Sociology of Comprehensive Schooling</u>, Methuen

Benn, C. and Simon, B. (1972) <u>Half way there</u>, Penguin

Benyon, L. (1981) 'Curriculum continuity', <u>Education 3-13</u>, vol. 9, no. 2
—— (1984) 'Investigation of the problems of continuity in the curriculum of primary and secondary schools', <u>Curriculum</u>, vol. 5, no 1

Bestwick, F.M. (1984) 'Core Programme at Bolsover' in Gorwood, B. (ed.), <u>Intermediate Schooling</u>, Aspects of Education No. 32, Institute of Education, University of Hull

Biggs, E.E. (1973) 'Forward and back - reflections from a decade of discovery mathematics', <u>Education 3-13</u>, vol. 1, no. 2

Blackburn, K. (1983) <u>Head of House, Head of Year</u>, Heinemann

Blackie, J. (1967) <u>Inside the primary school</u>, HMSO

Blenkin, G.M. and Kelly, A.V. (1983) <u>The Primary Curriculum in Action</u>, Harper and Row

Blyth, W.A.L. (1960) 'The Sociometric study of children's groups in English schools', <u>British Journal of Educational Studies</u>, vol. 8
—— (1965) <u>English Primary Education</u>, Routledge and Kegan Paul
—— (1984a) <u>Development, Experience and Curriculum in Primary Education</u>, Croom Helm

Blyth, W.A.L. (1984b) 'The English Middle School'
    in Gorwood, B. (ed.), Intermediate Schooling,
    Aspects of Education No. 32, Institute of
    Education, University of Hull
────── Cooper, K., Derricott, R., Elliott, G.,
    Sumner, H. and Waplington, A. (1976) Place,
    Time and Society 8-13 - Curriculum Planning in
    History, Geography and Social Science, Collins-
    E.S.L.
────── and Derricott, R. (1977) The Social
    Significance of Middle Schools, Batsford

Board of Education (1905) Suggestions for the
    consideration of teachers and others concerned
    in the work of the public elementary schools,
    HMSO
────── (1907) Report for the Year 1905-6 HMSO
────── (1913) Report for the Year 1911-12, HMSO
────── (1926) Report of the Consultative Committee
    on the Education of the Adolescent, HMSO
────── (1931) Report of the Consultative Committee
    on the Primary School, HMSO
────── (1943) Educational Reconstruction, Cmnd.
    6458, HMSO

Bossard, J.S. (1956) Parent and Child, University of
    Pennsylvania Press, Philadelphia, USA

Boucher, J. (1970) 'The New Mathematics' in Rogers
    V.R. (ed.) Teaching in the British Primary
    School, Macmillan

Boydell, D. (1978) The Primary Teacher in Action,
    Open Books

Brice, C. (1984) 'The Gateway Project at Holloway
    School, Islington' in Gorwood, B. (ed.),
    Intermediate Schooling, Aspects of Education
    No. 32, Institute of Education, University of
    Hull

Brighton Education Committee (1973) Middle Schools -
    Report of a Working Party of Teachers

British Broadcasting Corporation (1975) In-service
    education project for teachers: middle years at
    school, programme no. 9

Brooksbank, K. (ed.) (1980) Educational Admini-
    stration, Councils and Education Press

Brown, C. (1983) 'Curriculum management in the middle
    school', School Organization, vol. 3, no. 4

Browne, S. (1977) 'Curriculum: an HMI view', Trends
    in Education, Department of Education and Science

Bruner, J. (1960) The Process of Education, Vintage
    Books, New York, USA

Bryan, K.A. (1984) 'The Effectiveness of Different
    Forms of Intermediate Schooling' in Gorwood, B.
    (ed.), Intermediate Schooling, Aspects of
    Education No. 32, Institute of Education,
    University of Hull
—— and Digby, A. (1983) 'Pupil performance and
    school effectiveness', Westminster Studies in
    Education, vol. 6

Burrows, J. (1968) 'The Transition from primary to
    secondary education' in Bander, P. (ed.),
    Looking forward to the seventies, Smythe
—— (1969) 'Plans for Middle Schools and the Effect
    on the Classroom Situation' in Joint Four
    Conference on the Middle School, Joint Four
    Secondary Schools Association
—— (1978) The Middle School - High Road or Dead
    End? Woburn Press

Burstall, C., Jamieson, M., Cohen, S. and Hargreaves,
    M. (1974) Primary French in the balance, NFER

Button, L. (1976) Developmental group work in the
    secondary school pastoral programme, Department
    of Education, University College of Swansea
—— (1981) Group tutoring for the form tutor,
    Hodder and Stoughton

Camsey, S. (1981) 'A Junior-Secondary Transition
    Course' in Gorwood, B. (ed.), Intermediate
    Schooling, Aspects of Education No. 32,
    Institute of Education, University of Hull

Central Advisory Council for Education (1959)
    15-18, HMSO
—— (1963) Half our future, HMSO
—— (1967) Children and their primary schools, HMSO

Centre for Contemporary Cultural Studies - Education
    Group (1981) Unpopular Education - schooling
    and social democracy in England since 1944,
    Hutchinson

Clegg, A. (1969) 'The conception of the middle school
    in secondary reorganization in the West Riding'
    in Joint Four Conference on the Middle School,
    Joint Four Secondary Schools Association

Clift, P., Weiner, G. and Wilson, E. (1981) Record
    Keeping in Primary Schools, Macmillan - Schools
    Council

Cohen, B. (1976) 'Philosophical thinking and the
    middle years' in Raggett, M. and Clarkson, M.
    (eds.) Teaching the eight to thirteens,
    Ward Lock

Coleman, S. et al (1966) Equality of Educational
    Opportunity, U.S. Department of Health,
    Education and Welfare, Office of Education,
    Washington, USA

Collins, K.T. et al (1973) Key words in education,
    Longmans

Connell, W.F. (1967) The Foundation of Secondary
    Education, Australian Council for Educational
    Research

Cooper, K. (1976) Evaluation, assessment and record-
    keeping in history, geography and social science
    Collins/ESL for the Schools Council

Cox, J.E. (1984) 'Transfer from Primary to Secondary -
    a primary-school view' in Gorwood, B. (ed.),
    Intermediate Schooling, Aspects of Education
    No. 32, Institute of Education, University of
    Hull

Creasey, M., Findlay, F. and Walsh, B. (1983)
    Language across the transition - primary-
    secondary continuity and liaison in English,
    Longmans for the Schools Council

Croll, P. (1983) 'Transfer and Pupil Performance' in
    Galton, M. and Willcocks, J. (eds.) Moving from
    the Primary Classroom, Routledge and Kegan Paul

Culling, G. (1973) Teaching in the Middle School.
    Pitman

Cutler, V. (1984) 'Liaison between primary and
    secondary school', Secondary Education Journal,
    vol. 14, no. 1

BIBLIOGRAPHY

Dale, R.R. and Griffith, M. (1965) Down Stream: A Study of Failure in the Grammar School, Routledge and Kegan Paul

Daniel, M.V. (1949) Activity in the Primary School, Blackwell

Daniels, G.E. (1984) 'The role of the local authority adviser', in Spence, B.V. (ed.) Secondary School Management in the 1980s: Changing Roles, Aspects of Education No. 33, Institute of Education, University of Hull

Daunt, P.E. (1975) Comprehensive Values, Heinemann

Dean, J. (1980) 'Continuity' in Richards, C. (ed) Primary Education: Issues for the Eighties, A. and C. Black
—— (1983) Organising learning in the primary school classroom, Croom Helm

Delament, S. (1983) 'The Ethnography of Transfer' in Galton, M. and Willcocks, J. (eds.) Moving from the Primary Classroom, Routledge and Kegan Paul

Denton, B. (1975) 'The Development of consortia', Trends in Education, Department of Education and Science

Department of Education and Science (1966) New problems in school design: middle schools; implications of transfer at 12 or 13 years, Building Bulletin 35, HMSO
—— (1970) Towards the Middle School, HMSO
—— (1975) A Language for Life, Report of the Committee of Inquiry, HMSO
—— (1977) Education in Schools: A Consultative Document, Cmnd. 6869, HMSO
—— (1978a) Primary education in England: A survey by HM Inspectors of Schools, HMSO
—— (1978b) Comprehensive Education - Report of a conference at York, HMSO
—— (1979) Local Authority Arrangements for the School Curriculum, HMSO
—— (1980a) A framework for the school curriculum, HMSO
—— (1980b_ A view of the curriculum, Department of Education and Science
—— (1983) 9-13 Middle Schools - an illustrative survey, HMSO

BIBLIOGRAPHY

Dewey, J. (1938) Experience and Education, Macmillan

Dickinson, N.E. (1975) 'The Headteacher as Innovator: A Study of an English School District' in Reid, W.A. and Walker, D.F. (eds.) Case Studies in Curriculum Change, Routledge and Kegan Paul

Doherty, P. (1984) 'Moving on', Junior Education, vol. 8, no. 6

Downey, L.W. (1965) The Secondary Phase of Education. Blaisdell, New York, USA

Dutch, R.D. and McCall, J. (1974) 'Transition to secondary - an experiment in a Scottish comprehensive school', British Journal of Educational Psychology, vol. 44, no. 3

Findlay, F. (1983) 'Continuity and liaison in language', Education 3-13, vol. 11, no. I

Fisher, R.J. (1972) Learning how to learn - the English Primary School and American Education, Harcourt Brace Jovanovich, New York, USA

Fiske, D. (1978) 'Secondary reorganisation in an area - Manchester' in Department of Education and Science, Comprehensive Education, HMSO
—— (1980) 'Responsibilities, Power and the LEA', Local Government Studies, vol. 6, no. 6

Floud, J., Halsey, A.H. and Martin, F.M. (1956) Social Class and Educational Opportunity, Heinemann

Fowler, G. (1975) 'DES, ministers and the curriculum' in Bell, R. and Prescott, W. (eds.), The Schools Council: A Second Look, Ward Lock
—— (1977) 'Curriculum control: a review of the issues' in Glatter, R. (ed.) Control of the Curriculum - Issues and Trends in Britain and Europe, University of London Instutute of Education

Gagne, R.M. (1965) The conditions of learning, Holt, Rinehart and Winston, New York, USA
—— (1967) 'Learning research and its implications for independent learning' in Gleason, G.T. (ed.) The theory and nature of independent learning, International Textbooks, USA

BIBLIOGRAPHY

Gagne, R.M. (1971) 'Learning theory, educational media and individualized instruction' in Hooper, R. (ed.) The Curriculum: Context, Design and Development, Oliver and Boyd

Galton, M. (1983) 'Problems of Transition' in Galton, M. and Willcocks, J. (eds.) Moving from the Primary Classroom, Routledge and Kegan Paul

Gannon, T. and Whalley, A. (1975) Middle Schools, Heinemann

Ginsburg, M.B., Meyenn, R.J., Miller, H.D.R. and Ranceford-Hadley, C. (1977) The Role of the Middle School Teacher, Aston Educational Enquiry Monograph 7, University of Aston in Birmingham

Glatter, R. (ed.) (1977) Control of the Curriculum - Issues and Trends in Britain and Europe, University of London Institute of Education

Goldstein, H. (1980) 'The statistical procedures' in Tizard, B. et al 'Fifteen Thousand Hours' - A Discussion, University of London Institute of Education

Gordon, P. (1978) 'Control of the Curriculum' in Lawton, D. et al Theory and Practice of Curriculum Studies, Routledge and Kegan Paul

Gorwood, B. (1978) '9-13 middle schools: a local view', Education 3-13, vol. 6, no. 1
—— (1981) Continuity - with particular reference to the effectiveness of middle school experience upon upper school achievement in Kingston upon Hull, unpublished Ph.D. thesis, University of Hull
—— (1983) 'Curriculum continuity on transfer from middle to secondary school', School Organization, vol. 3, no. 3
—— (ed.) (1984) Intermediate Schooling, Aspects of Education No. 32, Institute of Education, University of Hull

Gwynn, J.M. (1960) Curriculum Principles and Social Trends, Macmillan, New York, USA

Haes, J. (1984) 'The Middle School Curriculum: Clash of Traditions or Unique Identity?' School Organization, vol. 4, no. 1

BIBLIOGRAPHY

Hallett, A. (1978) 'The slow learner in the comprehsive school: transfer at eleven anc subsequently', Journal of Applied Education Studies, vol. 7, no. 2

Halsall, E. (1973) The Comprehensive School, Pergamon

Hargreaves, A. (1980) 'The Ideology of the Middle School' in Hargreaves, A. and Tickle, L. (eds.) Middle Schools - Origins, Ideology and Practice, Harper and Row
—— and Warwick, D. (1978) 'Attitudes to middle schools', Education 3-13, vol. 6, no. 1

Harries, E. (1978) 'Curriculum continuity in the social studies', Education 3-13, vol. 6, no. 2

Harthill, R. (1977) 'Easing the transfer', Times Educational Supplement, 15.7.77

Hayling, H. (1970) 'Primary into secondary', Forum, vol. 13, ros. 1 and 3

Hecker, C.H. (1937) 'A Critical View of the Junior School' in The Year Book of Education 1937 University of London Institute of Education/ Evans

Her Majesty's Inspectorate (1977a) Aspects of Comprehensive Education, Department of Education and Science
—— (1977b) Mathematics, Science and Modern Languages in Maintained Schools in England, Department of Education and Science
—— (1980) Report on educational provision by the Inner London Education Authority, Department of Education and Science

Hill, C.J. (1972) Transfer at eleven - allocation in comprehensive and selective systems 1971-72, National Foundation for Educational Research

Hirst, P.H. (1969) 'The logic of the curriculum', Journal of Curriculum Studies, vol. 1, no. 2

Holly, J. (1977) 'Smoothing the path', ILEA Contact, vol. 5, no. 26

Holmes, E. (1911) What is and What Might Be, Constable

Hughes, M. (1968) 'The Changing Role of the Primary
    Teacher' in Thompson, R.H. (ed.) The Primary
    School in Transition, Aspects of Education No.
    8, Institute of Education, University of Hull

Hutchcroft, D. (1976) 'The Primary Impact', Times
    Educational Supplement, 6.2.76

Jackson, B. and Marsden, D. (1966) Education and the
    Working Class, Pelican

Jennings, K. and Hargreaves, D.J. 'Children's
    Attitudes to Secondary School Transfer',
    Educational Studies, vol. 7, no. 1

Johnson, D. et al (1980) Secondary Schools and the
    Welfare Network, Allen and Unwin

Jordan, J. (1981) The Transition from Junior to
    Senior School - Developmental Group Work in
    Junior School, Occasional Paper 2, Action
    Research Project, Department of Education,
    University College of Swansea

Kaye, D. and Hyson, P. (1979) 'From Primary to
    secondary - treat or trauma?' Spectrum,
    vol. 11, no. 2

Kerr, J. and Engel, E. (1980) 'Should science be
    taught in primary schools?' Education 3-13,
    vol. 8, no. 1

King, E. (1979) Other schools and ours (5th Edition)
    Holt, Rinehart and Winston

Kogan, M. (1973) 'English Primary Schools' in Fowler,
    G. (ed.) Decision Making in British Education,
    Heinemann
—— and Eyken, W. van der (1975) County Hall - The
    Role of the Chief Education Officer, Penguin

Lack, G.O. (1967) 'The schools' response' in Schools'
    Council, The Educational Implications of Social
    and Economic Change, HMSO

Lancashire County Council (1979) Active Tutorial
    Work, Blackwell

Lawson, J. and Silver, H. (1973) A Social History of
    Education in England, Methuen

BIBLIOGRAPHY

Lawton, D. (1969) 'Social Studies' in Schools'
Council, The middle years of schooling from 8
to 13 (Working Paper 22) Schools' Council
—— (1973) Social change, educational theory and
curriculum planning, University of London
Press
—— (1980) The politics of the school curriculum,
Routledge and Kegan Paul
—— (1981) 'The curriculum and curriculum change'
in Simon, B. and Taylor, W. (eds.) Education
in the Eighties - The Central Issues, Batsford
—— Campbell, J. and Burkitt, V. (1971) Social
Studies 8-13, Schools' Council Working Paper
39, Evans/Methuen
—— Gordon, P., Ing, M., Gibby, B., Pring, R. and
Moore, T. (1978) Theory and Practice of
Curriculum Studies, Routledge and Kegan Paul

Leeds City Council Department of Education (1983)
Continuity in Education

Lounsbury, J.H. and Vars, G.F. (1978) A curriculum
for the middle school years, Harper and Row,
New York, USA

Lowndes, G.A.N. (1969) The Silent Social Revolution,
Oxford University Press

Lyness, R.C. (1969) 'Modern Maths Revisited', Trends
in Education, Department of Education and
Science

McCormick, R. and James, M. (1983) Curriculum
evaluation in schools, Croom Helm

Mahoney, A. (1981) 'Little Fish in Large Pond',
Kent Education Gazette, vol. 61, no. 3

Makins, V. (1982) 'Hats off to my new school',
Times Educational Supplement, 5.2.82

Manning, D. (1971) Towards a Humanistic Curriculum,
Harper and Row, New York, USA

Marland, M. (1974) Pastoral Care, Heinemann
—— (1977) Language across the curriculum,
Heinemann

Marsh, L. (1970) Alongside the Child in the Primary
School, Black

Martin, D. and Buck, P. (1982) 'Bridging the gap
    between primary and secondary school' in
    Irving, A. (ed.) Starting to teach study
    skills, Edward Arnold

Maxfield, B. (1983) Computer-aided profiling,
    Further Education Unit, North Warwickshire
    College of Technology and Art

Michael, L.S. (1959) 'Articulation problems with
    lower school and higher education', Bulletin
    of the National Association of Secondary
    School Principals, no. 43, USA

Miles, M.B. (1964) 'On temporary systems' in Miles,
    M.B. (ed.) Innovation in Education, Teachers
    College, New York, USA

Ministry of Education, (1947) The New Secondary
    Education, HMSO
—— (1958) Secondary Education for All - A New
    Drive, Cmnd. 604, HMSO
—— (1959) Primary Education, HMSO

Mitchell, J. (1970) 'Freedom in the Junior School'
    in Rubinstein, D. and Stoneman, C. (eds.)
    Education for Democracy, Penguin

Moorhead, C. (1971) 'Missing Links: where 11-year-
    olds leap 100 yards into the unknown', Times
    Educational Supplement, 26.2.71

Moorhouse, E. (1971) 'The Philosophy underlying the
    British Primary School' in Rogers, V.R. (ed.)
    Teaching in the British Primary School,
    Macmillan

Morrish, I. (1976) Aspects of Educational Change,
    Allen and Unwin

Nash, R. (1973) Classroom Observed, Routledge and
    Kegan Paul

National Foundation for Educational Research (1969)
    Trends in Allocation Procedures, NFER

National Union of Teachers (1975) Middle schools
    (A Discussion Document), NUT
—— (1979) Middle Schools - Deemed or Doomed? NUT

BIBLIOGRAPHY

Neal, P.D. (ed.) (1975) Continuity in Education -
    EDC Project Five, City of Birmingham Education
    Department

Newsam, P. (1977) 'Transfer to a higher plane', ILEA
    Contact, vol. 5, no. 23

Nias, J. (1980) 'The Ideal Middle School: Its Public
    Image' in Hargreaves, A. and Tickle, L. (eds.)
    Middle Schools - Origins, Ideology and
    Practice, Harper and Row

Nisbet, J.D. and Entwistle, N.J. (1966) Age of
    Transfer to Secondary Education, University of
    London Press
    —— (1969) The Transition to Secondary Education,
    University of London Press

Norfolk Association of Middle School Head Teachers
    (1983) Discussion Document: Patterns of
    Liaison - Middle to Secondary

Northumberland Education Committee (1982) The School
    Curriculum 5-16 - A Statement of Policy

Oliver, A.I. (1977) Curriculum Improvement, Harper
    and Row, New York, USA

Organisation for Economic Co-operation and Develop-
    ment, Centre for Educational Research and
    Innovation (1975) Handbook on Curriculum
    Development, OECD, Paris, France

Orsborn, T. (1977) 'Talk about our problems', ILEA
    Contact, vol. 5, no. 25

Padley, R. and Cole, H. (eds.) (1940) Evacuation
    Survey, Routledge

Parkinson, M. (1970) The Labour Party and the
    Organisation of Secondary Education 1918-65,
    Routledge and Kegan Paul

Parkyn, G.W. (1962) 'The transition from primary
    to secondary school' in UNESCO, World Survey
    of Education, UNESCO, Paris, France

Partridge, J. (1966) Life in a Secondary Modern
    School, Penguin

Pearce, J. (1974) 'Planning for science and
    mathematics in the middle years: an overview'
    in Raggett, M. and Clarkson, M. (eds.)
    The middle years curriculum, Ward Lock

Pedley, R. (1964) The Comprehensive School, Penguin

Peirson, E.G. (1965) 'Training colleges in transition'
    in Cluderay, T. (ed.) The professional education
    of teachers, Aspects of Education No. 3,
    Institute of Education, University of Hull

Perkins, W.H. (1936) 'England' in International
    Institute of Teachers' Colleges, Education
    Yearbook 1936, Columbia University

Peters, R.S. (ed.) (1969) Perspectives on Plowden,
    Routledge and Kegan Paul

Philip, L. (1968) The effect of changes in the
    traditional transfer procedure in children's
    adjustment to secondary school, unpublished
    M.Ed. thesis, University of Aberdeen

Plowden, B. (1970) Children and their schools,
    University of Exeter Institute of Education

Popper, S.H. et al (1967) The American Middle
    School: an organisational analysis, Blaisdell
    Publishing Co, Waltham, Massachusetts, USA

Pring, R. (1978) 'Accountability' in Lawton, D. et al,
    Theory and Practice of Curriculum Studies,
    Routledge and Kegan Paul

Raison, T. (1976) The Act and the Partnership,
    Centre for Studies in Social Policy

Razzell, A. (1968) Juniors: A Postscript to Plowden,
    Penguin

Richards, C. (ed.) (1980) Primary Education: Issues
    for the Eighties, A. and C. Black
    —— (1981) 'The Primary Curriculum: perennial
    questions and current issues', Primary Education
    Review, no. 12
    —— (1982) 'Curriculum consistency' in Richards, C.
    (ed.) New directions in primary education,
    The Falmer Press

Richards, R. (1973) 'The swinging of a pendulum -
discovery science with young children',
Education 3-13, vol. 1, no. 1

Richardson, J.W. (1940) Problems of articulation
between the units of secondary education,
Teachers' College, Columbia University, New
York, USA

Richmond, W.K. (1978) Education in Britain since
1944, Methuen

Ross, A. (1969) 'Round-up on the whole curriculum' in
Schools' Council, The middle years of schooling
from 8 to 13, (Working Paper 22) HMSO
—— (1973) 'The whole curriculum of the middle
years', Forum, vol. 15, no. 3
—— Razzell, A. and Badcock, E. (1975) The
curriculum in the middle years (Working Paper
55) Evans/Methuen

Rowe, A. (1971) The School as a Guidance Community,
Pearson Press

Rundle, C.J. (1978) 'Transitional assessment'.
Journal of Applied Educational Studies, vol.7,
no. 2

Rutter, M., Maughan, B., Mortimore, P. and Ouston, J.
Fifteen Thousand Hours, Open Boks, 1979

Selby, C.H. (1977) APU - Questions and Answers,
Department of Education and Science

Sharp, J. (1975) 'Easing the move between primary
and secondary', Where? no. 102

Shipman, M.D. (1972) Children: A Sociological
Perspective, NFER
—— (1984) Education as a public service,
Harper and Row

Simon, A. and Ward, L.O. 'Anxiety, self-concept,
attitude to school and transition to the
comprehensive school', Counsellor, vol. 3,
no. 5

Simon, B. (1981) 'Why no pedagogy in England?' in
Simon, B. and Taylor, W. Education in the
eighties - the central issues, Batsford

BIBLIOGRAPHY

Skidelsky, R. (1960) English Progressive Schools,
    Penguin

Smith, D.J. (1981) 'Opinions of school, academic
    motiviation and school adjustment in the first
    year of secondary education: a pilot study in
    West Yorkshire', Educational Studies (Abingdon)
    vol. 7, no. 3

Spelman, B.J. (1979) Pupil Adaptation to Secondary
    School, Northern Ireland Council for Educational
    Research

Steadman, S.D. (1978) Impact and take-up project -
    interim report, Schools' Council

Stillman, A. (1984a) 'Some reflections on planning the
    transition in transfer' in Gorwood, B. (ed.)
    Intermediate Schooling, Aspects of Education
    No. 32, Institute of Education, University of
    Hull
—— (1984b) 'Transfer from school to school',
    Educational Research, vol. 26, no. 3
—— and Maychell, K. (1982) Transfer procedures at
    9 and 13, NFER
—— (1984) School to School, NFER - Nelson

Storm, M. (1979) 'Making Primary Progress',
    Times Educational Supplement, 7.12.79

Sumner, R. and Bradley, K. (1977) Assessment for
    transition, NFER

Taba, H. (1962) Curriculum development: theory and
    practice, Harcourt Brace Jovanovich Inc, New
    York, USA

Taylor, B. (1984) 'Local education authorities in
    England and the curriculum - a case for
    intervention?' New Era, vol. 65, no. 1

Taylor, G. (ed.) (1970) The Teacher as Manager,
    National Council for Educational Technology

Taylor, M. and Garson, Y. (1982) Schooling in the
    middle years, Trentham Books

Taylor, P.H. (1967) 'Purpose and structure in the
    curriculum', Educational Review, vol. 19,
    no. 3

BIBLIOGRAPHY

Thomas, S. (1979) 'Traumatic transfer', Junior
    Education, February

Times Educational Supplement, 'The Virtues of
    Necessity' (Leicestershire's 10-14 schools)
    Times Educational Supplement, 18.2.83

Usill, H.V. (1937) 'The Junior School and the
    Problem of Co-ordination' in The Year Book
    of Education, University of London Institute
    of Education - Evans

Vernon, P.E. (1957) Secondary School Selection
    Methuen

Walker, A.S. (1955) Pupils' School Records NFER

Walton, J. (1971) 'Continuity of Education and
    Teacher Control', Forum, vol. 13, no. 3

Walton, S. (1983) 'Junior to Secondary: Towards an
    Easy Transition', School Organization,
    vol. 3, no. 1

Warr, E.B. (1937) The New Era in the Junior School,
    Methuen

Weiner, G. (1978) 'For whose eyes only?' Times
    Educational Supplement, 15.9.79

Weston, P.B. (1979) Negotiating the curriculum: a
    study in secondary schooling, NFER

Whalen, T.E. and Fried, M.A. (1973) 'Geographic
    mobility and its effect on student achievement',
    Journal of Education Research, no. 67

White, J. (1975) The end of the compulsory
    curriculum' in The Curriculum (Doris Lee
    Lectures) Studies in Education, 2, University
    of London Institute of Education

White, R. and Brockington, D. (1983) Tales out of
    School, Routledge and Kegan Paul

Williams, V. (1975) 'Local education authorities and
    continuity of educational provision', Trends
    in Education, Department of Education and
    Science

Willcocks, J. (1983) 'Pupils in Transition' in Galton,
    M. and Willcocks, J. (eds.) Moving from the
    Primary Classroom, Routledge and Kegan Paul

Wright, N. (1977) Progress in Education, Croom Helm

Yates, A. (1971) The Organisation of Schooling,
    Routledge and Kegan Paul
—— and Pidgeon, D.A. (1957) Admission to Grammar
    Schools, NFER

Youngman, M.B. (1978) 'Six reactions to school
    transfer' British Journal of Educational
    Psychology, no. 48
—— (1980) 'Some determinants of early secondary
    school performance', British Journal of
    Educational Psychology, no. 50
—— and Lunzer, E.A. (1977) Adjustment to Secondary
    Schooling, Nottinghamshire County Council and
    Nottingham University School of Education

AUTHOR INDEX

AUTHOR INDEX

Simon, B. 42, 46-47,
    114-115
Skidelsky, R. 32
Smith, D. 183
Spelman, B.J. 13, 53,
    71, 80
Steadman, S.D. 116
Stillman, A. 12-13, 62-
    65, 68, 70, 78, 83,
    125, 133, 138, 157,
    191, 192, 194, 196,
    198
Storm, M. 7
Sumner, R. 10-12, 136,
    201

Taba, H. 116
Tawney, R.H. 18
Taylor, B. 153, 162-
    163, 209
Taylor, G. 124
Taylor, M. 86, 88, 92

Usill, H.V. 21

Vars, G.F. 5
Vernon, P.E. 29

Walker, A.S. 129, 133,
    200
Walton, J. 105-106
Walton, S. 185
Ward, F. 139
Warr, E.B. 21
Warwick, D. 93
Weiner, G. 131
Wells, H. 173
Weston, G. 3
Whalen, T.E. 13
Whalley, A. 64
White, J. 117
White, R. 8, 9, 210
Williams, V. 12, 42
Wilson, E. 131
Wright, N. 32

Yates, A. 29
Youngman, M.B. 8, 55-61,
    84, 108, 135